Academic Conversations

Academic Conversations

Classroom Talk That Fosters Critical Thinking and Content Understandings

Stenhouse
PUBLISHERS
Portland, Maine

**Jeff Zwiers &
Marie Crawford**

Stenhouse Publishers
www.stenhouse.com

Library of Congress Cataloging-in-Publication Data
Zwiers, Jeff.
  Academic conversations : classroom talk that fosters critical thinking and content understandings/ Jeff Zwiers and Marie Crawford.
        p. cm.
  Includes bibliographical references and index.
  ISBN 978-1-57110-884-5 (pbk. : alk. paper) -- ISBN 978-1-57110-922-4 (e-book)
  1. Thought and thinking--Study and teaching (Elementary) 2. Conversation--Study and teaching (Elementary) 3. Cognitive learning. I. Crawford, Marie. II. Title.
  LB1590.3.Z94 2011
  370.15'2--dc22
                                                                                    2011014790

Cover design, interior design, and typesetting by designboy Creative Group

Manufactured in the United States of America

PRINTED ON 30% PCW
   RECYCLED PAPER

17 16 15 14   9 8 7 6

Contents

Acknowledgments

We are deeply grateful for the tireless and brilliant work of so many teachers across the country who contributed ideas to this book. Special thanks go to Kim Yamashita, Dayna Yonamine, Patrick Hurley, and Octavio Rodriguez for their insights, patience, reflection, and exceptional teaching. Thanks also to Jenna Wachtel, Kristi Rallu, Rachel Spector, and Jennifer Bloom for the many insight-filled conversations about conversations.

Introduction

I didn't know what I knew until I talked about it.

—*Seventh-grade science student*

Since the dawn of language, conversations have been powerful teachers. They engage, motivate, and challenge. They help us build ideas, solve problems, and communicate our thoughts. They cause ideas to stick and grow in our minds. They teach us how other people see and do life, and they teach other people how we see and do life. Conversations strengthen our comprehension of new ideas.

Conversations are also powerful sculptors. They shape our identities, thoughts, beliefs, and emotions. We all have had intense conversations from which we walked away (or lost sleep) mulling over the ideas that we discussed. Conversations can leave us pondering and processing ideas for hours, days, and even years. These ideas, in turn, contribute to the inner dialogues that we hold in our heads throughout each day (Vygotsky 1986), which sculpt our thoughts—whether we like it or not.

More than we realize, we are the products of thousands of conversations.

As we worked in classrooms as instructional coaches and began to tap the teaching and sculpting power of extended, back-and-forth talk between students, an approach emerged that we called academic conversations. We then wrote down some of the ideas, stories, and examples, and hope that they will help you sharpen and deepen the learning that is already happening in each of your lessons. But be ready for a louder classroom.

What Are Academic Conversations?

Conversations are exchanges between people who are trying to learn from one another and build meanings that they didn't have before. Partners take turns talking, listening, and responding to each other's comments. Academic conversations are sustained and purposeful conversations about school topics. These topics vary widely, ranging from themes in *The Adventures of Tom Sawyer* to causes of the French Revolution, from the role of geography in culture to the debate on the use of stem cells. But regardless of topic or content area, in our classroom observations and analyses of transcripts we found five core conversation skills: elaborate and clarify; support ideas with examples; build on and/or challenge a partner's ideas; paraphrase; and synthesize conversation points. The diagram depicts how these skills, described in more detail in Chapter 2, are used to explore and focus on an academic topic.

Five Skills That Focus and Deepen Academic Conversations

These skills (some of which are also called discourse moves) work together to help students focus on and explore an important question, idea, or topic. You will notice most of these skills in your own conversations with colleagues and friends. And even though this book emphasizes paired conversations, these are skills that empower students to communicate well in a variety of situations, such as whole-class discussions, small groups, workplace meetings, social gatherings, and family interactions. These communication skills also align very well with the skills needed for high-quality academic writing and reading.

A Brief Background of Academic Conversation Work

In the years leading up to the writing of this book, we observed, as instructional coaches, many classrooms that used a wide variety of what were considered "best practices." We saw some students who were engaged and talking productively. But the other students, many of whom were English language learners (ELLs) and speakers of nonmainstream dialects of English, weren't talking much. And as we listened in to what students were talking about, we realized that they weren't having *productive* conversations. They could answer questions in short think-pair-shares and use memorized sentence starters to respond to the teacher, but they seldom took turns to negotiate meaning or dig into a topic. Students seldom co-constructed ideas, clarified thoughts for each other, or supported their opinions.

During our work with teachers, the focus on classroom talk intensified one day when we asked a fourth-grade student what she liked to do. Her eyes got really wide, and without hesitation, she emphatically said, "I *love* to talk!" This was quite true, but most of her talk, like that of others in the class, was not academic. And a handful of students in the class did not like to talk, especially in whole-class discussions. Many discussions and "conversations" were similar to this:

A: *Why did the author write this?*
B: To teach us about courage.
A: *Yeah, the guy was brave.*
B: Okay. What do we do now?

We then looked at the literature that argues for more and better student talk in classrooms, and we wondered if we could do something that tapped into students' passions for talking and also encouraged shy students to talk academically—and to each other. We had seen quite a few resources on teacher-led whole-class and group discussions, but we found few practical resources on training students to converse academically in pairs and small groups on their own.

Teachers whom we coached and their colleagues became interested in the topic of classroom conversations and joined the discussions, expressing their desire to improve students' oral language skills, critical thinking, and content understandings far beyond what tests required. Teachers also wanted a way to see students' learning that didn't show up in their writing or on multiple-choice tests. Teachers wanted to transform their classrooms into places where students initiated and maintained conversations, creating, shaping, applying, negotiating, and sharing academic ideas.

To inform our work with teachers and to write this book, we built on the extensive research and fieldwork on classroom discourse and cooperative learning. We often referred to the work of experts in this area, such as Courtney Cazden (2001), Roland Tharp and Ronald Gallimore (1991), Claude Goldenberg (1991), Neil Mercer (1995), Norman Fairclough (2003), John Dewey (1963 [1938]), Lev Vygotsky (1978, 1986), Mikhail Bakhtin (1981), Barbara Rogoff (1990), Mary Schleppegrell (2004), and Jerome Bruner (1986). The bulk of our work was done in language arts, social studies, and science classrooms. For conversation work in math, we recommend resources by Chapin, O'Connor, and Anderson (2009).

Audience for This Book

This book is most appropriate for teachers of language arts, social studies, history, and science in grades three through twelve. It is also meant for literacy coaches, special education teachers, curriculum specialists, and teachers of ELLs.

Parents can also benefit from this book. Many ideas in the following chapters can be used at home to improve conversations with toddlers, children, adolescents, and even spouses. The more and earlier that we have productive conversations with children, listening to their ideas, validating them, and clarifying them, the more practice children get at conversation skills and thinking. This prepares them for school interactions and thinking throughout life. Parents can use conversation strategies to talk about a story, an object, a TV show, animals, day trips, current events, and so on.

Objectives of This Book

This book attempts to equip educators to do the following:

» Teach students to converse in academic ways, using the five core academic conversation skills described in Chapter 2.

» Teach students content understandings and vocabulary through conversations, discussions, debates, and other oral interactions.

» Weave conversations into what teachers already do, every day. Teachers will be able to fortify lessons with authentic and extended conversations, including discipline-specific methods (e.g., case studies in the history chapter, creative writing projects in the language arts chapter, and labs in the science chapter).

» Train students to become more aware of how they think (metacognition) and to clearly express their thought processes to others.

» Use conversations as formative and summative assessments of a wide range of knowledge, skills, and engagement indicators.

» Build students' independence in facilitating their own academic conversations in pairs, small groups, and even whole-class settings. (Students will depend less and less on teacher prompts and guidance for their thinking and will become managers of their own ideas as they think together in conversation. Students will become prompters of one another's deep thinking, without relying on the teacher.)

» Build students' academic communication skills, which are the skills that tend not to be practiced in social situations outside of school, particularly in low-income homes and communities that do not speak mainstream dialects of English. (These highly valued oral skills are not emphasized in most state tests, curriculum programs, or intervention efforts, yet academic and professional success depends on them. They are major gate-keeper skills, and too many students who lack them are being stopped and turned away at this gate.)

Overview of Chapters

The first half of the book offers a wide-angle view of conversation and how it can be used across disciplines; the second half emphasizes specific disciplines and assessment. Chapters 2 through 10 contain multiple activities (denoted in the text by a pencil-and-paper icon) and examples of student conversations.

Chapter 1 describes the core principles of learning that provide a rationale for using and teaching academic conversation skills in the classroom. We delve into how students develop and learn through talk. Chapter 2 describes what teachers should do to prepare for conversation work. It outlines the five core conversation skills and behaviors. Chapter 3 presents activities to teach the skills described in Chapter 2. Chapter 4 covers the design of prompts and conversation tasks, and Chapter 5 includes specific strategies for teaching various conversation skills and for training students to hold advanced conversations across content areas. Chapter 6 focuses on how we can use conversation to build grammar and vocabulary, the two main gears of language.

One of the challenges of teaching conversation skills is that different disciplines have different rules and approaches for conversations. Chapter 7 highlights how conversation skills can be developed and used in language arts and English classes. It emphasizes conversations about literature and for writing analytical and persuasive essays. Chapter 8 covers conversations about history and social science issues, which can be used to develop students' critical thinking skills of debate, persuasion, interpretation, and application. Chapter 9 describes how to build scientific thinking skills through conversation, and how to build conversation skills through science. This chapter covers how to converse about scientific inquiry and experimentation, emphasizing the importance of connecting to previously learned science ideas to form hypotheses and foundations for claims. Chapter 10 describes how to use conversations as assessments, to show us how students are learning, the meanings they have built, and their abilities to make new meanings with another person. Conversations can show language skills, conversation behaviors, content knowledge, and even engagement. This chapter offers ideas and rubrics for formative and summative assessment of conversation as well as ideas for using conversation to assess reading, writing, and content understandings. Finally, Chapter 11 concludes with a synthesis of the previous chapters and offers practical suggestions.

At the end of each chapter we include a set of prompts that encourage readers to reflect on salient points in the chapter and begin to apply the ideas to their specific settings.

Like you, we are passionate about developing language, conversation skills, thinking skills, content understandings, and student character in classroom settings, especially in schools with high numbers of ELLs and speakers of nonprivileged dialects. We have worked extensively in urban settings with students who communicate in ways that do not neatly merge and align with the language of mainstream school and professional settings. These highly intelligent, motivated, and diverse students deserve classroom experiences that help them develop into deeper thinkers and clearer communicators. We hope that the following chapters will help you create such experiences.

Chapter 1
Reasons to Converse in School

> Conversations not only made us sound smarter,
> I think they actually made us smarter.

—Fourth-grade student

Most likely, you are already convinced of the value of using conversations to teach. But, just in case someone does ask why your classroom is so loud, here we provide some convincing reasons to offer in response. This chapter begins with a brief description of the need for more and better oral academic language in school, followed by advantages of classroom talk that we have grouped into five categories: language and literacy, thinking skills, content learning, social advantages, and psychological advantages.

The Need for Oral Academic Language

One possible reason for the lack of oral language development in school is the popular "Trivial Pursuit" view of learning (Perkins 1992), in which knowledge and intelligence are seen as an accumulation of routines and facts (we also refer to this as "game-show pedagogy"). Most high-stakes tests reflect this view, which in turn shapes curricula and classroom teaching practices. Yet, these days the facts are readily available on the Internet, they can change overnight, and they can be learned quickly. These days it is what you *do* with the knowledge that counts. Beyond just finding and memorizing the facts, an educated and productive person in today's world must be able to evaluate the facts and then *use* them for meaningful problem solving. Future workers need to know how to use a variety of critical thinking skills to build complex ideas and solve problems *with others*.

Despite their power, rich conversations in school are rare.

Oral language is a cornerstone on which we build our literacy and learning throughout life. Unfortunately, oral language is rarely taught in depth after third grade. Lessons dominated by teacher talk tend to be the norm in many classrooms (Corden 2001; Nystrand 1996). Of particular concern is oral academic language. Students from middle- and upper-class backgrounds tend to develop many academic aspects of English at home. When they arrive at school, they need to make only slight changes to their language to learn and show learning.

Sadly, academic talk is most scarce where it is most needed—in classrooms with high numbers of linguistically and culturally diverse students. These students (to whom we will refer as "diverse students" throughout this book) tend to speak nonmainstream versions of English and come from low-income backgrounds. Often, because of test-score pressures, diverse students are placed in classes that emphasize quiet practice of isolated skills and facts. Several studies have shown that teachers tend to give students from low-income backgrounds fewer opportunities to talk about content and engage in critical-thinking activities than teachers of higher-socioeconomic students (Cotton 1989; Lingard, Hayes, and Mills 2003; Weber et al. 2008). In one study, Arreaga-Mayer and Perdomo-Rivera (1996) found that ELLs spent only 4 percent of the school day engaged in school talk and 2 percent of the school day discussing focal content of the lesson. Nystrand et al. (2003) also found almost no effective dialogue in low-track eighth- and ninth-grade classes. These and other studies reflect the need for increased chances to talk and develop oral academic language in classrooms with diverse students.

Interaction Without Depth

In many classrooms, talking activities are used in limited ways, often just to check learning of facts and procedures rather than to teach or deepen understandings. We have seen many cases in which the following popular activities offered large amounts of interaction and language exchange (i.e., the room was loud) but did not take students to deeper levels of thinking and negotiation of meaning. Academic conversation work seeks to deepen and fortify these practices.

»   *Think-pair-shares.* On many checklists for effective and engaging lessons, think-pair-shares tend to consist of quick, surface-level answers and only one turn apiece by partners. Think-pair-shares (a.k.a. turn-and-talks) are more useful for quickly answering questions and to break up a long activity such as a teacher lecture. They usually lack depth and, when given more time, the chats quickly lose focus because students lack skills to stay on topic or extend it.

»   *Small groups.* We have seen many small groups in which students never negotiate meaning, never build on one another's ideas, just fill in charts, share their own answers to questions, allow one student to dominate and do all the work, and work alone next to one another.

»   *Answering with memorized sentence stems and frames.* Many classrooms have lists of language frames or sentence starters on the wall for students to use to answer questions. These are helpful in getting students started—that is, when the students understand what the frame means—but frames can be awkward during a conversation when students keep looking up at the wall or down at their notes to read them.

Electronic Communication and Computer Programs

Another need is created by current uses of certain electronic communication devices and computer programs. Even though we see the value of technology for learning and working, we are concerned by the lack of face-to-face communication that results from the use of such devices. Text-messaging, handheld games, online social networks, computer games, e-mail, and even cell phones have the ability to limit in-depth communication with other people. Granted, information is often exchanged, but exploration of a topic, the building of ideas, and emotional connections are often missing. As Putnam (2000) argues, we are experiencing a significant loss of social capital. This loss is characterized by a decline in the number of organizations, meetings, family dinners, and visits with friends. Face-to-face time is declining in schools, yet many professional folks beyond the walls of school, including employers, desire workers and colleagues with excellent oral communication skills. Moreover, popular modes of communication, such as video, podcasts, written texts, music, and images are mostly "one-way." They do not adjust their messages or negotiate meanings with their viewers, nor do such modes encourage students to think as much as a real partner in conversation can.

Developing Knowledge and Skills for the Future

Similar to the Trivial Pursuit/game-show approach is the brick-hauling model of teaching. Teaching is not meant to be like loading up a truck (a student's mind) with a large pile of bricks (facts) to dump out into a pile somewhere (standardized tests). Bricks are meant for building. True, they are necessary materials, but for them to be useful a builder must skillfully put them together over time to build something. In the same way, students must have academic knowledge available in their minds for thinking and conversation purposes. That is, students need things to think and talk about! Students should learn, for example, key events and people of the American Revolutionary War, geological forces, literary devices, and so on. At the same time, students must learn how to combine the facts and procedures, working with others to create products and solutions that are too complex to be tested with multiple-choice questions. In this way they will develop deep knowledge and expertise in a subject area. Facts become raw materials for building ideas, solving problems, thinking critically and creatively, communicating, and transferring concepts to novel situations. Conversation, as this book describes, can play a large role in developing these higher-level skills.

What are the academic skills that should be reinforced and emphasized? Many are on (but do not stand out on) state and federal lists of standards by grade level and subject area. Take a look at a typical standards list and highlight the verbs that ask students to do something. You might see terms such as *evaluate, distinguish, outline, summarize, analyze,* and *hypothesize.* Most of these are actually thinking skills that are often best developed in conversation. Moreover, some of these skills *need* to be developed in conversation, and if we remove this avenue, we weaken students' chances for academic success.

Another helpful place to look for the core skills that students need to learn is lists of the skills that employers desire and foresee desiring in the future. The skills and qualities in Figure 1.1 are a synthesis of several such lists. Some items on the list, for example, come from Tony Wagner's (2008) extensive interviews of organizations that intend to compete in an increasingly globalized world. Wagner, like many others, argues that many curricula, assessments, and teaching methods need to be drastically overhauled to develop students' high-leverage skills for the coming decades.

Take a look at Figure 1.1 and reflect on how evident these skills and qualities are in most classrooms' instruction. How often are they assessed in school? If we don't assess them or emphasize them, and then expect them in later years of school and work, what happens?

Figure 1.1 Skills and Qualities Desired by Employers

Skills	Qualities
<ul><li>Communicate effectively (#1 skill on most lists) (e.g., clearly listen, speak, and write complex and abstract concepts).</li><li>Ask insightful and critical questions.</li><li>Collaborate well with others (work in a team; lead and be led).</li><li>Solve problems logically, systematically, and creatively (define, plan, follow a plan, reflect, and improve over time).</li><li>Conduct logical, thorough research, and critically evaluate evidence.</li><li>Analyze, synthesize, prioritize, and organize ideas.</li><li>Weigh the relevance and importance of ideas.</li><li>Recognize bias.</li><li>See multiple perspectives on an issue and empathize.</li><li>Apply and generalize concepts to new domains.</li><li>Use technologies and visual literacy to learn, communicate, act, and produce.</li></ul>	<ul><li>Strong work ethic</li><li>Initiative</li><li>Flexibility/adaptability</li><li>Honesty</li><li>Professionalism</li><li>Loyalty/trustworthiness</li><li>Enthusiasm/encouraging of others</li><li>Willingness to learn</li><li>Emotional intelligence</li><li>Curiosity/interest</li><li>Cross-cultural understanding</li><li>Leadership</li></ul>

Adapted from Casner-Lotto and Barrington 2006; Hansen and Hansen 2009; National Association of Colleges and Employers 2007; Wagner 2008.

Even beyond these working-world skills and qualities, what else do students need for a successful life, to make the world a better place, to raise a family, to improve their communities, and to make positive changes in the world? What qualities do we want our own children to have? Some lists would probably include curiosity, concern for others, patience, altruism, and empathy. And, if these are important, we must ask if we are developing these in our curricula, assessments, lessons, and school environments.

Academic conversations can help to develop the highly important but under-tested skills and qualities just mentioned. Teachers can shape conversation prompts and mini-lessons to teach these skills throughout the year. One teacher even used these qualities as topics of student conversations. Students talked about what it meant to be loyal, honest, diligent, mature, motivated, and so on. As you read through this book and plan lessons, consider how to keep the development of these skills and qualities a high priority in student conversations. After all, our duty as teachers is to prepare, to our utmost abilities, each student for a successful life—no matter how misguided and disjointed the educational system is.

Academic conversations also align with the national Common Core State Standards that have been adopted by the majority of states in the United States. Students will be expected to collaborate in teams, express their ideas, and listen to one another as they communicate with purpose. They will be required to think critically together and express their thoughts in coherent ways for a variety of different applications. Here is a sample excerpt from the Common Core State Standards Web site:

> **Speaking and Listening: Flexible Communication and Collaboration**
>
> Including but not limited to skills necessary for formal presentations, the Speaking and Listening standards require students to develop a range of broadly useful oral communication and interpersonal skills. Students must learn to work together, express and listen carefully to ideas, integrate information from oral, visual, quantitative, and media sources, evaluate what they hear, use media and visual displays strategically to help achieve communicative purposes, and adapt speech to context and task. (Common Core State Standards Initiative 2010)

This and similar standards demonstrate the growing importance of teaching communication and conversation skills in school. The next section describes in more detail the advantages of using conversations to teach critical thinking and content, while at the same time building conversation skills.

Advantages of Conversation

Conversations offer a variety of advantages in different dimensions of academic and personal development, as described in the sections that follow. We have coded the advantages into different categories: language and literacy (LL), cognitive (COG), content learning (CON), social and cultural (SC), and psychological (PSY).

Conversation Builds Academic Language (LL)

People, especially children, internalize and develop language when they are immersed in it and when they use it for real purposes. Three processes are vital: listening, talking, and negotiating meaning (Krashen 1985; Swain 1995; Long 1981). Negotiating meaning means using nonverbal and verbal strategies to express, interpret, expand, and refine ideas and their variations in meaning in a conversation (Hernandez 2003). These three processes also apply to academic language, which is the set of words, grammar, and organizational strategies used to describe complex ideas, higher-order thinking processes, and abstract concepts most often encountered in academic and professional settings. Academic language tends to be used in lectures, textbooks, presentations, and workplace meetings.

Conversation fosters all three language learning processes (listening, talking, and negotiating meaning). Conversation allows students to practice the academic language they are absorbing and using from sources such as the teacher, texts, media, and peers. In a whole class, or even in a small group, students can lose focus. But in pairs, because students are engaged with one other person, they are more likely to listen and take in more challenging structures and words to make sense of them. They are also more likely to express their ideas with the more challenging language. Finally, in many conversations there is a healthy amount of repetition of ideas, which offers students a chance to say something again—better and clearer than the first or second time it was said. In a history classroom, for example, two students might have very different understandings of freedom and, as they negotiate its meaning with different partners, they will push themselves to use more precise examples and more advanced language each turn.

Conversation Builds Vocabulary (LL)

Being exposed to new words is important, but using them in authentic discourse is vital for lasting learning. When teachers with whom we worked compared the words used in conversation to those learned just for quizzes, they found that using new words in authentic conversation increased students' long-term learning of them. Through its use in authentic conversation and writing, a word becomes a familiar tool used to build ideas rather than just another term to memorize.. Conversations offer practice in using these meaning "tools" to construct and express a wide variety of ideas (Nystrand 1996).

Bakhtin (1986) argued that we learn words not from dictionaries but from other people; and the words carry with them the accumulated meanings of their previous users. It is vital for students to use new words in slightly new ways, transferring and tweaking and processing word meanings—stretching language to fit new situations. The process of making words fit new ideas makes the words stick in the brain, figuratively speaking. For example, the other day a student in a high school science class asked the teacher how to say "esta evidencia pesa más que la otra" (this evidence weighs more than the other) in the middle of a conversation with a partner.

This advantage should encourage us to create conversation tasks and experiences in which students *need* and want to use new words. See Chapters 4 and 6 for ideas on how to do this.

Conversation Builds Literacy Skills (LL)

Conversation builds oral language, which is a foundation for reading and writing (Roskos, Tabors, and Lenhart 2009). Conversation helps readers develop vocabulary, syntax, background knowledge, and thinking skills that authors of texts expect readers to have. It also helps students practice reading strategies such as predicting, questioning, summarizing, clarifying, connecting, and interpreting (Ketch 2005). For example, a student reading a history textbook can stop and talk to a partner about what she predicts the effects of the war will be, or her connections between war in the nineteenth century and war today. We have also seen conversations help students organize their thoughts, identify evidence in the text to support their opinions, and strengthen vocabulary and syntax needed for academic writing.

The language that happens in each person's head is the main set of tools for constructing meaning from texts and for writing. Conversations are opportunities to practice using such tools. As students talk about ideas from texts, they test their ideas and compare them to peers' ideas about the same text. Some points are confirmed while others are changed or discarded. In conversations, questions and inferences about the text are often explored and answered, and, as a result, comprehension of the text improves. An eighth grader remarked, "I never understood the book, so I never read it. But after talking to my partner about the chapter on atoms and stuff, I understood it finally. I even tried to read the next chapter on my own. But then I had to talk about it, too."

Conversation Builds Oral Language and Communication Skills (LL)

The development of oral language tends not to be emphasized in school. It is even less emphasized after third grade. Teachers have long lists of standards, assessments, and curricula based mostly on knowing, reading, and writing. Oral language is expected to serve other purposes. Yet the abilities to listen, express, and build meaning with others form a cornerstone for learning, one that must continue to be fortified every year, or the ever-expanding high-rise of learning that the foundation supports will fall down. After grade three, many nonmainstream English-speaking students are not immersed at home in language that aligns with the academic language of school. Their oral language growth depends mostly on oral language experiences in school, many of which are not focused on building oral language. Academic conversations intentionally immerse students in the oral building of ideas and the language that is needed to shape and support those ideas.

Many vital communication skills are not automatic in all students. Skills that adults might take for granted can be "hidden" until we make them visible and teach them to children. We realize that communication skills vary widely across cultures and groups. The skills typically valued in many mainstream academic and professional settings might be less often modeled in culturally and linguistically nonmainstream homes. For this reason, we must (a) realize and respect the differences, and (b) make extra efforts to teach the skills that students will need for higher education and work. Such skills include leaning toward your partner when conversing; making eye contact; using gestures and facial expressions to show understanding or puzzlement; and turn taking. These and other skills evolve through practice. All students can benefit from practicing conversation skills and carry these skills forward not only to support their immediate communication skills development but to also assist them in their adult lives.

The following list briefly describes several additional communication skills and values that conversations can foster.

Argumentation Skills. Many students do not see models of appropriate argumentation and persuasion skills at home, on the playground, or on TV. Classroom lessons offer a chance to observe and practice argumentation skills. Students learn how to compare what they are hearing from their partner with what they themselves are thinking and how to formulate their next response. They learn how to respectfully challenge others' ideas and respond to challenges to their own ideas. They practice coming to an agreement (or agreeing to disagree) and synthesizing their ideas.

Group Discussion Skills. Conversations tend to foster more student ownership of group and whole-class discussions. Students learn to talk to each other, not just through the teacher in an initiation-response-evaluation (IRE) format that is common in many lessons.

Listening. Conversation improves students' abilities to listen to academic messages. When they listen to one partner and are expected to respond and co-construct ideas, their listening skills sharpen. They learn to interpret intonations, facial expressions, silences, and other clues in a variety of different people.

Valuing talk and clarity. In conversations, students learn to value the process of talking with another person about deep and serious issues. They learn that talk is a powerful way to connect with others, to value them, and to understand the world. They learn that it is important to strive for clarity and that it takes negotiation of meaning to achieve it.

Conversation Builds Critical Thinking Skills (COG)

Critical thinking skills allow us to understand and overcome the many challenges and problems that we face. We want students to learn new thinking skills and develop existing ones to serve them in more challenging situations. As for those many facts that need to be learned, it is thinking about them and communicating them that helps them to be learned in lasting ways.

Oral interaction is one of the main avenues for developing critical thinking skills (Reznitskaya, Anderson, and Kuo 2007). These are the skills that tend to be used by experts in every discipline to build, shape, and challenge new and valued ideas. As Mercer (1995) describes it, "One of the opportunities school can offer pupils is the chance to involve other people in their thoughts—to use conversations to develop their own thoughts" (4).

There are many different lists of critical and creative thinking skills, including the famous taxonomy of Benjamin Bloom and colleagues (1956). Several skills that we have found to help students engage in academic tasks are recognizing and solving problems, inferring and predicting, gathering relevant information, interpreting themes and motives, evaluating evidence, comparing, seeing multiple perspectives, recognizing bias and ethical issues, applying ideas and skills to novel situations, and analyzing patterns and relationships. These skills and strategies to develop them are described throughout the following chapters.

Conversations tend to be much more complex than we realize. Ybarra et al. explain: "For example, a simple exchange of views between two people requires that they pay attention to each other, maintain in memory the topic of the conversation and respective contributions, adapt to each other's perspective, infer each other's beliefs and desires, assess the situational constraints acting on them at the time, and inhibit irrelevant or inappropriate behavior" (2008, 249). In each academic conversation a student must engage various habits of mind, quickly and in real time, often in response to what a partner says. Unlike writing or passive listening, conversation requires the skill of quickly processing and responding—without being able to push a button to forever delete a weak point or to move text around.

Conversations allow students to closely examine, scrutinize, criticize, validate, and shape the ideas being discussed. Such skills are vital in a democratic society. They allow students to own their ideas. If students are taught only to be consumers of information whose sole purpose in school is to raise their test scores, then they are less likely to be successful in high-level courses and jobs in the future.

Academic conversations develop students' intellectual agility (Brookfield and Preskill 2005). They learn to think in real time, to think on their feet. In conversation, students must be able to quickly process and respond to unanticipated comments, some of which might be very strong counterarguments. In conversations, students must continually compare their ideas to the ideas of others. And when students say their ideas out loud, they are open for critique and for development. This real-time cognitive agility is vital for future success.

Conversation Promotes Different Perspectives and Empathy (COG)

There is great value in getting to know other people's perspectives. This seems obvious, but it is not happening in many classrooms. Test-focused teaching in school and a texting-gaming-watching-TV culture outside of school tend to lower the chances for students to share and learn perspectives at more personal levels. In school, perspectives are often limited to those of the teacher and the textbook. Conversations encourage students to get to know each other and expose them to a range of opinions, ideas, and worldviews. A student can and should learn from every other classmate's opinions, experiences, and ways of thinking. And when students understand each other at deeper levels, many of their conflicts become smaller and fewer.

Talking with others allows their ideas to influence our ideas. All of our important ideas are unfinished. Throughout our entire lives we continue to shape our thoughts and theories through experience, reflection, and interaction with others. Each evolving big idea about life is packed with our biases, purposes, values, and past experiences. We have our own ways of organizing, categorizing, supporting, and using each idea. For example, in third grade you might have learned that animals adapt over time. In the years and decades that followed, you might have transferred the idea of adaptation into other areas, such as literature. Now, you might notice how characters adapt, or how literature adapts to its historical events and language. But your current conversation partner might have a different notion of adaptation. She adds examples from her life to your idea. When conversing about migration in a history class, she mentions how she adapted her personality when her family moved to a different state. She sees adaptation from a personal point of view, one that you haven't considered. Together, however, you expand the meaning of human adaptation. In conversation, partners transfer and expand their understandings of a concept as they explore one another's ideas.

Just telling two students to share their perspectives isn't enough for productive conversation. A partner must be interested, or at least show interest. The partner needs to respect the other person and value perspectives that might seem very different. In other words, I need to care about what you think and I need to believe that it is as valuable as what I think. To do this well, I need to listen. I need to step into your past and present shoes to consider what you feel. I need to empathize. When this happens, I see where your ideas are coming from, and vice versa, and we find common ground to share.

Finally, I can benefit greatly by learning others' views, but conversations (and all of school) should be about more than what *I* can get out of it. Conversations can help to counterbalance the "Look out for number one! Me first!" mentality that prevails in humans. Conversations can provide practice for students in thinking about what the partner needs, wants, values, and feels. In the long run, this is the kind of "skill" needed for solving the many social and political problems that students will face in the future.

Conversation Fosters Creativity (COG)

Creativity is often needed to solve problems or communicate a complex message, yet it has largely been squeezed out of most curricula these days. Creative writing decreases around fourth grade, and art and drama classes have given way to courses that are supposed to foster better test scores. We do not argue the obvious need for teaching and encouraging creativity in schools here, but we do argue that conversations can contribute to creativity in several ways.

First of all, conversations provide help in defining the problem or challenge. A partner's different perspective can also help with the brainstorming stage of the creative process, in which possible solutions are generated. A conversation can also be very helpful in the discernment stage, in which solutions are evaluated and decided. A partner can help another student see the flaws in one idea or the merits in another. For instance, in a sixth-grade science classroom, pairs were conversing about the pitfalls of different ways to prevent earthquake damage. Some ideas were too costly, while others did not take different types of earthquakes into account.

Conversations can even be designed with the stages of creativity in mind: define the issue; do needed research; brainstorm possible solutions—no matter how zany; discern which solution is most likely to work; and test and implement it (or communicate recommendations).

Conversation Fosters Skills for Negotiating Meaning and Focusing on a Topic (COG)

A key skill for learning and expanding one's language is negotiating differing meanings. Negotiating meaning, explained in more detail in Chapter 5, happens when two or more people adapt their differing ideas of a topic to come to a more shared understanding. Negotiation gets us on the same page, or at least on a page in between the two extremes. In classroom conversations, two important negotiation strategies that students develop are comprehension checking and paraphrasing. Comprehension checks are little phrases and words in our messages, such as *Right? Got it? Is that clear?* and *Understand?* These openings in the conversation allow a listener to question meanings of terms and concepts during the message. A listener can then paraphrase to confirm comprehension, using phrases like these: *So what you mean is . . . , In other words . . . , I think I get it. It's when . . . ,* and *Are you saying that . . . ?*

Staying focused seems to be getting more difficult by the day, given the myriad messages that are competing for students' attention, such as text messages, Web pages, e-mails, movies, advertisements, and so on. Textbooks and classroom activities seem to get less and less interesting and more challenging because they require extended focus. Conversations can help students build their focusing stamina. In addition to teacher modeling and guidance, students can use graphic organizers, students in the role of observers, and self-monitoring to maintain focus on a topic. For example, conversations helped one fourth-grade student who said, "Before doing this conversation stuff, I would listen to a partner and be thinking about lunch."

Conversation Builds Content Understandings (CON)

Students can learn and reinforce core content concepts from both talking and listening in conversations. The act of verbally sculpting and struggling with a big idea helps it stick in the mind. Over time, as students sculpt ideas with their evolving skills with academic language and growing vocabularies, their content understanding increases. But they need many chances to practice and many exposures to different students at different language proficiency levels. As Mercer writes, "Information can be accumulated, but knowledge and understanding are only generated by working with information, selecting from it, organizing it, arguing for its relevance" (1995, 67).

Conversation helps students to refine and enrich their knowledge (Alvermann, Dillon, and O'Brien 1987). Hearing another's ideas or perspective on an issue challenges each student to take a closer look at his or her own ideas and perspectives. When two or more people converse, their ideas mix and interact to create new knowledge. Talkers walk away from the conversation with much more than they could have thought up on their own. Like flowers that rely on bees to pollinate them, we need the ideas of others for our minds to thrive. Calkins writes that "talk, like reading and writing, is a major motor—I could even say *the* major motor—of intellectual development" (2000, 226). The more students expend mental energy to clarify and verbalize their emerging ideas, the more language and thinking they use in the process. They are doing more than regurgitating information or selecting answers for points. They are taking ownership of ideas. They are using additional parts of the brain to sculpt and resculpt the ideas for and with a real audience. These processes foster learning that endures.

In conversations, students often become teachers of one another. A student will teach a partner what he or she is thinking. The process of teaching, as teachers know, forces a person to focus, to dedicate lots of mental energy to the concept, to understand it on multiple levels, to clarify it, and to learn it through and through. A ninth-grade math student told us, "I didn't know how to solve equations well enough to teach it, but then when we worked together to come up with a mini-lesson, we got good at it. I think the teacher should have paid us."

Conversation Cultivates Connections (CON)

Much of what we are teaching our students in school and how we are teaching it, especially to our linguistically diverse students, is too disconnected. Because of intense pressures to raise test scores, many schools inundate students with isolated practice activities and imitation test items on a myriad of facts and grammar rules. However, learning needs to be meaningful, coherent, deep, and connected.

Conversations help students connect thoughts to build ideas that are much bigger and more relevant than snippets of knowledge needed for most tests. In the metaphorical story about two stonecutters who are asked what they are doing, one answers, "I am cutting this stone into a perfectly square block," and the other answers, "I am building a cathedral." The second worker uses each day to build something significant. We argue that we should want students to take both perspectives and then add a third: to be the designers of the cathedral. Students can and should be part of real content-area issues and solution building. This can happen as schools design more assessments and curricula that encourage creativity and connections to the world.

Although we might think that conversations last just a few minutes, they often last weeks, months, or even years. A single conversation is often a short slice that forms part of a "long conversation" that builds on previous meanings (Mercer 1995). This may seem a bit abstract, but most teachers have learned much from these long-lasting conversations in which ideas have built up over time. Our teaching and curricula need to keep long conversations in mind. If we don't, the winds of a busy life easily scatter the many standards being learned by students.

Conversation Helps Students to Co-construct Understandings (CON)

Understanding comes from working with ideas, not just regurgitating facts and answers. Conversations allow students to work with new facts and words to build their own theories, opinions, and mental models. Ideas last longer when they are products of shared mental labor. When students shape knowledge, they are more likely to own it. If you paint a picture, for example, you remember the details and its meaning much better than if you were told to memorize the scene from someone else's painting. When construction workers build a house, they learn to use the tools very skillfully and in a variety of settings. Similarly, students learn from working with knowledge to construct ideas. The ideas come to life, reminding us of Alfred North Whitehead's comment, "We must beware of inert ideas, i.e., ideas that are merely received into the mind without being utilized or tested, or thrown into fresh combinations . . . Education with inert ideas is not only useless: it is above all things, harmful" (1929, 38).

Conversations allow for the building of a rich foundation of communal backgrounds and shared experiences. In individualized learning, each student has only his or her own background to build from. But with lots of conversation, a classroom has a wide range of experiences and connections upon which to build new learning.

Conversation Helps Teachers and Students Assess Learning (CON)

Conversations allow students to show what they know and can do. Through conversations, students can see what they have learned and still need to learn. Teachers can observe students working in pairs or have conversations with students to see what they have learned or need to learn. For example, a seventh-grade language arts teacher, upon observing students converse about themes in *The Giver* (Lowry 2006), realized that students were missing several key themes and evidence from the book. She also noticed that they were strong in building on each other's ideas, but weak in synthesizing points at the end. (See Chapter 10 for more ideas on assessing with conversations.)

Conversation Builds Relationships (SC)

When students are provided the opportunity to converse with other students with whom they might not normally interact socially, walls come down and new relationships can be forged. Students begin to find their commonalities while at the same time they learn to appreciate their different perspectives. The experience of getting to know another student's thoughts and views can provide an entry point into new friendships and a way to clear away obstacles to a positive relationship.

A powerful relational aspect of conversation is caring. When someone takes the time to listen to us, use our ideas, say things like, "Great idea," "I like that," "Tell me more," and so on, we feel good. This is advantageous in two ways: (1) conversation gives practice in caring about another person's ideas and thoughts—an immensely vital yet untested skill in life; and (2) when a partner cares, it makes the recipient feel valued and cared for.

Almasi et al. (2004), studying 412 K–3 students, found that the peer discussion treatment group developed fewer socially isolated students and fewer social stars. We also found this leveling of social status in our own research with fourth and eighth graders (Zwiers and Crawford 2009). Several fourth-grade students mentioned to us that they became friends with other students after just a few paired conversations. Some students said that they had had few friends before the conversation work started, even after years of being in the same classes. One student said, "I made friends with kids I never thought I would even talk to, or want to talk to."

Conversation Builds Academic Ambience (SC)

It is a wonderful experience to hear students excitedly discussing the content of their core curriculum and making connections to their own lives and experiences. Once students are encouraged to converse about the content of their lessons, their entire school experience becomes more connected and integrated, including their social interactions on the playground and those in the classroom. When students are encouraged to make and discuss connections, they begin to do this naturally, and school becomes a place of continual learning, not simply segmented time devoted to individual subject areas. One student even said, "I think about things a lot more when I know I am gonna talk about it with another student."

Conversation Makes Lessons More Culturally Relevant (SC)

Culture has a powerful influence on shaping language, learning, and thinking in society. Many diverse students come from backgrounds in which they learn through lots of interaction. As Mercer and Littleton state, "A sociocultural perspective raises the possibility that educational success and failure may be explained by the quality of the educational dialogue, rather than simply by considering the capability of individual students or the skill of their teachers" (2007, 4). We agree, but such thinking contradicts many current "direct instruction" and test-score-raising practices. A cultural lens encourages us all to place a much higher priority on understanding how students think, learn, and communicate in order to develop academic skills and content. It forces us to think about the whole person and about how to strategically teach for students' long-term academic, social, and emotional gains.

A key cultural issue that arises is the variety of conversations that can and should happen. Each culture, community, and home might use conversations in different ways. One person's idea of a conversation, academic or otherwise, might differ significantly from that of another person. Diverse students might hear a wide range of academic conversations in their homes that take different paths and use different moves than what are expected at school. As Shirley Brice Heath, in her seminal study of language learning in homes and schools of differing communities, found, "There is a deep continuity between patterns of socialization and language learning in the home culture and what goes on at school" (1983, 56). When these continuities don't exist, students often struggle. For example, at home a child might not hear extensive use of examples to support ideas but at school might be expected to use examples to support ideas.

Conversation Fosters Equity (SC)

Equity means providing underserved students extra experiences, resources, knowledge, skills, and language so they may gain equal access to future educational and professional opportunities. It means acceleration. Many diverse students come from homes and communities with language and communication styles that are very different from those of mainstream schools. Mainstream students might have thousands more stories read to them and many more conversations about the stories. These conversations will tend to use more school-like terms and features. Conversations in school can increase students' exposure to the language and thinking of texts.

Language, whether used by a pair of students in the classroom or at international peace summits, is a powerful tool. People use language to influence others, establish dominance, and defend their beliefs and rights. We want our students to have and use the tools of language to even the playing fields—to share their ideas, defend their opinions, and change the many unjust cycles that are perpetuated by current policies and practices. If we neglect to cultivate students' language skills, positive change will not happen. Cummins explains, "For example, it has been argued by many theorists that the vision of our future society implied by the dominant transmission models of pedagogy is a society of compliant consumers who passively accept rather than critically analyze the forces that impinge on their lives" (1994, 47). It seems that many current teaching approaches, especially in classrooms with high percentages of diverse students, promote dependence on authority, passive involvement, and short-term learning. Academic conversations can counteract these effects by empowering students to be more independent in voicing and shaping ideas.

Conversation Develops Inner Dialogue and Self-Talk (PSY)

Some of the most important "conversations" that we can have don't involve other people. We often have conversations with ourselves. We talk to ourselves silently about a wide range of mundane and deep topics. Classroom interactions can have a positive influence on our students' inner conversations over time. Just as it is important to say thoughts out loud and to organize them into logical sentences, it is important to get students into the habit of coherent thinking. This means that we must engage students enough so that they walk away conversing with themselves. Just as what we hear from others shapes us, the many things that we say to ourselves sculpt us over time.

As Routman points out, "All learning involves conversation. The ongoing dialogue, internal and external, that occurs as we read write, listen, compose, observe, refine, interpret, and analyze is how we learn" (2000, xxxvi). The external dialogue (conversation with others) cultivates the internal dialogue (thinking).

Conversations with others shape "inside-your-head" conversations. Vygostky (1986) highlighted the importance of inner speech and the fact that children have powerful inner dialogues. If you spend much time learning a new language in another country, you notice that after a while the new language starts popping up in your head at odd times. It is being absorbed, and the brain begins to use the language to make sense of all that is happening. This is less obvious with our first language, but this still happens. Our brains grab on to the language around us and use it to make sense of the day's thoughts and feelings. We dialogue with ourselves as language forms a stream of thoughts all day and even at night. You are likely having a dialogue with yourself about this text right now. You might be asking questions, or even having an inner dialogue on whether you hold inner dialogues or not.

Knowing this, we can be strategic about the language and ideas that shape students' minds. We can provide learning experiences that students mull over well after class. We can improve students' inner dialogues in order to cultivate their thinking skills and conceptual understandings. We can provide them with and immerse them in academic language that they can use for their inner dialogues. Two powerful ways to build these inner dialogue abilities and self-talk are listening to conversations and holding conversations. The back-and-forth negotiation of meaning in conversations provides loads of rich language in which students can be immersed and engaged.

School experiences, classroom conversations, and teacher language have a profound impact on the thinking of students. Students often begin to hear the teacher's voice inside their heads. Recently, during a conversation with a teacher about this topic, a student walked in and the teacher asked her, "When you read, do you ever hear my words in your head?" She replied, "Oh yeah, big time. When I stop reading I start asking questions like you do. You know, why did the author write this, and how this connects to my life. It's creepy, but I think it helps." Over the years, we want students to develop helpful inner conversations and thinking habits of generating multiple ideas, questioning them, and evaluating them. And we have to be ever-reflective and watchful of what we say.

Conversation Fosters Engagement and Motivation (PSY)

Many students like to gossip and chitchat; they like to be social and engage with others. Even though it is a bit more work to have an academic conversation, much of the social motivation is already there. One day we asked three sixth-grade girls who were very engaged in conversation what they were talking about. They said, "The book we were talking about in class." We thought they were kidding. "Really, we were debating if we thought it was right for him to stay in the house or leave." We asked, "Wow, why are you still talking about it?" One girl said, "We didn't have enough time in class to finish, and this type of talking is fun, almost as much as gossip." Getting them to practice academic talking and thinking outside of class like this excites teachers and accelerates learning. Such talk shows students that conversations can be valuable in life. Through conversation, students see that it is interesting to learn from others, wrestle with ideas together, change minds (of others and their own), and build and apply ideas to their lives. Such interactions can intrinsically motivate students to learn (Taylor et al. 2003). Students become energized by thinking together with others.

Students often prefer to talk in pairs and small groups where it is safer to make mistakes and where they can talk more. In pairs, students are even more motivated to listen because they need to show their understanding in order to respond; they do not want to offend the partner by not listening.

Finally, conversations are often unpredictable. Unpredictability, as in stories and movies, makes conversations more interesting. We don't know what our partner is going to say, and vice versa, and we look forward to some surprises as we talk.

Conversation Builds Confidence and Academic Identity (PSY)

Being listened to and having our thoughts valued is important at all ages. Moreover, the skill of valuing other people's thoughts is highly beneficial in life. Too many adults do not value the ideas of others, and many do not know how to express how they value others' ideas. We can train students to value others' ideas and to respond by saying things like this:

Great idea! Let's write it down.
Wow, I hadn't thought of that. That makes sense.
Brilliant. Tell us more.
Juan had a great insight about how . . .

Conversation Fosters Choice, Ownership, and Control over Thinking (PSY)

Academic conversations allow students to connect to and choose ideas from their own backgrounds and experiences. Such conversations give value to students' diverse background experiences and cultures. As students build ideas from their own life experiences, they become lifelong learners who, when they face new situations, compare, assimilate, and accommodate the new with what they already know.

In building their conversation skills, students build their potential for extending talk with more capable peers and adults. Their confidence as communicators and thinkers increases. For example, in our work, students expressed that they felt more confident to talk and initiate rich conversations with older students and adults (Zwiers and Crawford 2009). This confidence is a key factor in fueling engagement in future academic interactions.

Barron and Darling-Hammond (2008) argue that we should give students authority to identify and address significant problems and challenges in a discipline. This means trusting students to collaboratively wrestle with ideas and go much deeper than memorizing standards or facts for tests. In fact, we have seen some teachers encourage their students to make a real difference in a field of study—to be change agents and shapers of the discipline rather than just consumers and assembly-line workers. Can a fourth grader shape current historical thought about the influence of the American Civil War? When the teacher's answer to this question is *yes*, great things will happen in that classroom.

Conversation Builds Academic Identity (PSY)

Identity formation is a large yet less visible part of schooling. In our research, students who conversed more and more over time gradually assumed what can best be described as academic identities. In fact, many students reported feeling smarter and more capable in their ability to talk about what they were learning (Zwiers and Crawford 2009). This formation of academic identity has a tremendous benefit for students' confidence in school, abilities to express their thinking in writing, and willingness to contribute their ideas to class discussions.

Conversation Fosters Self-Discovery (PSY)

Conversation can help students to uncover and clarify their opinions, interests, perspectives, and even their talents. As we talk with others, we more clearly see what we think about the topic. We understand our own point of view, how well it is supported or not, and how important the topic is to us. A comment from a partner on a new insight might spark an interest in us that wasn't there before. One student commented, "I didn't know I was interested in history until I started talking about it. Just memorizing it is boring." Moreover, when a partner encourages us and expresses interest in our ideas, we can discover talents in a discipline that we didn't know we had. As many famous people have remarked, "One conversation changed my life." How many genius-level talents are never discovered by our students as they sit silently in classrooms around the world?

Conversation Builds Student Voice and Empowerment (PSY)

Conversation topics often stem from issues that are generated by the students as they engage in dialogue. Paolo Freire (1970) calls these issues "generative themes." Freire states, "Students, as they are increasingly posed with problems relating to themselves in the world and with the world, will feel increasingly challenged and obliged to respond to that challenge . . . Their response to the challenge evokes new challenges, followed by new understandings; and gradually the students come to regard themselves as committed" (62). Students' generative themes, ideas, connections, questions, and conversations can then form a foundation for larger projects and classroom activities, such as debates, persuasive letters to government officials, participation in community meetings, and so on. When ideas come from students, they own their learning, hear their own voices, and build up their roles in a democratic society.

Paired Conversations Are Powerful

Finally, in this book we emphasize paired conversations for several reasons. First, pairs allow half of the students in a class to talk at any one time. Class time is precious; students get much more practice talking and listening when face-to-face in pairs. Second, pair work forces a partner to focus on and listen to what the other is saying. We all know people, perhaps even ourselves, who don't always listen closely if we are in a group where we can rely on others to do the real listening. Third, most students are afraid to share in whole-class settings and will share as little as possible. Fourth, pairs can teach each other, creating a community of acceleration and independence.

After watching many hours of video of teachers and students interacting, often in whole-class discussions, we noticed that many of the great prompts that teachers said could have been said by students. We can prepare students to be continual teachers of one another, prompting each other to think. This is advantageous because we know the power of one-on-one teaching, and if we equip students with these teacher-like skills, we can accelerate the overall learning in the class. Finally, students need to learn how to engage in extended face-to-face conversations in life. Most of their conversations will be with one other person.

Reflections

1. Have a conversation about the same topic with three different people. Compare the ideas that emerge. Compare the skills and moves that deepened and moved the conversation along. Evaluate what you learned.
2. Have conversations about three different topics with the same person at different times. Reflect on the differences and similarities.
3. Pick a content area and write down and discuss the top five facts, top five concepts, top three skills, and top three qualities that you want your students to know and have in that content area by the end of the year. How do you assess these things? How can you emphasize them enough during the year for student success?

Chapter 2
Getting Started with Academic Conversations

> It was weird. When we finished talking, we had a totally new idea.

—Sixth-grade student

Teachers are often concerned with how to get all of this conversation work started. This can be more challenging than it should be, mainly because many teachers and students have become accustomed to certain ways of "doing school" that are contrary to conversational (i.e., louder and deeper) approaches. For this reason, we work extra hard in this chapter to help teachers break some molds and begin teaching effective conversation skills.

You can prepare by holding several casual conversations with students about what they are reading and learning. Get to know how students think and how they talk about their thinking. Get a rough idea of how well and how often your students use the core skills described in this chapter. You might even record several pairs of students as a preassessment to inform your lesson planning and to have something to compare to at the end of the year.

You can also read other resources on classroom conversation and discussion by authors such as Dixie Lee Spiegel (2005), Maria Nichols (2006), Courtney Cazden (2001), and Neil Mercer (1995) to reinforce the importance of conversations and how they should be used in class.

Structured Interaction Practice Activities

There are many activities that can help students interact in structured ways and prepare them for more independent conversation work. Structured interaction activities are not quite conversations and allow students to work on communication skills with extra supports in place. The supports might include providing the content to be discussed, talking to different partners, or physically moving to show one's stance on an issue.

Stand and Converse

Make numbered cards for the number of students in your class. Have students count off (numbers 1 through 26, for example). Pull six different cards and have students with those numbers stand up. Model and explain two conversation starters that students can ask each other to keep their conversation going (e.g., "Can you elaborate on . . . ?"). Ask an initial question or prompt to get the conversation going (e.g., What was a theme that emerged in this story? How can statistics lie? How do you know something is living?). The lowest numbered student of the six selected begins talking and then sits down. The student with the next highest number prompts for elaboration from the first student, adds an idea, and then sits down as well. The student with the third highest number continues the routine, and so on until each of the six students has taken a turn. The rest of the class can then add to the discussion.

A variation is to have the six students form a circle and pass a ball of string, holding on to the end, each time a person talks. By passing the string back and forth as they take turns talking, they make a web.

Take a Side

Students pick a side of an issue, get up, and stand on different sides of the room (adapted from Wilhelm 2002) depending on their choice. For example, one side of the room can represent a pro opinion and the other side a con opinion. Some students might want to stand toward the middle of the room as if on a continuum line, but they should have solid reasons to be there (e.g., they have evidence for both perspectives). They need to pick a side off the center point and be able to justify that side over the other. Students then tell students near them why they chose to stand where they are (e.g., "Even though it is true that . . . , I chose this side because . . .").

Have students move to the opposite side and argue for that side with peers. Finally, have students share what the person next to them shared. Examples of prompts include *Are you in favor of genetic engineering? Is honesty always the best policy?* or *Should the U.S. president have one six-year term?* You can also weave into prompts academic language terms such as *long-term effects, negative influence, short-term advantages, evidence, risks, drawbacks, outweighs,* and *ramifications.* Explain the terms as you clarify the prompts, and encourage students to use these highlighted terms as they talk.

Conversation Lines and Circles

Conversation lines and circles allow students to practice new language patterns with different partners and get needed repetition of grammar and vocabulary. Students get to improve their responses when they talk to different partners about the same prompt. Before starting, create or brainstorm with students several interesting (perhaps controversial) prompts, such as *Why is there war? How are bacteria different from viruses? What is a black hole? Why was this character important in the story?* and *What would life be like without algebra or geometry?*

In the line version, students line up facing one another (two or four separate facing lines), and, after discussing their responses, one line moves to change partners. The end student of the moving line who is not paired walks to the other end of the same line to face a new partner from the opposite line. For the circle version, students stand up and make two circles with equal numbers in each, one inside the other, with the students in the inner circle facing the students in the outer circle. Give the prompt and have students discuss their responses with the partner facing them. They can take notes, if needed. After a short time, tell the inner circle to move two people to the right and talk with a new partner. You can give the same prompt or a new one. Encourage students to use academic language from the walls of the classroom and from their notes. At the end, students can synthesize as a whole class the information discussed.

The First Days

The integration of academic conversation into your teaching should start in the beginning of the year. Many of the skills take a year to build, as do the relationships that support rich conversations. Here are some suggestions for the first days.

Discuss the Purpose of Conversation Skills

Students need to know what is expected of them, especially with a new set of skills that can't be constantly monitored by the teacher or graded late at night. Ask students about their conversations with friends, parents, and teachers. Ask those who like to talk why they like to talk, and ask those who don't like to talk why they don't like to talk. Brainstorm how talking might help them learn. Some of the advantages discussed in Chapter 1 should come up.

Emphasize to students that in peer conversations they are able to take more ownership of ideas and learning. Inform them that you will be trusting them to work hard to stay focused when they talk. Sometimes you will monitor them, sometimes not, and still other times you might ask for written responses to their conversations. Remind them that gossip and chitchat do not help them learn.

Go Over What Conversation Is and Is Not

You can make an anchor chart or checklist of what conversations are and aren't. Many conversation behaviors and skills are described later in this chapter. Students (and adults) often think of conversation as an argument to win. Their zeal to argue often prevents them from going deeper and from learning. They need to realize that conversation is the process of bringing your ideas to the table, sharing them, and shaping them as you listen to the ideas of another person. All partners should walk away with new ideas. Rather than winning, the goal is learning. Even if it is a persuasive (two-sided) conversation, the overarching goal should be learning through healthy debate.

Model Bad Conversation Behaviors in a Drama or Fishbowl Setting

You can make a video or have students from a different class come in and model certain behaviors that stop or ruin a conversation. For example, you might dramatize these behaviors: go off on a wild tangent about your uncle; lean way in and start gossiping; criticize a partner's idea; answer with one word and do not clarify; look around a lot; lean back and look bored; check your phone; nod your head but do not paraphrase; share your own unrelated idea instead of building off a partner's idea; give a bad example; and so on. In later mini-lessons, of course, you will model the good conversation skills described in the next section.

Emphasize the Ongoing Habit of Sticking to the Destination, the Purpose, the Main Topic

Academic conversations are opportunities to take a verbal journey with others. And journeys have destinations. It is very tempting to veer off the path. It takes much less mental work to jump around to different topics. This happens to all of us, but the trick is to get back on the path quickly. The skills and behaviors described in this chapter will help students stay on (and return to) the path. Hopefully, each year of school they will become more and more independent in their use of these skills so that the skills become lifelong conversation habits.

Establish Shared Conversation Norms

You likely have created and used posters of norms before. Such posters help students as they talk, but students also need to have others (peers and teacher) observe and provide feedback, and they need to self-assess right after they converse. Remember to develop a norms poster over time and with the help of students. Just slapping a finished poster up on the wall achieves little. Here are a few example norms that you and your students might generate for your poster.

» We listen to each other.
» We share our own ideas and explain them.
» We respect one another's ideas, even if they are different.

» We respectfully disagree and try to see the other view.
» We let others finish explaining their ideas without interrupting.
» We try to come to some agreement in the end.
» We take turns and share air time.

Some teachers use little chants to remind students of key norms for holding effective conversations (some with hand motions), such as "Focus! Listen! Link, build, dig!" or "Value, Respect, Support, Connect!"

From the posters and chants you can create self-assessment checklists for use after conversations. See Chapter 10 for more details on self-assessment.

Five Core Skills of Academic Conversation

In our research and work with teachers we identified five core skills that make conversations more academic:

1. Elaborate and clarify
2. Support ideas with examples
3. Build on and/or challenge a partner's idea
4. Paraphrase
5. Synthesize conversation points

These five core skills, also called conversation moves, overlap considerably, and some are used more in certain types of conversation than in others. When conversing about academic topics, these skills usually don't come naturally: students tend to not elaborate, not support their ideas, not build and focus on one idea, not paraphrase along the way, and not synthesize at the end. And because these skills don't come naturally, we need to—and get to—work on them in school.

Figure 2.1 provides ideas for teaching the core conversation skills emphasized throughout this book. (The appendix contains another version of this graphic called the Academic Conversation Placemat. See Chapter 4 for more on using the placemat.) The symbols and associated hand motions reinforce each skill for all learners, especially those who like to make visual and kinesthetic connections. Some teachers, in warm-up activities, point to a symbol and have students quickly do the hand motions and practice a sentence frame or two on a current topic of the lesson. The frames eventually become automatic: when students hear them and practice them enough in various mini-lessons and activities, they will use them more and more naturally.

Figure 2.1 Core Academic Conversation Skills, with Symbols, Hand Motions, Prompt Frames, and Response Frames

Conversation Skills (with symbols and hand motions)	Frames for Prompting the Skill	Frames for Responding
Elaborate and Clarify *(Pull hands apart)*	Can you elaborate on . . .? What do you mean by . . .? Can you tell me more about . . .? What makes you think that? Can you clarify the part about . . .? Can you be more specific? How so? How/Why is that important? I'd love to hear more about . . . How does that connect to . . .? I wonder if . . . How so? Can you unpack that for me? I am a little confused about the part . . .	I think it means that . . . In other words, . . . I believe that . . . An analogy for this might be . . . It is important because . . . It's similar to when . . .
Support Ideas with Examples (from this text, other texts, the world, and life) *(Point thumb and three fingers up and place palm of other hand on top like a table; or point one index finger to the tip of the pinky of the other hand)*	Can you give an example from the text? Can you show me where it says that? What are examples from other texts? What is a real-world example? What is an example from your life? Are there any cases of that? What is the evidence for that . . .? Like what? Why do you say that? How do you justify that? What does that look like? Such as? What would illustrate that? Why is that a good example?	For example, . . . In the text it said that . . . One case showed that . . . An example from my life is . . . For instance, . . . According to . . . An illustration of this could be . . . On one occasion . . . In this situation . . . To demonstrate, . . . In fact, . . . Indeed, ... such as . . . Have you ever . . . ?

Build On and/or Challenge a Partner's Idea	What do you think about the idea that . . .?	I would add that . . .
 (Layer hands on each other and build up)	Can you add to this idea? Do you agree? What might be other points of view? What are other ideas? How does that connect to the idea . . . ? I am not sure if this is relevant, but . . . How can we bring this back to the question of . . . ?	I want to expand on your point about . . . I want to follow up on your idea . . . (To challenge) Then again, I think that . . . Another way to look at this could be . . . Yet I wonder also if . . . If_____, then _____ What struck me about what you said is . . .
Paraphrase *(Move both palms toward each other)*	I'm not sure that was clear . . . I can't remember all that I said. How can we relate what I said to the topic/question? What do we know so far? What is your take on what I said? I don't know. Did that make sense? What are you hearing?	So, you are saying that . . . Let me see if I understand you . . . Am I right in hearing you say that . . . ? In a nutshell, you are arguing that . . . In other words . . . What I am hearing is . . . Essentially, you think that . . . It sounds like you are saying that . . .
Synthesize Conversation Points *(Start both arms out wide and then cup them into a ball)*	What have we discussed so far? How should we synthesize what we talked about? How can we bring this all together? What can we agree upon? What main points can we share? What was our original question? What key idea can we take away?	We can say that . . . The main theme/point seems to be . . . As a result of this conversation, we think that we should . . . How does this sound . . . ? What if we . . . ? The evidence seems to suggest that . . .

Three important principles frame the five conversation skills:

1. Each skill is actually a double skill: (a) appropriately prompting the partner to use the skill *and* (b) effectively responding to a partner's prompting.
2. Each skill requires good listening. Good listening means working hard to understand what the other is saying, keeping track of ideas, being aware of the whole conversation, being aware of what is not said, and interpreting a speaker's tone and body language.
3. The overarching purpose of all the skills is to focus on, deepen, explore, negotiate, and co-construct ideas vital for content learning. Each conversation should have a destination and make progress toward it. Each conversation should apply core thinking skills and key principles of the discipline.

Skill 1: Elaborate and Clarify

Elaborating provides more important information about a topic or idea. The elaborator should be aware of the amount and detail of the information that needs to be shared to make the point clear. Likewise, a listener should know when more information is needed. This often happens when a speaker introduces a general, complex, muddy, or abstract topic without much detail. For example, when a speaker says, "She was a very important person in that time period," most adults would ask for elaboration or explanation, or would ask why and how. For younger students, prompting for elaboration often simply means saying, "Tell me more about . . . ," which is fine because students thereby show that they want to hear more. Two things then happen: the listener shifts the focus from his or her own thoughts to show interest in what the partner has to say, and the listener gets to hear more language.

It is important to teach students to say, "Can you elaborate on . . ." rather than just, "Can you elaborate?" because this forces the asker to pick out a certain part of what the speaker is saying and give it a name. For example, asking "Can you elaborate on your reasons why you think he altered the documents?" demonstrates that the asker has been listening and wants to move the conversation deeper. Moreover, when an asker is not specific and instead says, "Can you elaborate on that?" you can teach the speaker to respond, "Elaborate on what?" This forces the asker to be more specific and process what he or she is listening to.

Elaborating with Analogies

One type of advanced elaboration and clarification is an analogous illustration from a different area. A recent example was a group of boys who used the analogy of playing soccer to describe a theme from a non-sport-related story. They all could relate to the feeling of having missed an easy goal, which illustrated the theme of working hard in spite of failures. No student named a particular incident, but used the helpful phrase, "It's like when . . ." for general cases: "It's like when

I was in fifth grade and . . ." In a way, using analogy is another level of connection; a more figurative and theoretical level. It is extremely common in academic speeches and texts in later grades.

Questioning to Clarify and Probe

Students need to ask good questions to get conversations going and to keep them going. In fact, one of the highly ranked skills wanted by employers is asking good questions. A good question sparks conversation, brings up issues that have not yet been addressed, looks at different perspectives, and addresses big-picture and long-run issues. Questioning also shows others that you genuinely care about what they think and say.

Train students to ask the right questions at the right time and to facilitate as teachers might do. A well-placed question at a certain time can focus and extend the conversation.

I wonder, how . . . ? (or, why . . . ?)
That's true, but how . . . ?
And how can we connect that to . . . ?
What do you think about . . . ?
Why do you think that is?

Elaborating and Clarifying with Examples

Often, when asked to elaborate, a person uses examples. Examples are concrete instances or members of a category. Examples are a natural way to explain or illustrate general, complex, or abstract concepts. These concepts and their examples are commonly accepted (i.e., generally not up for debate). For example, a student might mention independent variables, and when her partner asks her for an example, she clarifies by giving examples of independent variables from a recent lab on plant growth (e.g., amount of sunlight, amount of water, etc.). Other concepts that can be illustrated with examples include exothermic reactions, omnivores, democratic principles, alliteration, transitions, anthropomorphism, and technology.

If the concept's examples are not commonly accepted and are up for debate, then partners need to use the next skill, supporting an idea with examples.

Skill 2: Support Ideas with Examples

A student must learn to use examples to strengthen a debatable idea or argument. Examples are often used as *evidence*, the broad term used for any specific information that logically supports a hypothesis or perspective. For instance, if one student starts and says that human greed has defined the borders of many nations, his or her partner could ask for examples as evidence in support of the idea. Most of the evidence used to support ideas in academic conversations is in the form of examples.

Students should learn to use four main types of examples. The order is important here, because many students tend to jump straight to examples from their own lives and run out of time to talk about examples from texts or the world, which tend to be more powerful and challenging. Encourage students to think of examples in the order listed, at least initially.

1. Examples from the text
2. Examples from other texts
3. Examples from the world
4. Examples from one's own life

Use Examples from the Text

In schools where there aren't plenty of students who are models of proficient mainstream English, the text can serve as a model of academic language, especially if you build "going back into the text" as a habit each day, each year. Students often discuss a text that they have just read or are reading. When they prompt each other for examples to support ideas, the first place to look should be the text. This is important, because students tend to want to connect to their lives. Connecting to their lives is fine later on, but students seldom get back into the text if they launch into their own life examples first. Students should start with the text, and you can scaffold their use of text examples with sentence starters such as *Based on what the character said here, . . .* , *In the text, let's see, the exact wording was . . .* , *This means that . . .* , or *Remember the part where . . .*

A common challenge for students is finding the best quotations from the text to logically support their ideas. In a strategy that we call "quotation negotiation," you post several themes, opinions, or main ideas around the classroom and read them out loud to students. Each student receives a slip of paper (or two) with a quotation from the text. Students then pair up and converse with five different people to decide and justify under which theme their quotation should go. They need to argue for the best place for the quotation.

Use Examples from Other Texts

Students should learn to prompt for and provide examples from other texts read in and out of school, as well as "texts" such as TV shows, movies, Web pages, and artwork. Students can then evaluate the value of the examples as they converse. For example, we observed one student who used a photo he had seen the week before in history class as an example of the struggle described in the narrative he and his partner read in language arts class.

Use Examples from the World

Much of what teachers strive for in school is for students to connect ideas learned in school to the world outside, to how things work and how people behave. As you use and encourage the use of examples from the world, you train students to be continually observing and "reading the world" (Freire and Macedo 1987, 35) to synthesize, making links that can serve them throughout life.

For example, a student referred to a recent attack by a mountain lion as an example of the clash between people and nature in science class.

Use Examples from One's Own Life

The most natural form of example that pops up in conversations is from one's own life. It is usually easier and more interesting (at least for the talker) to use examples from one's own life than to find supporting examples from the text or world. Students knowingly or unknowingly prefer to fill talking time with summaries and personal examples. This is natural, and it can be very helpful for understanding and remembering the topic, but life examples should always stay connected to the topic and the text in some way.

Young students, in particular, can lose focus quickly when they share their life examples. Train them to take a few seconds (and give them a few seconds) to think about whether the example will help deepen the conversation or take it too far away from the text. Will it be too entertaining, distracting, or tempting for other students to make similar comments? When you lead discussions, model for students how to set aside unhelpful examples. If an idea has lots of potential, but doesn't fit in right then, teach students to write it down and bring it up later. This process of evaluating the usefulness of examples and other ideas that pop into our heads—and parking them for later—is a key skill that many people never develop.

Support an Idea with Reasons

Often, people support an idea with reasons, which are less abstract than the main argument but not as specific as examples. However, reasons usually need examples to support them as well. For instance, if a student argues against nuclear power, he or she might give reasons such as high risk of contamination, viability of other forms of energy, and high costs of waste disposal. These reasons should then be supported with specific examples and statistics.

In order to help students build their abilities to produce and evaluate solid reasons, it is helpful to have a class discussion on bias, correlation versus causation, sample size, comparing apples and oranges (e.g., lives vs. money), and basic logic (e.g., If A is a member of group B and all Bs are hungry, then A is hungry). These are common elements of reasoning that students must grasp to think critically about how well an idea is supported by a reason posed by a partner.

Explain the Strength of an Example

An important skill associated with the use of examples is explaining why the examples are used and how influential they are. Students need to evaluate and often argue the strength or "weight" of the example's support of an argument or hypothesis. You must therefore model and scaffold for students how to think along abstract continua and even how to visualize examples as weights on a balance scale. This helps students see that certain types of examples have more evidential weight than others, according to common societal and professional scales. For instance, a student might have several weak examples for his position on global warming, and his partner should question their value and prompt him to explain their value in conversation. He might then explain how strong the correlation is between temperatures and the increases in use of fossil fuels.

As students engage with one another and negotiate the weights of examples, their minds become sharper and stronger.

Skill 3: Build On and/or Challenge a Partner's Idea

You might have noticed that students often just "popcorn" out ideas without connecting to the ideas of other students. Students need to learn to build on a partner's idea and/or appropriately challenge it.

The *co-* in collaborate, cooperate, and co-construct means *together*. This means building up ideas, which is why we used the brick house as a symbol in Figure 2.2. In a conversation, your next idea should build on, connect to, or logically challenge what your partner just said. Your idea should not be a random idea tossed out to smother or replace your partner's idea. We must teach students to address, respect, and build on every single partner utterance. In other words, no popcorning—or brick-piling.

Figure 2.2 Piles of Random Thoughts Versus Constructed Ideas

Many students (and adults) tend to limit their perspectives to the first idea that comes to them. They then defend it with full force before considering other points of view. But much of life is subjective and full of conflicting perspectives, solutions, and opinions. Many good ideas come from others. The sooner students are taught to encourage, respect, value, and build other perspectives on any given topic, the better. Students should have the mind-set of building, not competing or winning. They should want to know what others think, and not just fixate on saying what they themselves think. As much as possible, encourage students to *genuinely* seek to understand what others are thinking and feeling.

Zoom In and Pick a Point

Often, a conversation partner shares several points or ideas in one turn. Teach students as they listen to try to zoom in on a point that best maintains focus on the topic and moves the conversation along. This could be a point of agreement or disagreement. A partner, for example, might use a quotation from a character to support the proposed theme of denial in the story. The partner might agree and elaborate on that quotation, providing another similar line from the story to support the idea.

Connect Ideas

A student should also build by linking a partner's idea to previous ideas, thoughts, texts, other conversations, interests, world issues, and examples. Some of the links should be to ideas in the same conversation. This all requires a good working memory. Students can bring up what has happened before in class, the world, or their own lives to use as material for conversations. This might include referring to notes or graphic organizers.

As students converse, they must learn to keep track of important ideas in the class, the text, and previous statements by a partner or classmates. The ability to remember linkable ideas varies, of course, but you can train students to make more and better connections as they converse, read, and write.

Stay Relevant

When students do bring up ideas, they need to demonstrate a good "filter" for relevance and logic. They should share notions of what is relevant to the topic as they talk (Barnes and Todd 1977). This means that students must be able to discern whether the idea or example helps support or extend the topic, or whether it is off base and needs to be set aside. Students also need to self-filter and prune ideas before sharing out loud. We teachers do this more than we think. A connection pops up into our heads during class discussion, and we quickly decide if it will help or if it will distract and get students off on some wild tangent that will not end until the bell rings for lunch. One strategy, if students are not sure of the relevance, is to start with, "I don't know how this fits, but what about . . . ," and then to be open to the partner saying, "Let's table that for now."

Challenge an Idea

You likely hear plenty of students challenging other students in different ways in school. The goal with classroom conversation is to teach respectful and productive challenging skills. Much learning can result from the energy of conflict and controversy, as we know, but we must be tactful. Sentence frames can help, but often when things get most interesting, the respectfulness erodes. Have students practice taking different sides in short pair-shares and practice responding. You can role-play a person who is inwardly angry but responds with respect to an opposing view. (Also see the two-sided information gap conversation activity in Chapter 7.)

Adapt an Idea

Another part of building is adapting. By this we mean that conversations are alive, somewhat like an active child: you never know where it is going, and often you have to follow, adapt, and make new plans. One middle school teacher, Erin Dillane, tells her students, "Sometimes in conversation another person says your idea, or the conversation goes in a different direction and you have to let your idea go. Be flexible." Many students are used to saying their idea—getting it out there—but not listening to others' ideas, not building. These students need to adapt, be flexible, be open to new ideas, and be ready to do the hard work of building on each other's thoughts.

Skill 4: Paraphrase

Paraphrasing is the skill of keeping track of what we are hearing, organizing the speaker's points, and describing what we understand in our own words. It requires some selection and inference. We "read" the speaker's tone and emphasis and see what is important to them. This helps us select key points for our paraphrased version of what the speaker said. We also might highlight the points that relate most to the main topic of the conversation.

Paraphrasing serves multiple purposes. First, it helps conversation partners negotiate meaning. The listener synthesizes important points, which sometimes contradict each other, and paraphrases them back to the speaker. The speaker can then clarify if that was the intended message. And because no two people have experienced the world exactly the same way, such negotiations and clarification are much needed. "A speaker can never transmit information to a listener that will be understood in exactly the same way as the speaker conceptualizes that particular piece of information" (Raban 2001, 33). Even identical twins must negotiate meaning.

Second, the person paraphrasing can shape or guide the speaker's key points to stay focused on the conversation's main topic. The listener can choose a point or two that relate the most or dig the deepest and can bring those points up in the paraphrase to maintain the conversation's focus. Third, paraphrasing is great practice for listening and creating chunks of key points. This chunking can help students' comprehension of future oral and reading experiences. Fourth, a good paraphrase shows that a person is listening and understanding what the partner is saying. Anyone can nod their head, but to paraphrase what a partner just said shows true listening. And finally, even if a listener doesn't paraphrase out loud, it is a great listening and comprehension habit to develop.

Skill 5: Synthesize Conversation Points

Ideas, useful and not, float around during a conversation, and it takes skill and practice to keep track of the ideas and combine the useful ones. Synthesizing conversation points means remembering, highlighting, and fitting together key ideas from the conversation into a coherent thought statement. It is the process of taking the many paraphrased chunks, fitting them together, weeding some out, and whittling them down into a shared conclusion.

A synthesis can be a rich part of the conversation, because to form it, students need to negotiate ideas that they discussed in order to come to a consensus. Or they might "agree to disagree" on the final synthesis. Both are worthy outcomes and prepare students for thinking and talking in future classes, jobs, and life. A key supporting skill for synthesizing is recognizing the unimportant points and pruning them out of the synthesis. Synthesizing also is supported by and builds skills of organizing, prioritizing, and shaping abstract ideas into a summarized form.

Leave enough time at the end of each conversation for students to think back and gather their ideas together into a synthesis. Ask them to think about the most important points and how they can apply or generalize ideas to make them interesting and useful in life. You can have them summarize on paper first, individually, then talk with each other to negotiate their synthesis. The joint synthesis can also be written down as a record of the conversation. You can circulate to see which syntheses might spark a rich whole-class conversation.

A synthesis solidifies the conversation's purpose and greatly increases the chances of the ideas being remembered and learned.

Behaviors of Effective Conversation

Conversation is much more than talking and listening. There are many manners, behaviors, and nonverbal signals that play key roles. These behaviors tend to become habits as a result of home and community interactions. But for students who have been less immersed at home in communication behaviors valued at school, teachers need to teach such behaviors in class in order to accelerate their development. These behaviors include the following:
   » Appropriate eye contact (not always looking down or away or past the person—and not constantly staring either)
   » Facing one another (with whole body)
   » Attentive posture (leaning toward the partner)
   » Nodding head to show understanding
   » Appropriate gesturing (not rolling eyes or sighing or looking bored with folded arms, and so on)

> » Laughing, smiling, looking surprised, showing interest
> » Using "keep talking" tactics (*Uh huh, Wow, Interesting, Hmm, Yes, Okay, I see, Go on, Really? Seriously?*)
> » Silence (to allow thinking and time to put thoughts into words)
> » Prosody (changing voice tone, pitch, volume, and emphasis)
> » Interrupting (by agreeing, asking for clarification, or using nonverbal signals)

Attitudes for Effective Conversation

Perhaps the hardest conversational dimension to teach and model is attitude. The following attitudes and dispositions are needed in addition to the skills and behaviors described in the preceding sections:

Humility. It is tough to have a good conversation with a know-it-all. We prefer to converse with others who admit they have things to learn, that their knowledge is incomplete, and that they can learn from others. Humility is being open to new ideas and to having one's mind changed—it is knowing that our opinions have limitations (Brookfield and Preskill 2005). For students who have high status in a classroom and know it, humility means they might need to be less visible and more patient and to see other students as teachers.

Thoroughness. This is the attitude that keeps students exploring and deepening ideas and creatively extending conversations. It means to look at all perspectives and possible solutions and to work together to accomplish the task with the highest quality possible. "Can we do better?" should run through students' minds as they work.

Respect. It's essential to respect each other, especially when opposing viewpoints are being discussed. Respect is a foundational attitude that supports conversations at all levels. In addition, it deepens as students have more opportunities to talk with one another. We have encountered many students who report that their thoughts and attitudes towards their peers have shifted dramatically as a result of respectful academic conversations.

Positivity. The positive attitude that great learning can happen through conversation is vital. Some students approach school and their peers with a negative attitude. Enthusiasm stems from positivity.

Interest. Too many people seek to be interesting when they should seek to be more interested. Many "interesting" people know or think they are interesting, and therefore talk too much. *Interested* people, on the other hand, are interested in what other people say. They want to work with, build from, and encourage others' ideas. And if both partners are interested, good conversation happens.

Conversation Diversity

Conversations are very diverse. No conversation between students at any given moment is the same, nor is a conversation the same between the same two people at different points in time. Yet, the conversation skills, the behaviors, and the attitudes described in this chapter are effective in most conversations. Look for the skills (which are more evident in transcripts than behaviors and attitudes are) in the following excerpt from a fifth-grade conversation on a book about the challenges faced by Ruby Bridges, one of the first African American girls to attend an all-white school, in 1960.

1	*Monica:*	What did you like about the story?
2	*Luís:*	I think we are supposed to talk about what it means.
3	*Monica:*	Okay. What did it mean?
4	*Luís:*	Ruby was brave.
5	*Monica:*	Can you elaborate on that?
6	*Luís:*	She was scared, but kept walking past those angry people. Then she was alone with the teacher. That's scary, too.
7	*Monica:*	Yeah, I don't think I would've kept going. I once had some old man scream at me and I stayed away from that store for weeks. I wanted to spit on him. But then it was crazy; Ruby prayed for those people who hated her!
8	*Luís:*	Why'd she do that?
9	*Monica:*	I don't think screaming back at them would've helped. Maybe they wanted her to yell at them so they could have reasons to not like her.
10	*Luís:*	So you're saying, she would've become like them.
11	*Monica:*	Yeah, I guess. So, how do we sum this up?
12	*Luís:*	Ruby was brave by walking past yelling people. She forgave them to not be like them. We should forgive people like that, like that old man that yelled at you.
13	*Monica:*	And not give in. She could've stopped going to school and forgiven them, but she didn't.

All five conversation skills are evident in this excerpt. In line 2, Luís redirects to focus on the story's meaning and not on what they liked. Monica then asks for elaboration in line 5 to expand and give shape to the idea presented in line 4. In line 7, Monica uses an example from her life to build on Luís's elaboration. Luís then asks a probing question about cause and empathy in line 8, and Monica produces a possible hypothesis, which is followed by Luís's paraphrase in line 10. Finally, in lines 12 and 13 the students negotiate a synthesis.

These fifth graders didn't have this conversation out of the blue. Their teacher trained them to use conversation skills through a variety of lessons throughout the year. When asked what helped them do so well, the teacher said, "Starting this conversation work early on and infusing it into most of my lessons during the year."

Reflections

1. Think of challenges that might occur as you try to implement more conversation in your classes.
2. Think of possible topics in your discipline that could be used as cases to discuss and build conversations around.
3. Consider the thinking skills that you would like to emphasize when introducing academic conversations.
4. Think of two students and write an ideal conversation between them. Think about what you want them to think about, say, and emphasize. This can then shape your teaching.
5. Hold conversations with other adults about texts, news events, and meaningful topics. Take mental or even real notes. Reflect on how the conversations developed, veered, or stagnated. Try some of the conversation skills described in this chapter. You might even try using the stems from Figure 2.1 (or the Academic Conversation Placemat in the Appendix) as you converse.
6. Which skills, behaviors, or attitudes do *you* need to work on?

Chapter 3
Lesson Activities for Developing Core Conversation Skills

The book was only so-so, but our conversations about it were awesome.

—Fifth-grade language arts student

The conversation skills and behaviors described in Chapter 2 should be woven into the content you are teaching—not taught in isolation or out of context. Chapters 3, 4, and 5 were written to help you do this. They describe how to strategically improve conversations so that students build their academic communication skills as they build their content understandings.

The activities in this chapter are categorized under the five core conversation skills introduced in Chapter 2, but most of the activities develop more than one skill, at no extra cost. The activities can be used in mini-lessons to develop skills that you have assessed to be most needed in your class. Some of the activities can be used in the early stages of conversation work (described in Chapter 2) and others are for use throughout the year as needs arise and as conversations evolve.

Activities for Skill 1: Elaborate and Clarify

This section describes several activities that you can use during lessons to cultivate students' abilities to elaborate and clarify ideas in their conversations.

Clarifying with Analogies and Metaphors

Students should learn how to borrow, create, and understand analogies and other figurative devices used to explain ideas. Gather analogies and metaphors from various sources, including speeches, textbooks, articles, and other places to discuss with students. Ask questions such as, *Why did the person use this analogy? Where does the analogy break down?* and *Is there a better analogy for this?* Have students look for analogies in everything they read and watch.

Challenge student pairs to come up with their own analogies for concepts and processes that you are teaching. For example, they might compare a character's motivations to those of a bee looking for honey, or a nation's foreign policy to an old and cranky person, or an ant colony to a factory. You can tell students that they will be helping you to teach the concept next year by giving you analogy ideas to use with your future students.

Converse About Graphic Organizers and Manipulatives

Graphic organizers provide a visual display of ideas that can help students organize and deepen their conversations. Semantic maps, Venn diagrams, story maps, data tables, diagrams, 3-D persuasive seesaws, strange objects, and visual organizers all provide a scaffold for talk and chances to elaborate, probe, and question. When filling in a semantic map on Christopher Columbus, for example, a partner might question the writing of the word *hero* in one box. The writer then needs to respond with some elaboration and rationale. Or in science, a partner might need to clarify how to construct a complex molecule using manipulatives such as Lego pieces. Remind students that a high-quality conversation is the priority—not filling in the visual organizer. Examples of visual organizers are found in the following chapters.

Opinion Continuum

Pick three or four two-sided issues about which students could have opinions. Cut fifteen 8 1/2-by-11-inch sheets of paper in half the long way and draw a continuum line across the paper, with the opposing perspectives on each extreme (students can make these, too). Figure 3.1 shows an example of this. Give half of the students a continuum sheet. Students with sheets meet with nonsheet students, and the nonsheet students share their opinions with their partners. The sheet holder asks questions to clarify the nonsheet student's opinion. The nonsheet student elaborates and justifies his or her opinion with examples. The nonsheet student signs his or her name on the continuum at the point that matches his or her opinion. Students should not be directly in the middle. Students then rotate to new partners. After gathering three or more signatures, or when you indicate, each sheet holder must sign his or her name on the continuum and provide elaboration and justification to a nonsheet partner. If there is time, sheet students can share out what their partners argued and whether they were swayed by the conversations. If there is time, you can start over, with the nonsheet partners becoming sheet students.

Figure 3.1 Sample Opinion Continuum

Variation: After student conversations, draw a continuum on the board and stand in front of it. Call on students to share their opinions and move left or right, depending on the arguments offered by the students. You can also have students or an administrator move along the big continuum, as they are convinced by students on each side of the issue.

Journal Jumpstarts

Use journal writes to fuel and build students' thinking before conversing. If you are getting the vibe that students don't have enough material ready in their minds to converse, have them write down ideas beforehand in their journals. They can respond to open questions generated by them or by you. Prompts might include the following:

> *The author is trying to teach us that . . .*
> *A question I keep having about this book is . . .*
> *This reminds me of another story . . .*
> *I wonder why the author . . .*
> *This history text is biased because . . .*
> *This science concept is important to our future because . . .*

Students can also fill in graphic organizers or create drawings to jumpstart their conversation ideas.

Activities for Skill 2: Support Ideas with Examples

This section describes several activities that you can use during lessons to cultivate students' abilities to prompt for and generate useful examples, evidence, and logical reasons to support ideas in their conversations.

Hunting for Deep Quotations

In this activity students prepare for their conversations by looking for "deep" and thought-provoking parts of a text as they read. Students might not have any themes in mind, so they are simply looking for parts that make them stop and think. Later they can think about themes that emerge—themes for which the quotations might be supportive examples. Along the way, students might generate thought-provoking questions, which can also help them generate themes. Students can put the quotations onto cards and try to sort them with a partner or small group. They can group them into themes or other categories. This visual manipulation helps them prepare for supporting their ideas in conversations.

Planning Their Conversations on Paper

Writing down what they will talk about forces students to sort out the relevant from the ir-relevant and to organize their thoughts before they share them with a partner. It provides some silent thinking and language practice before the actual conversation. Students can then use the notes, if needed, during the conversation. Writing might take the form of two-column notes, Venn diagrams, quick paragraphs, charts, semantic maps, drawings, and so on.

Students might even fill in a conversation planning form, like the one in Figure 3.2. This form, or any variation of it that you might choose, helps students to generate and organize their thoughts before they converse. They can fill it in individually or together. Planning on paper also shows students the importance of organizing ideas in conversations.

Figure 3.2 Conversation Planning Form

CONVERSATION PLANNING FORM		
Prompt, topic, question:		
Connections (Examples)	**Causes** (Examples)	**Interpretations, Opinions, Ideas** (Examples)
Comparisons (Examples)	**Effects** (Examples)	**Applications** (Examples)
Ideas after the conversation:		

Teach Terms That Trigger the Need for Examples

Academic messages often use abstract category words, such as *aspects, processes, factors, variables, issues, systems, terms, advantages, outcomes,* and *activities.* You can teach students to use these words and to ask for examples when they hear these words. Your class can generate its own list.

When the terms arise, highlight them on a poster. Ask questions that contain them, model how to use them, and provide examples for them automatically when you are talking and explaining. Train students to ask questions such as, *Can you give me a couple of examples of the factors/aspects/ issues that you mentioned?* and *What is an example of that?*

Supportive Examples Practice

This activity offers students a chance to quickly generate examples that support an idea, perspective, or argument. You and/or the class provide an idea or theme statement, and students tell each other examples from the text, other texts, media, their lives, the past, the present, and the future. They can also generate counterexamples. Finally, students can discuss whether the theme is valid or not, based on the strength of the examples.

Students can use the graphic organizer shown in Figure 3.3 to organize and spark their generation of examples. Students can also use the following starters:

For example	*As stated in*	*In fact*
According to	*The author stated*	*The text shows*
To illustrate	*For instance*	*As evidence of*
Another example	*A salient example*	*Specifically*
Such as	*Consider*	*Let us take the case of*

Figure 3.3 Graphic Organizer for Supportive Examples Practice

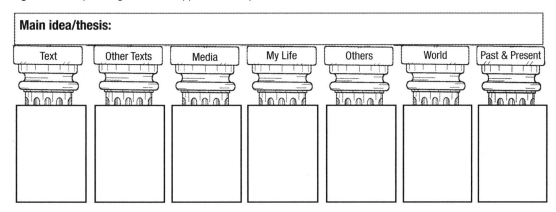

Evaluating the Support of Examples

Teachers sometimes ask the question, "Is that a strong example?" This is an important question, and one that all students should ask themselves and one another, but it is not easy to answer without some extra teaching. How do we know if an example is helpful or not in supporting an idea? In any society, and in each discipline, there is an amorphous set of values that students must learn in order to evaluate the support of ideas in a discipline. Students must learn to judge the value of each idea and example as they read, listen, and talk. For example, in social science, students must learn that the data from a few convenient people is likely less valuable than data from a random sample of many people.

Students can practice evaluating the support value of examples in conversations using the graphic organizer shown in Figure 3.4. First, write an idea or opinion in the top box. This could relate to a theme, interpretation, hypothesis, or inference. Second, as a class, generate a list of examples and put them below the arrow boxes or off to the side. Third, model and discuss with the class the level of support or weight that each example gives, and write it in the corresponding arrow: Weak Support, Some Support, and Strong Support. (Instead of using the organizer shown in Figure 3.4, you could also make a continuum and put examples along it with sticky notes.) Finally, have students come up with their own ideas with examples and then discuss them in pairs as they fill in the support arrows.

Here is a brief example from a sixth-grade history class.

Esteban:	Okay. Our opinion is that the Spanish were greedy. What's an example?
Leslie:	They sailed to America.
Esteban:	But maybe it was just to explore. Let's put it in the weak arrow, for now.
Leslie:	How about beating the Aztecs and looking for their gold? That's a strong example, I think.
Esteban:	I agree. It's strong because they only wanted gold and killed for it.

Figure 3.4 Organizer for Evaluating the Support of Examples

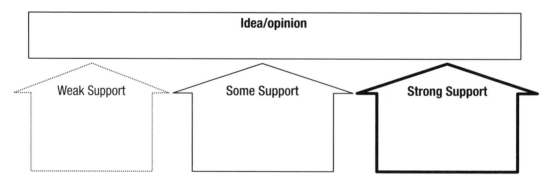

Students can use this simple visual tool while conversing to abstractly measure or weigh the value of certain examples. After they finish, they can see what kinds of patterns emerge, asking why some supporting examples were weak and why some were strong.

Activities for Skill 3:
Build On and/or Challenge a Partner's Idea

This section describes several activities that you can use during lessons to cultivate students' abilities to build on and challenge ideas in their conversations.

Idea Building

This activity trains students to build on the previous idea mentioned in a conversation. Students use small slips of paper as "bricks" to build up the idea. The graphic organizer shown in Figure 3.5 can be used for this activity. For example, if one student brings up the idea that humans are causing global warming, write that big idea in the oval. Students should then fill in bricks that support, relate to, question, or add on to that idea. Bricks that don't relate well should be placed to the side.

As they share their bricks, students should use appropriate idea-building language, such as *I would add that . . . , To piggyback off your idea about . . . , I also have an example of that . . . , Some people might say that this . . . , This is important because . . . ,* and *Yet some might argue against this because. . . .*

Figure 3.5 Graphic Organizer for Idea Building

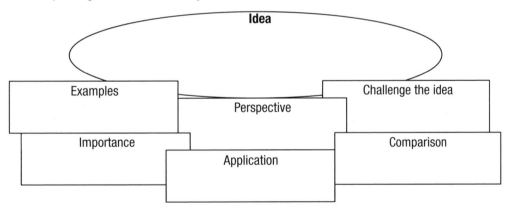

Conflicting Texts and Quotations

Choose two or more texts that contradict one another. These might be opinion articles, historical accounts, interpretations of scientific data, and so on, on the same topic. Or they might be quotations that conflict. For example, in history class you might give two quotations that contradict one another from the same person. Abraham Lincoln had several, and John Smith told the story about his capture by Pocahontas's tribe two different ways at different times in his life. Many folks offer conflicting reviews of novels, films, and current events.

Have students converse about the conflicting texts and come to a consensus on what they mean or why they conflict. Each student can take a text and argue for it. Or both can work together to build up the most reasonable interpretation for the clash. Here is a sample conversation:

Samuel:	I think Lincoln was more interested in the Union than in abolition of slavery.
Ali:	What do you mean?
Samuel:	Well, there is a quote that says he will preserve the Union, even if slavery is needed.
Ali:	Then he also says how bad slavery is in other quotations. He is famous for abolishing slavery and being one of the greatest presidents. Do you really think that?
Samuel:	Well, people can cover up their real beliefs to get what they want, even their whole life.
Ali:	I don't know. Maybe he changed his mind over time. People can do that, too.

Two-Minute Opinion Share

With students in pairs, assign one student to be A and one to be B. Describe a controversial issue and have students think about their opinions for a minute. Then call a letter and have the person assigned that letter begin, describing his or her opinion for one minute, backed by examples and evidence. The other student must take the opposing side of the issue. Students should challenge one another's evidence, solicit examples, and ask for elaboration. They can try to come to a consensus in the third minute.

A whole-class variation of this activity is to have students divide into two groups and to place the groups on different sides of the room. Each group acts together as one partner. When one side responds, the other has thirty seconds to gather their thoughts. Each student on each side can only talk once, and they should remember to work on the skill of appropriately challenging the other group's ideas. Students can work on other skills using this activity as well.

Practice Norms for Controversial Conversations

Johnson and Johnson (2009) suggest setting up clear norms for participating in controversial conversations in the classroom. Politeness and respect can fade quickly when emotions and competitiveness emerge. Many students (and adults) see models of resolving controversy at home and in the media that are not academic.

As with most checklists and rubrics, we suggest that you build controversy norms checklists with students and clarify and role-play each point. A few suggestions for items that you might have on checklists are included here.

- I am critical of ideas, not of people.
- I strive to confirm that I value others, even if I challenge their ideas.
- I know that I am valuable even if others criticize my ideas.
- I converse, disagree, and challenge in order to learn, not to win.
- I listen respectfully to all ideas, even if I disagree.
- I work to understand all sides and perspectives of an issue.
- I change my mind when evidence and reason convinces me.

Activities for Skill 4: Paraphrase

This section describes several activities that you can use during lessons to cultivate students' abilities to paraphrase in their conversations.

Understand and Organize as a Listener

One of the listener's jobs is to understand. Listening is hard work that demands mental discipline, much like reading. It means setting aside one's own thinking and controlling one's urges to interject. As Palmer (1998) shares, "When I suspend, for just a while, my inner chatter about what I am going to say next, I open room within myself to receive the external conversation" (135). Remind students that, just as reading is hard work, so is listening. Listening also demands mental endurance and multitasking. A listener must keep track of the key ideas shared as well as the surface and under-the-surface meanings. The listener needs to decide if the speaker is making sense, if examples are valid, if the conversation is remaining focused, and so on.

Listeners need to signal when they don't understand. They need to use facial signals and need to ask the right questions. Many students have played the game of school long enough to know that they can nod their heads and maintain eye contact to feign listening while they think about something very different. This becomes a habit that happens even in paired conversations.

In front of all students, verbally share a three-minute argument and don't allow students to take notes. You might argue that you think Germany was not entirely to blame for starting World War I or that global warming is caused by humans. Have students remember the main points that you mention, and then have them compare those points with a partner. You can also have students listen to recorded speeches and messages related to the content they are learning. We know several teachers who have students paraphrase portions of chapters that are read aloud to them. The more academic oral language that students listen to and process in their own words, the better they build the skill of paraphrasing *and* the better they internalize the content.

Paraphrase Cards

This activity serves several purposes. It teaches equity of voice, paraphrasing, and organization of ideas. Partner A holds five or six blank sharing cards for Partner B. When Partner B shares an idea, Partner A writes down a paraphrased version of the message and puts it down in front of them. They can organize the cards later, if needed. If one partner shares too much, it will be obvious, and the partner who shared less will need to share more.

Interview Grids

Another way to practice and develop paraphrasing skills is to have students quickly answer questions and have partners paraphrase the answers on paper, preferably in small boxes. The interview grid is a matrix used by students as they go around the room talking to each other. On the top are academic questions that should require long-ish answers, which makes them better for paraphrasing. Figure 3.6 is an example of a grid used in middle school science. Notice that the prompts (compare, explain, argue) require thinking.

Figure 3.6 Sample Interview Grid

Name	Compare bird and insect adaptations	Explain how crocodiles have adapted	Argue why dinosaurs became extinct
Silvia	Birds and insects can escape by flying.	Fast in water; sharp teeth	Meteor started an ice age
David	Some bugs smell bad; others can sting you.	They eat everything; camouflage	Smoking
Safiye		Very tough skin; they look like logs	They got diseases and ran out of food.

Students must listen, then verbally paraphrase to the student just interviewed, then paraphrase the idea in writing on the grid. When most spaces are filled in, students share ideas orally with other students in small groups. They must expand the paraphrased notes into complete sentences. Students get to hear similar ideas several times, reinforcing the thinking and vocabulary. Encourage students to use target terms and grammar such as *Because they . . . , On the other hand . . . , nucleus, nutrients, camouflage, adapt, differ, developed, traits, evidence, chloroplast,* and so on. To finish up, students can briefly share some of their paraphrased ideas with the class.

Activities for Skill 5: Synthesize Conversation Points

This section describes several activities that you can use during lessons to cultivate students' abilities to synthesize the key points of their conversations.

Parking, Promoting, and Pruning Ideas

Parking distracting thoughts. Train students to write down thoughts that might be useful later, or to "park" them (Nichols 2006). Tell students that you, as a teacher, park your thoughts often, during every lesson and conversation. Many different ideas pop up that you are about to share, but you don't share them because only a few help to support the focus of the discussion or the point of the lesson. You might write some down, and others just drift away.

Promoting. Some of the greatest ideas never get shared. Many brilliant students are very shy and reticent to share, even in pair settings. Exhort students to share and promote their ideas. Granted, it is vital to set up an environment where students value one another's ideas. You can even offer up examples of historical figures who came up with "crazy" ideas like airplanes, cell phones, freedom, equality, visiting the moon, and so on.

Pruning. Students also need to learn to discard (prune) thoughts that are likely to be unhelpful. Train students to preprune their own ideas and tactfully prune others' unhelpful ideas from the flow of the conversation. If a brick in the wall doesn't fit, it must be discarded, because it is heavy and it is taking the place of other more useful bricks/ideas. Some ideas distract, some lead off to dead ends, some bog us down, and some are just not logical or relevant enough.

Converse at the Computer

Conversing side by side with another person at one computer can build a range of skills. First, if using the Internet, students can train themselves to stay focused on a topic as they navigate the wide range of links that can often lead students off topic. This parallels what can happen in a real conversation (not near a computer), in which our own path of mental "links" takes us off topic. Students must learn when to hit the Back button on the computer and in their minds.

Conversing at a computer can also build online literacies and other critical thinking skills. For example, a vital online skill is evaluating the usefulness and credibility of a Web site. In looking at a site for evidence, two students can converse, for example, about the value of the information to support their idea that Christopher Columbus was motivated by greed. They can analyze the source, authors, visuals, text quality, and relevance. They can converse about the site's motivation for existing, its possible biases, and its commercial or political motives.

Students can also take part in online discussions and converse about how they might respond (as one person) on a blog or discussion board or other platform. Thus, they are "double-conversing," on one level with the world and at a different level with each other, face to face.

Skill-Based Roles for Group Conversations

Even though you want students to use all of the essential conversation skills as they talk, at times you can tell them to emphasize a certain skill in order to hone it. For example, in a group of four, one student can be the focuser, another the builder, another the elaborator and example person, and the last person the paraphraser and synthesizer. Of course, they can all do these tasks along the way, but the role gives them extra concentration on that skill. Students can also use cards with prompts and sentence starters on them, as described in Chapter 2. We have even seen students take on roles for half the time, then abandon them and do all roles in the second half of the conversation.

Conversation Mini-Lessons

A mini-lesson introduces a skill and allows students to practice it in a short amount of time. Here are some basic components of mini-lessons:

Analyze and dissect. You can analyze good and bad conversations in fishbowl-like settings. You can also look for behaviors in videos and dissect written transcripts. Together, create a checklist of good conversation skills and behaviors. Ask the class what is wrong, what is needed, what is effective, and what might help. Eventually you will generate a set of norms that can take the form of a poster or anchor chart.

Model. Teacher modeling, while important, loses its luster quickly. When students model, their classmates often listen a bit longer, and it gives the modelers a chance to be teachers. Prepare several pairs of students to model how they talk about a text. You might preplant conversation moves that you want them to use and that you want to emphasize in your mini-lesson. You might bring students up to model how you ask them for their ideas and then build on them. You and the class can then add the modeled skill to the conversation poster or checklist that you are developing as a class. You can also model a longer conversation between you and the rest of the class, in which the whole class acts as your partner. Model the skill you are working on and have the students do the same as a group.

Scaffold. Scaffolding provides a helpful metaphor for the process of building students' independence in an area of learning (Bruner 1978). For conversation skills, this means that you or a more capable peer models a skill and gradually reduces support over time as the learner practices and develops independence. You might use think-alouds, conversations with students, and analyses of conversation models (written and oral). Much of the scaffolding involves observing and providing feedback as students are working in pairs and groups.

Practice and build independence. Have students practice in "pair-plus-one" groups. The third person is an observer who provides feedback and extra support as the partners converse. Eventually, students practice in pairs and self-monitor. Then throughout the year, work to build students' independent communication skills. Use a scaffolding approach that supports their skills less and less during the year. Every day, observe skills and behaviors in a variety of settings to see what students need to work on the next day or week. This formative assessment will often lead to differentiated instruction to meet individual needs in different areas. Hold conversations with individual students. Let them practice their emerging conversation skills with you. Resist the temptation to control the conversation, and allow them to guide and decide, to ask questions, and to facilitate.

Pairing Techniques

There are times when you can strategically pair students and other times when you want random pairings. We recommend both diversity and continuity. That is, each student should interact with all other students over the course of a month or two; yet each student should also talk with the same partner over time in order to build longer conversations. To strategically pair students, consider who works well with whom, who challenges whom, and who doesn't work well with whom. Create a chart or cards with pairs on them and have students practice short conversations or pair-shares. The following strategies are various ways you can assign pairs:

Find your partner. Create pair cards, such as states and capitals, multiplication problems and answers, famous first and last names, events and their years, sentences missing words, split-up sentences, abstract ideas with concrete examples, and so on. Hand these out and have students find their partner to converse. Another variation, using a deck of cards, involves pairing red numbers with red numbers and black numbers with black numbers (e.g., five of hearts meets with five of diamonds).

Clock partners. Draw a clock on a piece of paper and lines that extend from each number. You will likely just use the 3, 6, 9, and 12 for only four paired meetings. Each student quickly circulates, talks with four other students, sets a time to meet for each one, and writes the corresponding name for each of the times. Make sure they are different names. At different times throughout the day, when you want to have a conversation, tell them, for example, "Meet with your three o'clock partner!"

Interview grids. Give each student a grid on a piece of paper and have them take their grids around as they talk to other students. On the grid, the left column is for student names and the top row has several prompts or questions. Students interview other students and write down a summary of their responses. They move on to talk with another student to fill in another row. This is often a warm-up or cool-down activity.

Flexible grouping. You can also mix up and group students according to the following: primary language, language proficiency level, need to work on the same skill, background knowledge, student choice, interest, or random grouping. You can also pair by abilities, pairing the student with the "highest" ability in a certain skill to a "midpoint" student. For example, you can temporarily rank all thirty students for a particular skill, then pair number 1 with 16, number 2 with 17, and so on. It is important to know your students well and observe how they work with other students over time.

Reflections

1. What activities not described in this chapter do you or your colleagues use to develop conversation skills?
2. What are the most unnatural or challenging conversation skills for students? Why?
3. After using some of the activities described in this chapter, how would you modify them to meet your students' needs?

Chapter 4
Designing Effective Conversation Tasks

This chapter answers questions that might have emerged as you read Chapters 2 and 3, such as *How do I know a conversation is effective? How do I create effective conversation prompts?* and *How can I improve the quality of conversations during each lesson and throughout the year?* The first part of this chapter describes seven features of effective conversation tasks. These are features to keep in mind in the creation of prompts and in the refinement of conversations during lessons. The second part of the chapter describes four different bases, or starting points, for designing powerful conversation prompts.

Features of Effective Conversation Tasks

Academic conversation tasks should have the following features, which help in the ongoing refinement and improvement of conversations in class:

1. Require both partners to talk.
2. Require critical and creative thinking.
3. Take advantage of controversies and conflict.
4. Recognize and reduce ambiguity.
5. Encourage thinking based on principles, laws, and approaches of the discipline.
6. Build in opportunities for transfer of knowledge and skills.
7. Provide choice and ownership.

Given that conversations take time and energy, they should be as educational as possible. As you observe and design conversations, keep in mind the features described in the following sections. Designing effective conversation tasks is an ever-evolving process. Sometimes the prompt needs to change; sometimes you need to intervene and help students while they are conversing. Academic conversation tasks become more effective when the following features coexist.

Feature 1: Require Both Partners to Talk

The task design should require both students to talk in roughly equal amounts and to negotiate meanings at appropriately challenging levels. You will notice that most of the prompts in this book have "focused open-endedness." Focused open-endedness allows students to form different ideas on a topic, defend them, and negotiate them. This means that teachers and prompts should encourage students to explore ideas, not just reach a quick consensus. You want students to wrestle with meanings—because easy answers, one-sided arguments, and unsupported ideas simply waste your students' precious time.

Feature 2: Require Critical and Creative Thinking

Conversations should help students develop critical and creative thinking skills. Critical thinking tends to be focused, zooming in on an argument, dissecting it, and evaluating its worth. Creative thinking tends to be divergent, generating a range of ideas and possible solutions, some of which seem outlandish but provide raw material for effective solutions. Good conversations can have both critical and creative thinking. You can teach creativity strategies such as brainstorming, taking different perspectives (e.g., taking the perspective of a glacier in science class), using analogies, visualizing, and using different tools and media, such as diagrams, drama, art, and freewriting.

You can also use conversations to teach critical literacy. As information piles up on the Internet and in other media spaces, students must be increasingly critical and discerning, even skeptical. As they question sources and consider possible biases, they learn to learn. Barron and Darling-Hammond argue that teachers should "encourage students to define problems and treat claims and explanatory accounts, even those offered by 'experts,' as needing evidence" (2008, 32). As students question sources and argue for their value or lack of value, they have powerful conversations.

Feature 3: Take Advantage of Controversies and Conflicts

Life is rife with controversy. Conversations can give students plenty of practice with persuasion, argumentation, and resolution of issues. Tell students that disagreement is a natural part of living and communicating with others and that the process of negotiating conflicts with others promotes lots of learning and skills that are useful in the future. As Johnson and Johnson point out, "By structuring intellectual conflict in a lesson, instructors can grab and hold students' attention and energize students to learn at a level beyond what they may have intended" (2009, 37). That is, conflict tends to motivate students to learn more about the topic, focus more, retain more, think more, and do more.

Develop a classroom mind-set that welcomes controversy and challenge. Disagreement shouldn't be avoided (Sams and Dawes 2004); it is a golden opportunity to negotiate meaning and dig into a topic and its different sides. Students should learn how to work toward logical agreement, and not just accept the view of the majority perspective. Discussions on concepts such as peer pressure, standing out, rebelling, and conforming are helpful ways to begin. It is important to teach students to fully explore different ideas, solutions, and perspectives as well as the reasons that support them. Teachers must stress to students that they should avoid two things: (1) quickly complying, conforming, and taking one side without thinking and (2) pigheadedly defending one idea over others. Train students to play devil's advocate at times and to logically disagree with counterarguments, especially when it seems that the majority are complying too quickly.

Unfortunately, most people do not like others to disagree with them. It takes an especially academic mind-set to remove oneself from the emotion of controversy and see its value for learning. Some leaders are famous for saying that they like to surround themselves with folks who disagree with them. Such challenges create dialogue, spark stronger arguments for making decisions, and often generate new ideas altogether.

Feature 4: Recognize and Reduce Ambiguity

Where ambiguity exists, there is a need to clarify. Ambiguity exists in many areas of life and school, and you can use it to train students to clarify and be extra explicit. Questions such as *What does that really mean?* or *What does this mean in this case?* help students see the importance of clarifying academic ideas. It also helps them see how meanings, especially of abstract ideas, can vary widely across people and settings. In order to clarify, teachers often use examples, which help students build the skill of identifying examples, comparing them, and evaluating them. For example, a conversation topic might be, *With your partner, clarify what we mean by loyalty. What does the text have to say about it? What are examples of it?* Students might also clarify concepts such as adaptation, democracy, probability, proof, love, happiness, progress, truth, bias, peace, community, religion, and so on.

Feature 5: Encourage Thinking Based on Principles, Laws, and Approaches of the Discipline

Experts in a discipline use core ideas of their field in their work and in conversations about their work. Core ideas include principles, laws, and approaches. Examples include: adaptation, democracy, greed, symbiosis, gravity, balancing equations, DNA, bias, perspective, motivation, power, time, isolating variables in an experiment, and so on. Experts know why they use certain procedures and know when to alter such procedures by applying principles to the situation (Mercer 1995). A task should encourage students to understand, explain, and use core principles to accomplish it. Students, for example, should know how to convert a fraction into a decimal, why the procedure works, and how it is useful in life.

Therefore, teachers should emphasize the overarching "umbrella" principles, laws, and approaches of the discipline to design conversations. One of the most useful gifts you can offer students is a set of solid frames for constructing their thinking and their conversations in each subject, in school and out of school. Even though the list of these umbrella principles for each subject is long, here are a few:

- Language Arts: interpreting the deeper meanings about life in a text and applying them to the past, present, and future; comparing works by one author or works from one time period; analyzing the use of literary devices to engage a reader
- History: evaluating the accuracy and bias of sources; interpreting the past to understand and teach about the present and future; applying causes from the past to predict present-day issues; empathizing with historical characters; applying social science and psychology to social events
- Science: hypothesizing causes and effects; asking why something happens; designing experiments that isolate variables; applying physical and biological principles to observations; using visual ways to show information (charts, graphs, pictures)

These big ideas, principles, and concepts make conversations much more interesting, authentic, and engaging. Such conversations should be infused throughout the curriculum.

Students tend to approach school and its topics with preconceived ideas of how the world works. If not significantly challenged or engaged, students will tend to learn what is needed for the test and then revert back to preconceived ideas (National Research Council 2000). Conversations that focus on big and interesting ideas tend to engage students and help them build on or challenge their preconceptions. Learning often happens when students' preconceptions about important ideas in a discipline are challenged, wrestled with, and changed.

Feature 6: Build in Opportunities for Transfer of Knowledge and Skills

A, if not *the*, major goal for classroom learning is being able to transfer skills or knowledge to new problems or situations. That is, students should learn how to use the ideas and skills learned in one class in other classes and in the real world. You can build such transfer into conversations. Before transferring, students should build solid understandings and skills of the content area. For example, in one class a teacher may want students to first understand the nature of sacrifice to gain freedom, a major theme in the novel they are reading. This can be clarified in an academic conversation. Then, in social studies class, the students might have another conversation about how people throughout history sacrificed their lives and homes for freedom. As students experiment with these types of transfer and application, they become more and more expert not only in a specific area but also in making connections across essential ideas and disciplines.

Feature 7: Provide Choice and Ownership

One of the powerful aspects of conversations is that they give students choice of how they shape and direct the conversation. When students take these different conversational directions, they might go places that you or they never thought they would go. They might explore ideas that were not in your or their notes. Clarify the different types of choices that students have as they converse:

- » To disagree with a partner
- » To support a partner's idea and add to it
- » To delve into a topic in depth
- » To ask questions and challenge current thought
- » To refer to a source or text to add to the conversation
- » To add a bit of humor
- » To go in different thinking-skill directions: interpretation, application, connection, compare, cause and effect, perspective, and so on.
- » To make meaningful connections

You should strive to support and build student independence each day and each year. When students are given the ability to choose a relevant topic and learn how to discuss it, they gain a stronger sense of agency, the conviction that they can think on their own and act to accomplish their goals. As you seek to foster conversations that allow students to explore ideas beyond and beneath the typical teachings of textbooks and tests, you cultivate students' sense of agency and independence as learners. Along the way, you "control for quality" of content learning and thinking skills development through extensive observation and written evidence.

Creating Academic Conversation Prompts

All conversations happen for a reason. In a café with a friend, you might just converse for the pleasure of sharing ideas or interpreting the latest life events. In the working world, you might converse in order to clarify and solve problems. In the academic world, you might converse to explore ideas, expand them, and solve problems. In class, you need to make sure the reasons for conversations are clear to get the most out of conversation time. A powerful initial prompt helps to energize, focus, and shape a conversation. Good prompts and topics are based on many factors, such as standards, curricula, student interests, current events, and school focuses.

In this section we describe four bases for developing an effective initial prompt for academic conversations: a deep question that drives a unit or discipline; a thinking skill that students need to use in the discipline; a task or product that shows students' learning; and a life experience that connects to the learning. These four bases can also overlap. You might have a core question, which is based on a thinking skill, which leads to the completion of a task or product. An example of this might be the prompt *Who was more right, the loyalists or patriots? Cocreate a persuasive poster based on your conversation.* For each prompt that you and your students craft, consider how interesting and real-world-esque it is. That is, would real people (normal adults and students) want to talk about the topic? For example, the prompt *Choose one of these topics and discuss it with your partner* is too flat and vague. Why should people discuss this at all? Instead, give some thinking depth and purpose to each prompt.

First and foremost, each of the bases must align with the standard and objective(s) of the lesson. State and district standards, and the more recent Common Core State Standards, offer a wide range of challenging skills and concepts that students must learn. These standards should be used to form unit and lesson objectives and, in turn, to create prompts for academic conversations. Once you have clarified the lesson objectives (for content, thinking, and language), you can craft prompts based on the four bases. Eventually, you want students to come up with their own great conversation prompts.

Base Prompts on a Deep Question

Deep questions that we have used in language arts lessons are *Why did the author write this?* and *What did the character show us about human nature?* For history texts we have used *Why is this important in history?* and *What were the ultimate effects of this event/person?* In science we have used *Why did this happen?* and *What would happen if. . . .* These questions allow for some opinion and support and some zooming in and out between general principles and concrete examples.

To create the initial prompt based on a question, consider some general guiding questions: (1) Does the question connect the current text to the essential understandings (big ideas) of the unit? (2) Does the question leave room for multiple perspectives, abstract ideas, and negotiation of meanings? (3) Is the question one that you would like to talk about with your friends or colleagues?

Students can generate their own deep questions with bookmarks and posters. Early on, you can provide the initial questions to get the conversations going. But quickly encourage students to generate their own higher-level questions and prompts. One fifth-grade teacher has students ask questions during reading using a bookmark based on different levels of thinking (Figure 4.1). You can choose different thinking skills to put on the bookmark or poster, such as evaluating, comparing, empathizing, and so on. Before conversing, students choose one question or synthesize several related questions in order to initiate their academic conversation.

Figure 4.1 Ideas for Conversation Prompt Bookmarks or Posters

Evaluate/ Choose	Empathize	Apply	Infer (cause and effect)	Interpret
Which is most . . . ?	How did they feel about . . . ?	How does this apply to . . . ?	Why did this . . . ?	What is the meaning of . . . ?

Use student wonderings. When students' ideas and questions are valued enough to be used as teaching prompts for conversations, students feel valued. Students tend to be more engaged when they pose their own questions and set out to answer them. You might have students put questions up on the wall or fill a "Wonder Bucket" with their big questions on slips of paper. Then choose the questions that will spark conversations.

Give students the space and freedom to wonder. Yet for some, wonder is not easy to foster. Some students have turned their interest and wonder levels way down for many subjects in school. Wonder comes from modeling, from using engaging curriculum, and from presenting real-world issues, dilemmas, and problems. When students get into the habit of wondering and voicing their wondering, conversations thrive.

Play the "deep question challenge." Have a challenge set up in which you train students to come up with conversation-worthy questions about any text or topic. They can evaluate their questions against a checklist that they create with you, and even prioritize them. The checklist might include items such as "has different perspectives; is interesting; makes you think; is a question that keeps coming up in history; is useful in my life." Sample questions include the following: *Was she biased when she wrote this? What did they have to gain by starting the war? How can we stop modern slavery? Should we allow genetic engineering? Do modern technology advances equal progress? Should the main character have lied or not? What should we learn in school?* and *Can statistics lie?*

Have students display and discuss which of the questions are most likely to get a good conversation going. Often conversations result from talking about and clarifying the question— even before the "official" conversations begin!

Use question-charged quotations and statements. Effective conversations can result from questioning the meaning of a quotation or statement. A quotation can come from a famous person or from a text. It might even be a commonly held truth or belief. The statement should incite students to respond with some emotion, shock, or anger that the idea would be said or believed. Here are some examples:

» "My paramount objective in this struggle is to save the Union, and is not either to save or to destroy slavery. If I could save the Union without freeing any slave I would do it, and if I could save it by freeing all the slaves I would do it." —Abraham Lincoln

» "If you want a symbolic gesture, don't burn the flag, wash it." —Norman Thomas

» "I know not with what weapons World War III will be fought, but World War IV will be fought with sticks and stones." —Albert Einstein

» "It has become appallingly obvious that our technology has exceeded our humanity." —Albert Einstein

» "Out, out, brief candle! Life's but a walking shadow, a poor player that struts and frets his hour upon the stage and then is heard no more: it is a tale told by an idiot, full of sound and fury, signifying nothing." —Shakespeare (*Macbeth*, Act V, Scene V).

» "Democracy is the road to Socialism." —Karl Marx

» "The world has a cancer, and that cancer is man." —Merton Lambert

» "Childbearing [should be] a punishable crime against society, unless the parents hold a government license." —David Brower

» "The best argument against democracy is a five-minute conversation with the average voter." —Winston Churchill

» "We only have to look at ourselves to see how intelligent life might develop into something we wouldn't want to meet." —Stephen Hawking (warning that we should avoid contact with aliens)

» "The Constitution is what the judges say it is." —Former Supreme Court Chief Justice Charles E. Hughes

Common questions used to analyze a quotation might be: *What made the author say or write this? How does it fit into the text or historical context? Do people hold these views today?* and *What are points that support the different sides of the issue?* Try out these prompts on different quotations and see what happens.

All along, you must remember that the goal is to have students generate their own initial questions and prompts, similar to or better than the prompts that you would pose to them. You can model how to choose the most conversation-worthy questions by collecting them from students and thinking aloud as you consider them. You can then have students evaluate or rank the questions they think would be best to prompt deep conversations.

Base Prompts on a Thinking Skill

Prompts can come from core thinking skills that you are developing in your courses. You might refer to the chart of key skills in Figure 1.1 in Chapter 1 as you design these prompts. Several language arts, history, and science skills and prompts are described in more detail in Chapters 7, 8, and 9. You can also create your own chart of thinking skills and associated prompt starters and have students quickly choose from that list for classroom conversations. Of course, more than one thinking skill will likely be used in any extended conversation. We include examples of two thinking skills and associated prompts in Figure 4.2. These skills can also overlap with major questions of the discipline.

Figure 4.2 Sample Prompts Based on Thinking Skills

Thinking Skill	Sample Prompts
Interpret	What does the author mean by . . . ? Why do you think the author wrote this? What is a major theme in this . . . ? What did it mean when . . . ? What does this character teach us about life? What are other interpretations?
Identify causes and effects	Describe the role that he/she played in . . . Identify the primary causes and effects of . . . Was it causation or correlation, in the case of . . . When was the turning point? What brought this on? What were the long-term effects?

A visual way to scaffold the focus on thinking is to use the Academic Conversation (AC) Placemat shown in Figure 4.3 (an expanded, full-page version of the placemat is in the appendix). In the AC Placemat you can brainstorm ideas for conversation topics based on the thinking skills in the top dotted box. This allows you and students to choose and create a topic that is rich enough for a conversation. The topic or prompt you generate goes in the center oval. Recently we met with a teacher who was teaching the roots of the U.S. Constitution. Instead of just naming and describing the main influences that shaped the Constitution, the teacher had students evaluate which of the influences were more important and why. They started by reading about the factual content that they needed to learn in order to talk about the roots of the Constitution. Then they used the AC Placemat to plan conversations that would challenge their skills of evaluation, persuasion, and communication.

Throughout the year, as you observe student conversations, you can take note of and emphasize the skills that they need to work on. Students can use the placemat to take notes and to remind them of the skills they can use to keep the conversation going.

Figure 4.3 Academic Conversation Placemat

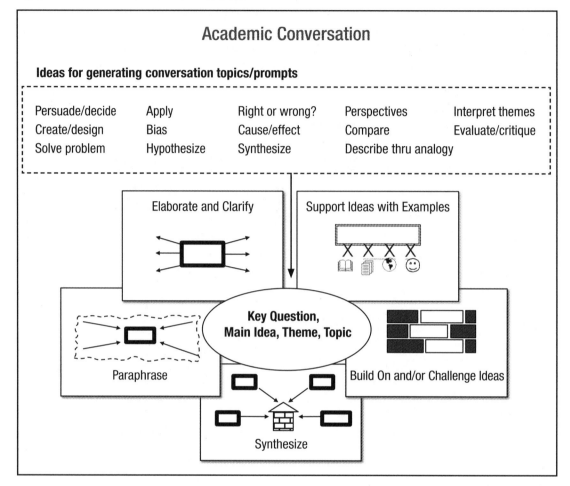

Base Prompts on a Product or Task

Another way to generate a prompt and give purpose to conversations is to give students a task to accomplish or a product to create. Students learn through authentic talk that has a productive purpose. It is important to have students converse (just talk) for a portion of the time before starting the hands-on work. Students often like to jump into the project without talking and digging into ideas, but it is the talking and negotiating that will foster quality when they do engage in the work.

Often, engaging conversations come from talking about connections between school and the real world. For example, one teacher had students talk about the theme of the story they were reading and then converse about how to create a drama that would show the theme through scenes. The conversation had two parts: (1) to come up with a life lesson from the text and (2) to figure out an effective way to communicate the life lesson to an audience. Two students decided that the theme in the story was sacrifice. They discussed various ideas for teaching this theme to younger students and decided to use drama in the form of a movie trailer with narration. They worked on it for two days and then presented the trailer to a younger class.

Similarly, another eighth-grade teacher had her students, in pairs, ask second-grade students what their favorite book topic was, collaborate to write and illustrate a children's book on that topic (with a moral lesson in it), read the book to the student, and present the book to him or her. The eighth graders then collaborated to write two responses to literature essays on their own and another pair's stories.

You can transform much of what you teach into tasks that might exist in the real world. Many topics and concepts in all disciplines can be shaped into engaging problems and tasks that foster more motivation and ownership of learning. For example, an objective such as learning to summarize might be turned into this task: *You are working at a publishing company and the director has asked you to write a synopsis for an advertisement of this book without giving away the ending. It needs to be* . . . [add assignment requirements for length, and so on]. In science, to learn and show learning about adaptation, students might be asked by a museum director to create an exhibit that shows eight different types of adaptation. Older students might be asked to write an article predicting how humans will change in the next 50,000 years. Students might address the problem of eradicating malaria as they learn about parasites in biology; they might write letters to the president suggesting ways to end wars and terrorism; they might write to authors to suggest a theme for a future novel or write an editorial on how statistics were misused in a recent newspaper article, and so on. Other ideas are presented in Figure 4.4 and in the chart titled "Conversation-Worthy Performance Tasks by Discipline" in the appendix.

Teachers who use tasks to build conversation skills often comment that working on such skills increases the quality of the final product and, because students are engaged in the tasks, the conversation practice is more authentic than quick "turn and talk" sessions during a teacher presentation. As we mentioned in Chapter 1, conversations help students see other ways of thinking and doing things, while they also challenge and strengthen one's ideas. Therefore, when conversing about tasks, students are training to do two very important real-world things: to collaborate and to create.

Figure 4.4 Thinking Skills, Prompt Ideas, and Sample Conversation Excerpts

Possible Thinking Focuses	Tasks with Conversation Components That Require and Show the Thinking	Sample Conversation Excerpt (after several minutes of developing the idea)
Interpret theme; Empathy and perspective	• Write a drama, role-play, movie, or screenplay. • Respond to a film or video as a critic.	"Well, we want to show the audience the theme of sacrifice." "So, let's come up with an example that we can role-play." "From my life . . . "
Determine importance, analyze, categorize	• Design a test or quiz. • Create a role-play card game. • Make a chart, table, or graph.	"What categories go on the chart?" "How about geology?" "You mean geography." "I don't think it's important enough."
Cause and effect	• Design a museum display. • Create a poster. • Fill in a graphic organizer.	"We need to put in the religion." "Why?" "Because it, like, helped them build up their civilization." "How so?"
Interpret theme, analyze character development	• Create/draft a children's story (use a story map).	"We should teach them not to bully." "Could we have a bully get bullied?" "Or we could have him get punished." "Okay, let's decide. What is more common? What will teach a lesson?"
Problem solve, apply ideas	• Design a business plan. • Design an experiment.	"How are we going to see if it is sunlight or fertilizer or the temperature?" "We keep all variables the same except one and we test it." "You mean just change one thing?"
Persuade, apply ideas	• Create an advertisement for the idea discussed in text (a magazine ad or billboard).	"We need to convince people that they will benefit from giving money to the shelter program." "I disagree. I think we should convince them it is the right thing to do."

Cause and effect, identify bias, perspective	• Write an article in an ancient newspaper about the decline of civilization, its reasons, and suggestions for improvement.	"We should include causes of decline." "Like what? Bad government? No democracy?" "Yes, but we need real evidence."
Identify ethics	• Write a persuasive article. • Prepare for a debate.	"We think animals have rights to not be tested." "It's not ethical to cause them pain." "What about animals we eat?"

Base Prompts on Life Experiences

Learning that endures often happens in real life. The decontextualized nature of many classroom lessons doesn't always help ideas to stick and doesn't tend to develop enduring thinking skills or language. We can, however, learn from others (a core thread in this book), and we can creatively craft more real-world-like experiences that give students something to converse about. Some of the most memorable learning can come from real experiences and conversations about them. Remember that the conversations (before, during, and after an experience) can be as important—or even more important—for learning as the actual activity. The following are some examples of ways to integrate academic conversations with real-world-like experiences:

Shared experiences. We know teachers who have students do atypical activities, such as go blindfolded for thirty minutes, sleep on the floor, ask others for money, be accused of a theft, wear strange clothes, take a field trip, and so on. Following the activity, students share their thoughts and feelings with a partner, connecting the event to the lesson topic.

Case studies. While typically used in upper grades and higher education, case studies are powerful in younger grades as well. A case is any account based on real-world events that students can analyze and discuss, as experts might do. The activity can have different approaches: diagnostic (as in the medical field), judicial (as in legal decisions), or problem-based (as in business or science). For example, a fifth-grade teacher uses cases to teach environmental science. Students read the cases and converse to prepare brief role-plays of the case. They present to the class, and then the class breaks into groups to converse about the case they just saw.

Simulations and role-plays. Acting offers a chance to empathize with people and understand events through others' perspectives. Drama is engaging and provides great raw material for rich conversations. A math teacher might have students act out a long word problem; when they converse about it afterward, they have actually acted out the problem or seen it happen already. A history teacher might act as a dictator for a week and use the thoughts and feelings that emerged in students to foster conversations about democracy, rights, and so on. In a simulation game about the events leading to World War I, students might act like the heads of the nations involved. A science teacher might put elements from the periodic table on the backs of students' chairs. Students learn about "what element they are" and how they react with other elements (students) around the room. A language arts teacher might have students create role-plays based on story events. Students converse to choose the most meaningful parts to act out and to create the script, the actions, props, and so on.

Reflections

1. What types of conversations are most interesting to your students? How do they start?
2. Think of a topic for a future lesson and come up with the four different types of prompts that could spark academic conversations about it.
3. Write a model conversation transcript that has the seven features of effective conversations described in the beginning of the chapter.

Chapter 5
Training Students for Advanced Conversations

> I never realized how much was involved in a good conversation.

—*Sixth-grade teacher*

This chapter provides ways to train students to have in-depth conversations across subject areas and grade levels. It includes strategies for using visual organizers, asking effective questions, honing thinking skills, and solving communication problems. It is meant to answer many of the "How do I do this with dozens of real students?" questions that may have emerged as you read earlier chapters.

One of the greatest gifts you can give your students is the set of skills needed to productively collaborate with others. Granted, students might be in for a shock if they enter your class after spending previous years in classrooms that were focused on memorization and right answers (i.e., game-show pedagogy). But as they realize that you are looking for their ideas, not just memorized answers, students feel safer to share even the beginnings of an idea or opinion. As students converse and share their thoughts, they expand their ideas, sharpen their thinking skills, and learn to clearly communicate—a three-for-one bargain.

Students need a lot of training and practice to get their minds into decathlon-like shape for academic conversation. When conversing, a person uses a variety of thinking skills all at once, akin to mental multitasking. For example, you might converse with a friend about a current political issue. As you listen, you summarize what she says in your mind, question what she means by freedom, formulate a response with an example, predict how she will respond, evaluate her evidence, and decide whether you should disagree or not. These all happen automatically and in a split second. Most teachers have honed these abilities for decades. In this chapter we describe these advanced skills in order to help you help your students develop them in less time than you did.

Train Students to Take Conversation to More Academic Levels

Figure 5.1 is useful for showing students the levels they should try to reach in their conversations. Ideas for hand motions are included in parentheses on the left side of the figure. Level 1 is the surface, where many conversations remain. This consists of retelling events or stories, relaying information, social exchanges, and basic chatting. In Level 2, students generate a meaningful, often abstract or inferred, idea based on information that arose in Level 1. In Level 3, students support the idea(s) in Level 2 with examples, elaborations, connections, and explanations. Then in Level 4, students generate other ideas, evaluate them, and use persuasive argument to decide which is the most valuable. You can use Figure 5.1 as a poster and/or a self-assessment checklist. You can practice digging down to or even starting at deeper levels. For example, you might give a pair of students two conflicting themes to support and then argue.

Granted, there are many types of academic conversations. Figure 5.1 shows only one model to get you thinking about what they might become. Notice the extra thinking and negotiation of meaning in Level 4. Students work together using negotiation and thinking skills to create a final "product" in the form of an idea. You can modify this visual as needed for use as an anchor poster.

Each response is pivotal in an academic conversation. Students should use each turn to build and deepen their conversation, using the five skills described in Chapter 2 in combination with other critical thinking and communication behaviors of the discipline. Students should know where each conversation is going and the best moves to take them there. One way to help them make their responses more academic is to use conversation observations and transcript analyses. These can model for students how to make the next utterance as useful, appropriate, interesting, probing, professional, mature, and technical as possible.

Train Students to Facilitate Conversations in Teacher-Like Ways

Many teachers know how to foster effective whole-class conversations and squeeze the most learning into them. They ask deep questions at the right times, keep the conversation focused, notice when students are confused, and build ideas upon ideas. They employ the skills in Chapter 2 and work very hard to get students to verbalize their thinking. However—and this is one of the big threads of this book—teachers can and should train students to do these same things: to use teacher-like skills in their own conversations. We harp on this point because, when analyzing many transcripts of teacher-led conversations, we often write in the margins, "Student should/could say this." Students should gradually become independent of teacher control of conversations. The following are some of the teacher-like skills that students should learn to use:

Figure 5.1 Levels of Thought Within a Conversation

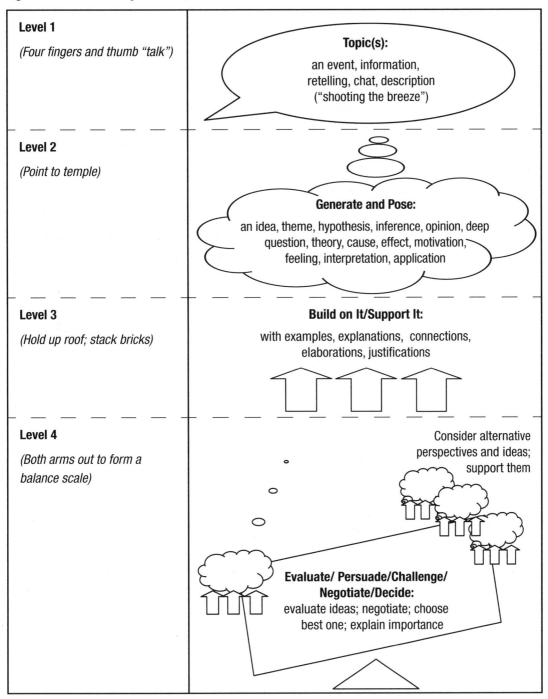

Level 1	
(Four fingers and thumb "talk")	**Topic(s):** an event, information, retelling, chat, description ("shooting the breeze")

Level 2

(Point to temple)

Generate and Pose:
an idea, theme, hypothesis, inference, opinion, deep question, theory, cause, effect, motivation, feeling, interpretation, application

Level 3

(Hold up roof; stack bricks)

Build on It/Support It:
with examples, explanations, connections, elaborations, justifications

Level 4

(Both arms out to form a balance scale)

Consider alternative perspectives and ideas; support them

Evaluate/ Persuade/Challenge/ Negotiate/Decide:
evaluate ideas; negotiate; choose best one; explain importance

Teaching points. Teachers are always looking for "teaching points" in student comments, along with ways to extend discussions, go deeper, and highlight the big idea in the lesson. You can train students to use partner responses as ways to get deeper and more academic. When a partner is shocked or humored by something, students can ask probing questions or connect it to modern life. Students can come up with prompts, some of which are as simple as: *Why? What does that mean in this case? What is a modern example of that?* and *Why is that important?* Other teacher-like sentence starters include: *Why did the author . . . ? What are our next steps?* and *What are we trying to say here?* We have seen many conversations go deeper with such prompts, prompts that at the same time show that the questioner is valuing what the partner says.

Pauses. Students should learn to pause during talking or pause before taking a turn. The pause allows the partner to think about what was said, to paraphrase, and to respond. It allows the speaker to stop and think about what to say next. Of course, the listener must also not use every pause to jump in and speak; a pause is sometimes needed for thinking and perhaps asking a probing question.

Students teach. In most conversations, some teaching happens. One person explains his or her ideas or knowledge to another, "teaching" the partner, in a sense. As one student teaches, both students learn. You can also have a third student act as a mediator, like a teacher who listens to the conversation and intercedes at key points.

It helps to equip students with other teacher-like skills, several of which are included along with sentence starters in Figure 5.2. The skills are on the left and possible things to say are on the right. Teachers should model these conversation skills and sentence starters in whole-class discussions, groups, and individual conversations with students.

Train Students in Different Types of Academic Conversation

It helps to be aware of different overlapping types of conversation that are useful for classroom learning. Two or more types might happen in the same conversation, and they can all happen across the content areas. Here are some conversation types:

Build and explore ideas. Building and exploring an idea means to analyze, highlight, explain, uncover, and understand a complex or abstract idea. It means to put heads together and build out and up from an undeveloped thought. For example, if a student brings up a new

Figure 5.2 Teacher-Like Conversation Skills That Students Should Learn

Teacher-Like Skill	Possible Things to Say
Pose a thought-provoking question to get the conversation going or make it go deeper.	Why . . . ? How . . . ? In your opinion, . . .
Let the partner say as much as he or she can; encourage the partner to think aloud.	That's interesting, please keep going. Tell us what you are thinking. Tell me more about . . .
Keep the goal or topic in mind; get the conversation back on track; maintain focus.	What are we trying to do? What is our goal? Remember, our central question is . . .
Value others' thinking; remember what a person said earlier and connect to it.	Great idea! Let's write that down. Connecting back to what you said about . . ., we can . . . Do you think that . . . ?
Don't pick one side of an issue; be impartial and inquisitive; encourage open-mindedness and value different perspectives.	Then again, we need to remember . . . What about . . . ? What are other points of view?
Question a source; challenge an idea.	Where did that evidence come from? What makes that a reliable source?
Generate theories, big ideas, and truths about the world, history, life, and so on.	We might interpret this as . . . One theory could be that . . .
Clarify another person's or your own idea (when you see wondering faces and wandering minds).	Interesting, so what you are saying is . . . In other words, . . .
Paraphrase, emphasizing that the idea helped to move the discussion forward.	Okay, so you are saying . . . That helps us. Juan highlighted that . . . Let's build on this.
Be specific, clear, brief, and sincere.	Specifically, I mean that . . .

connection between war and Darwin, the conversation can add layers to this idea, challenge it, and think of examples, counterexamples, relevance, and similar ideas. The students work together and add to, shape, or gently challenge each other's contributions.

Debate issues. Some of the most educational conversations involve the arguing and negotiating of differing ideas. This type of talk includes several skills that are highly valued in many societies. These include the ability to constructively criticize ideas, consider well-supported points, question the quality of claims, and make joint decisions (Mercer 1995). Even first graders can and do use language for related purposes (e.g., "That's not fair!").

Solve problems. In classes such as math and science, much of the emphasis is on solving problems. Interestingly and importantly, much of the conversation in the real world is about solving problems, improving conditions, making decisions, and so on. Students can converse through various problem-solving steps, checking on each other, and adding ideas that the partner may not have considered. At times there might be some debate about which way to proceed or whether a solution is the most appropriate.

Teach and learn. Teach-and-learn conversation happens when one student knows information or a skill and needs to teach the partner. You have likely seen both how well and how poorly many students teach their peers. They may just quickly tell partners the answer, tell them what to do, or do it for them. You can teach students how to teach in one-on-one settings, knowing that all students will be in the role of teacher and student at different times. And you can also remind students how much teachers actually learn and remember from teaching a concept to others.

Train Students to Perceive When Their Listeners Don't Understand

Many people, young and old, don't always perceive their listener's grasp—or lack of grasp—of what is being communicated. They just keep talking. Teachers need to train students to be keenly aware of their partners' understanding while they are speaking. The partner might have missed a word, or the message might be long and the speaker might need to stop to allow the listener's brain to chunk the information and paraphrase it. The speaker might see a confused look and ask, *Does that make sense? Is that clear?* or *What do you think?* The speaker should do little comprehension checks along the way.

In pairs, students often become temporary teachers of whatever they are expressing. Student A is trying to "teach" student B what she feels is her possible explanation of why the author of a text was biased, for example. Just like adult teachers, students need to make their language comprehensible. They can do this in many different ways. Emphasize that communicating academic ideas is often hard work. Saying it once might not be enough. Just verbalizing it might not be enough. Students might take out a piece of paper during a conversation to create a visual representation of an abstract concept; they might even get out of their seat to act out what they are trying to say. The key is for students to recognize when their listeners are having trouble understanding and pause to take steps to explain more clearly.

Train Students to Ask Useful Questions

Questions linger, push, and energize thinking. They open up the mind rather than shut it down. Questions help students to be creative, hypothetical, empathetic, and humble—all of which are qualities that will help them later in life. In fact, many employers put "asks good questions" in their top five qualities for new hires. Here are several types of questions that students should be able to produce.

Questions That Sustain Conversations

Questions that sustain good conversations are often of the clarification and focusing nature, such as *What do you mean by . . . ? How does that connect to our question of . . . ?* and *Why is that important?* When a partner says, "I agree," students should ask the partner why. A simple, well-placed "Why?" or "How?" can be powerful. In fact, we have seen the continued asking of a simple "Why?" bring students to the foundations of the human psyche, historical processes, scientific laws, and themes in literature. Other questions include *How can we apply this in the future? What do others think? Why is it relevant? What makes something relevant or not?* and *What is logic?*

Prepare students for responding to partner questions that will seem like challenges or criticisms of their ideas. Students must be able to accept and answer such questions with respect, though they might be caught off guard or feel threatened. With a classroom spirit that encourages inquiry and exploration, this should not be a problem.

Questions That Explore Ideas

Student exploration of concepts and ideas is missing in many curricula. Students are often asked to memorize definitions, but not come up with their own definitions. Students need to repeatedly explore and apply the meanings of core concepts such as truth, loyalty, right, wrong, peace, freedom, balance, humanity, democracy, justice, history, bias, proof, gravity, time, and love, to name a few. In order to explore meanings as they converse, you can train students to ask questions such as these:

> » *What does _____ mean? What does it mean for those people, in that time, for us these days, and so on.?*
> » *What does _____ require?*
> » *Is it possible to be _____ and (<u>antonym of term</u>) at the same time?*
> » *What are good and poor examples of _____?*
> » *Is it possible that she was _____, yet she had other motives?*

Questions That Linger

One of your goals should be to get students to come up with deep questions *at the end of* a conversation, a lesson, a school day, and so on. You want them to go out the classroom door with something to ponder. Pondering often leads to more focused and strategic thinking and problem solving, which leads to learning. A question can linger in a person's mind, motivating them to talk about it with others, to think deeply about it, and to look for answers *on their own time and not for points*. When this happens, one question becomes much more educational than a long string of answers.

Train and encourage students to ask deep questions. When they do ask questions that make everyone think, get excited. Write them down. This motivates students to keep generating such questions inside and outside of school. Here are a few additional ideas for developing students' questioning skills:

- Put up on the wall a chart that lists different thinking categories you are shooting for during the year (e.g., empathy, bias, application to life, comparison). Model the types of questions that go in each category. Have students fill out large cards with their questions about a topic you are studying. As a class, decide under which category each question goes and evaluate the depth or engagement value of each question for a conversation.
- During a class discussion, stop periodically to have everyone write down an important question. Have several students share their questions. Vote on one that best continues or deepens the discussion.
- Read a variety of texts and have students generate homework, quiz, or test questions that they think would be most interesting to answer.

- Give questioning skills tests. These are tests that give the answers and require students to come up with good questions for them. You can discuss with students a rubric for the types of questions you are looking for. Then you can give a practice quiz or two with answers on them and score the questions as a class. Another option is to have students come up with the answers, which will take the form of key knowledge, concepts, skills, or quantitative results in math and science. You can then give a compilation to the whole class or trade the student-made tests between groups.

Questions That Require and Inspire Higher-Order Thinking

Since 1956, when Benjamin Bloom and his colleagues created their leveled taxonomy of thinking skills, educators have made much progress in understanding the realm of cognitive skills. There are many different taxonomies and skills floating around the literature. We lean toward the notion that once you are below the surface level of recall and memorization, thinking skills get deep and messy. They often support one another. Therefore, we tell teachers to not worry so much about levels, but to focus on several core thinking skills and work on them throughout the year in a variety of topics. Examples of these skills and their question and prompt stems for specific subject areas are found in Chapters 7, 8 and 9.

Train Students to Negotiate Meaning

Many ideas and decisions in life are not right or wrong, black or white, or multiple choice. They are abstract, complex, dynamic, fuzzy, and made of words that mean different things to different people. Negotiation means to modify your meaning in response to a partner's differing meaning on the same issue. As shown at the top of Figure 5.3, Student A might have one idea and Student B another. As they converse, they form a mutual understanding by conceding some points and adding others from the partner. You can liken it to bargaining: "I give up this point about . . . and you give up your point about . . . I will add your point about . . . if you add my point about . . ." As Figure 5.3 shows, the final idea will seldom be a perfect overlap, but the result is shared understanding (and lots of academic talk and thinking). The object is not to win, but to understand and build stronger ideas that are less black and white. This process is exhibited in this excerpt from a fifth-grade language arts class, in which students are discussing the book *The Giver* (Lowry 2006).

Figure 5.3 Negotiation of Meaning

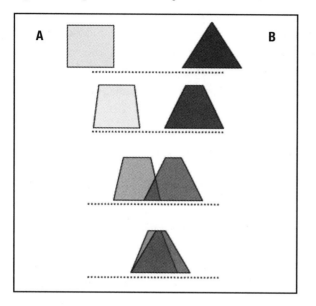

Sandeep: I think it's about showing how evil humans can be.

Tasha: Why do you say that?

Sandeep: Because all those memories are described.

Tasha: So, if all those things are so bad, what is wrong with those people who want to make sure the children don't know that stuff? I don't want to know all that stuff.

Sandeep: We are better off knowing our past, even if it's bad.

Tasha: Everything? There are a lot of horrible things that even we don't know about; they would give us nightmares and, I don't know.

Sandeep: Well, maybe some stuff shouldn't be passed down to us. But we need to learn, too, from mistakes.

Tasha: Okay, maybe, but what bad things should we know about? What will help us learn and not do that stuff?

Sandeep: I don't know, maybe things like nuclear bombs, you know, and war.

Tasha: Okay, but maybe not the gory details.

One of the keys to effective negotiation is seeing the other person's perspective(s). By knowing what the other person is thinking, you can predict what they consider to be important. You can be more empathetic, which tends to make the other person more willing to work with you to come up with a negotiated solution. See the section titled "Considering Multiple Perspectives" in Chapter 7 for more information.

Train Students to Encourage and Compliment

Positive comments to a partner during and after a conversation are powerful on several levels. Such comments can show that the listener understands and is interested in what the partner is saying. The listener can also show that he or she trusts the partner's ideas. Even though practicing encouragement and compliments can sound a bit contrived, it is effective. Many students are not accustomed to building up others. Just saying, "This was a great conversation" is not enough. Whether in pairs or in whole-class settings, a person needs to be specific in order to reinforce conversation behaviors. Comments often need to be modeled and highlighted by teachers early on. Comments might be similar to these:

> » *I loved the way you built off my hypothesis that the main character had selfish motives for leaving.*
> » *This conversation was effective because you helped keep it focused.*
> » *Wow, nice job. I liked how you made sure all four of us got chances to speak.*
> » *When someone asked a question, you all paused to think before sharing.*
> » *I appreciated how you supported your idea with evidence from the book.*
> » *I liked how you disagreed in a respectful way.*
> » *I liked how you listened with your eyes and head; you were very interested in what I was saying.*

Descriptions of encouragement and support can be put, if needed, into the self-assessment checklist or rubric that students use after conversing. Students can write down notes of encouraging comments and go over them when they reflect on the conversation.

A related skill is making others feel important. We often have heard people praise those who make others around them feel important. We want students to do this, too. Even though it is natural to do the opposite (make ourselves feel more important than others), we can train students to make others feel important in conversations through compliments, expressions, and comments. Collect these comments, if you can, and share them. You will likely notice a major improvement in classroom climate as these comments emerge.

Train Students to Maintain Logical Flow, Connections, and Depth of Thought

Conversations can be very challenging because, rather than being linear as many written texts are, conversations tend to be recursive, cycling through ideas and returning to those that are most interesting and relevant (Spiegel 2005). Conversations should focus on a topic to give it depth, but many conversations also explore various subtopics, move back and forth between ideas, address conflicting points of view, and even move into different topics entirely.

Here are several student-friendly reminders based on the analogy of driving a car:

Stay on (or near) the road! Keep tangential ideas from hijacking the conversation. Teach students to "keep within sight of the road" when they do veer a little bit. For example, you might tell a quick story about your cousin that relates to the topic, but you can't start recounting his whole life story. Staying on topic takes work. It is hard work to prune away all the semi-related thoughts that quickly stream in as others talk.

Don't lose your keys! Unlike the reading process, in conversation it is hard to look back at the exact details of what was said four minutes ago or four days ago to use it to construct meaning. Students should learn to take notes on key ideas or figure out a mental trick to keep track of them. Train students to respond to the general question, *What do you think?* with *About what, specifically?* This forces the questioner to choose a key point.

Stop to get your bearings. Every few minutes, students should take a moment to think and paraphrase their ideas so far. You, the teacher, can encourage practice of this with a "midway pause" in which you say, "Okay everyone, stop to bundle up the meaning you have so far. What have you done? What do you still need to discuss?"

If it stalls, get out and push or ask for help. Before stopping the conversation or moving on to a new topic, students should try to develop current ideas as much as possible. They should seek to develop ideas into theories and profound insights. Partners should keep asking if there are other perspectives, examples, and related ideas. They can ask a peer or the teacher for an idea jumpstart. One idea is to put the ideas or theories in the center of a semantic map and see how many different branches they can add: examples, applications, details, questions, and anything else that supports the idea.

Train Students to Recognize That an Abstract Idea Needs Support, Elaboration, and/or Examples

A student might bring up a theme or an abstract idea as a result of his or her interpretation of the text. Teachers need to train students to feel unsatisfied with short, one- or two-word abstract ideas. Ideas such as bravery, love, freedom, rights, and power could mean many different things to different people. Eventually, a talker should elaborate without prompting, feeling uneasy about just offering a short, general, abstract answer. Even when prompts seem a bit awkward, they are still very useful at extending conversations, as seen in the following conversation about a chapter in a fourth-grade history textbook.

José:	Why do you think the author wrote this?
Juan:	To show how they suffered and how they lived and to show the history of the Chumash people.
José:	Can you elaborate?
Juan:	Okay, Native Americans were sent to missions and they were forced to work there, and many died.
José:	Can you give an example?
Juan:	Well, they were like slaves in farms and then they got European diseases.
José:	I don't know what it meant that they disappeared all together. What idea does that give you?
Juan:	How they disappeared?
José:	Yeah.
Juan:	I think that when they were forced to go somewhere else and didn't have medicine to heal them, maybe they died.
José:	So you think that they didn't have medicine to cure the people that were sick? Okay. In the future I just hope that the Native Americans will still be on this land like they are today, but I don't think it was fair to be treated that way.
Juan:	The main idea seems to be that it is a lesson not to be selfish, or force people, but it's a lesson to be . . .
José:	To be fair.
Juan:	Yeah, to be fair.

Train Students to Be Leaders and Team Players

In a recent conversation, a friend in the business world mentioned the importance of both leadership and "followship." Conversations can train students to develop both qualities. In a conversation, a student can work on the leadership skills of guiding the conversation, keeping it focused, clarifying and defending ideas, and being patient with others. Followship involves listening, building on a partner's idea, and allowing and helping the partner to shape the conversation. Students should learn how to work together as a team, play different roles, and respectfully lead and follow the directions of others.

Train Students to Think and Talk Like Experts

One objective during the course of schooling is to train students to think more and more like experts in various disciplines. In order to have more expert-like conversations, students also need to know *why* experts in each discipline talk and *what* they talk about. Think about what happens in conversations between literary critics, between scientists, between mathematicians, between historians, and so on. Write down some ideas for the why and what in the content area you are teaching.

Zoom In and Out

A key feature of expert-like thinking is being able to zoom in and out, that is, to go from general to specific (or from specific to general), from theory to practice, from abstract ideas to concrete examples. One must be able to zoom out and refer to the big ideas and general principles of the discipline in conversations. For this reason, students need to know the big laws, truths, theories, principles, themes, and essential understandings that frame the discipline. Then students must learn and practice how to apply these big ideas to specific ideas in conversations. For example, they might zoom out as they refer to conservation of mass in chemistry, adaptation in biology, irony in literature, and bias in a history text. Students must learn to apply principles to new data and evidence.

See Patterns

Another thinking skill used by experts is seeing patterns and relationships. Experts look for patterns that confirm what they already know about the discipline. For example, a historian might look at several primary sources and see a common pattern of biased accounts. Experts also look for new patterns and relationships. They might use this to formulate new theories and insights about the field. For example, an astronomer might see data that suggests gravitational waves are stronger in some parts of space and then form a theory based on this data. Students need to get into the habit of seeing patterns and either confirming or creating theories for them. They might read several short stories about Colonial America and see common character traits. They might read different accounts of McCarthyism and formulate a theory about human psychology. They might read several books by the same author and pose a theory about the author's past.

Use Sentence Starters

Another way to get students thinking and talking academically is by giving them sentence starters (also called stems or frames). Many teachers already have posters of effective sentence starters on the wall. Teachers notice that students use the starters initially, but then during the conversation the talk seldom contains the starter language. Students don't (and shouldn't) look at the wall all the time while they are in face-to-face conversations. Here are several ideas for encouraging students to use the language in sentence starters:

- *Have students use starters in writing.* Before they converse, have students use the starters in writing. Usually, teachers use conversing (or allow it) in order to get a good piece of writing produced. This strategy uses writing to help scaffold better conversations.
- *Offer points for using starters.* Give students points for using the stems in conversation. You can use an honor system or have a third observer. In this way students nudge themselves a bit more to use the stems; the observer can even support them by whispering possible starters or pointing to one on a piece of paper.
- *Model the starters as much as possible.* The more students hear the language stems in real use, the more they will use them.

Remember, sentence starters are just a start. Students should not be looking up at the wall at the end of the year, nor should they be just answering questions in pairs in preparation for tests. They should be using the starter language throughout their academic conversations.

Weave Academic Conversations into Lessons

Conversations can be powerful ways to reinforce, deepen, and clarify learning during lessons. We have seen successful teachers use them in all stages of a lesson.

Here is an example of how one teacher weaves conversation into her lessons:

1. Students have an initial academic conversation to predict the topic and meaning of the text, using several quotations and key words from the text, along with the title.
2. The teacher reads aloud the first part of the text, stopping at times to think aloud and discuss the purpose of the text, predictions, connections to life, and questions. The teacher might personalize, but doesn't linger too long on personal connections. She molds them into examples for supporting higher-level themes.

3. Student pairs silently read the rest of the text, stopping at agreed points to write down conversation ideas. They can stop twice to converse about the text.

4. The whole group holds a discussion to generate possible topics for extended academic conversations. This is the time to build up background knowledge, vocabulary, and ideas that will fuel conversations. The class generates ideas to work with and negotiate—not answers to simply repeat during the paired conversations.

5. The teacher and a student model a conversation skill in a mini-lesson or fishbowl.

6. Student pairs hold academic conversations (sometimes these are also used to generate ideas for writing).

7. Students write and provide peer feedback.

8. Students read each other's writing and have academic conversations about the ideas in the written pieces.

Conversations allow students to stop to process and clarify meanings. You must decide when this is most needed in a lesson. You don't want students talking the entire lesson. The key is to think about where you want students to stop and think and verbalize what they are thinking. A lesson needs to flow, but it needs to stop at times or it flows too quickly and the learning doesn't stick.

When Conversations Deteriorate

Teachers must also train students to overcome common obstacles to effective conversation. Students need to learn to avoid and notice common conversation damagers, some of which are listed in the left-hand column of Figure 5.4. Possible solutions are listed in the right-hand column.

Figure 5.4 Obstacles to Effective Conversations and Possible Solutions

Obstacles	Possible Solutions
Laughing at your partner's answer or making fun of it, rolling eyes, and so on	Conduct a mini-lesson and role-play to show effects of such behaviors.
Popcorning— when partners bring up many ideas that don't connect or build on previous ideas	Have students, in a fun way, say whatever comes to their mind to show how they don't connect. Have students use a semantic map to make sure ideas connect to a central idea.

Talking too much	Remind students that partners can only listen so much. If they talk too much, the partner gets overwhelmed with too many ideas, and often stops listening or loses the train of thought. Have students use talking chips or cards (students put a chip or card in when they talk; stop when they run out of chips). Train students who are listening to interrupt with a paraphrase ("Wait, so you are saying that . . .") to begin their own turn.
Being off-task; talking about unrelated topics	Have students paraphrase: "So far, we agree that . . . we disagree that . . . you argue that . . ." Require exit-ticket summaries or another product that shows learning after conversing.
Being overly argumentative; trying to win; getting angry or frustrated	Remind students of norms; train students to take uncommon perspectives and respect those who do so; use role-plays to show good and poor argumentation.
Conversation stalls	Allow silent time for thinking. Paraphrase: "Okay, our goal is to . . . So far, we know that . . . We have established that . . . You believe that . . ." Have students stop and write down their thoughts so far.

Reflections

1. Analyze transcripts of whole-class discussions. What do the teacher and students say and when? What makes it go deeper? Shallower?
2. What are the most challenging skills to train students to use? Why?
3. Design a lesson with academic conversations in it. Have a colleague critique it and provide feedback.

Chapter 6
Developing Academic Grammar and Vocabulary Through Conversation

> Language a would mess be grammar without.

—*Ninth-grade student*

This chapter focuses on grammar and vocabulary, two vital gears of language that work together to clearly communicate messages. As in other chapters, this chapter is two-way, describing how to use conversation to build grammar and vocabulary and how to use grammar and vocabulary to improve conversation skills.

Building Academic Grammar Through and For Conversation

Grammar is the organization of words, phrases, and sentences. In most cases, there are many ways to organize one's message. Over time, students learn from home, media, school conversations, and texts the kinds of grammar that are expected—what "sounds right"—in each setting. As Dunn and Lindblom argue, "What they need is the ability to communicate effectively with people in all kinds of contexts for all kinds of purposes . . . Pretending that grammar rules provide a smooth, toll-free road to economic success is a harmful myth" (2003, 45). Therefore, we can and should teach students how to analyze language for clarity; and along the way, we provide them with additional ways to express their advancing thoughts.

Grammar is highly rooted in one's oral language. If the ability to form coherent thoughts in different grammatical ways is already in one's head, then reading, listening, and writing challenging texts becomes more automatic. Ehrenworth and Vinton (2005) argue that we should teach grammar in order to "increase power, opportunity, and voice; to teach habits of fluency, inquiry, and experimentation; to engage students in such a way that this knowledge and these habits are sustaining and flexible" (14). The challenge, of course, is to teach grammar in engaging ways.

A good converser must be able to determine the importance in a message by figuring out the main actors, actions, and circumstances (Schleppegrell and de Oliveira 2006). The message usually contains a variety of grammatical devices to link, compare, add detail, emphasize, and clarify. Both partners need to condense (i.e., chunk) ideas that come up in the conversation as they build meanings. To do this, many students still need to build up their grammatical muscles.

Teach High-Leverage Grammar

Through mini-lessons, you can teach the grammar that is commonly used to communicate academic messages in conversations. We seldom consciously apply grammar rules to answer questions or to speak. So, rather than getting too bogged down in the vast mire of grammar rules and exceptions, you can be selective and teach some of the "high-yield" academic grammar rules described in the following sections. These should be taught through real communication as much as possible. A conversation can be a part of each mini-lesson to allow students to practice the new grammar.

Complex Sentences

Complex sentences have an independent clause and one or more dependent clauses. The independent clause usually has the main subject and main verb. Dependent clauses add detail or explanation to the main clause in the sentence. A dependent clause starts with either a relative pronoun (e.g., *that, who, whom, whose, where, when,* or *which)* or a subordinating conjunction (e.g., *although, after, despite, because, since, before, whether, until, if, how, once, when*). (See the section titled "Sentence Building" later in this chapter.) Some sample sentences are listed here, but others are found in the activities later in the chapter.

Language Arts: *When they discovered footprints by the lake, Luke began to believe that he would see his uncle again.*

History: *Geography played a key role in the isolation of local languages, which still share only a few words.*

Science: *In order to cover their escape from predators, some species of squid have developed capabilities to create a cloud of ink.*

When you listen to a complex sentence, you will notice that the speaker presents dependent (subordinate) clauses in a lower volume and tone, with a slightly quicker pace and less emphasis.

For example, read this aloud: *Although he had planned for every contingency, the lack of oxygen at the top weakened his ability to communicate with the others who accompanied him up the mountain.* You likely heard yourself slow down and emphasize the middle clause (*the lack of oxygen at the top weakened his ability to communicate with the others*), which carries the main subject and action or state. The first and third clauses provide extra information. Reading with emphasis on the key parts of the sentence helps readers to focus on the important information and thus to better comprehend the text or oral message. Likewise, as students use complex sentences in conversation, they should practice this emphasis on the main clauses.

Transitions and Connectives

Transitions and connectives are the glue and mortar words that are important in writing and speech in order to maintain coherence and flow of meaning. These are often used at the beginnings of sentences to connect them to previous sentences. Here are main categories and examples of transitions and connectives:

» Cause and effect: *For this reason, since, but, then, therefore, thus, because*
» Additional examples and information: *for example, in addition, also, besides, another, moreover*
» U-turn clauses/comparison: *on the contrary, nevertheless, however, although, at the same time, then again, on the other hand, yet, but, instead of*
» Sequence: *first, second, then, last, finally*

Pronouns

Students, in talking and writing, tend to overuse pronouns. For example, "It said that she wanted her sister to find her picture of her before she tells her friend about what happened to her." Students should learn to be extra explicit in academic settings, to predict when the use of a pronoun might be confusing, and to use the same term or a synonym instead of the pronoun. Students must also learn to ask for clarification of pronouns when they hear them used by partners. This will train partners to not overuse pronouns.

Terms That Qualify, Soften, Hedge, and Express Uncertainty

Life is often all or nothing for students. It is full of extremes, and their speech often mirrors this thinking: "I'll die if he says that again!" "There is no chance of winning!" "All students are furious at the principal." When this type of speech enters the academic realm, students don't sound very academic. There are always—check that—*usually* exceptions to all-or-nothing statements. Train students to listen for all-or-nothing terms and call their partners on such terms.

You should also train students to express uncertainty by speculating, qualifying, and using hedge terms. This avoids their falling into all-or-nothing traps to which others will react. Expressing uncertainties helps students to approach a topic with humility and inquisitiveness. To do so, students need to learn to use hedging terms such as *might, may, could, would, possibly, most, some, evidence suggests that, likely, tends to, often, seldom, perhaps, probably, sometimes, many, few, rarely, can, most, occasionally, apparently,* and *theoretically*. For example, instead of saying, "The evidence shows that humans are causing global warming," a student should say, "The evidence in this report *suggests* that humans are causing global warming." Qualifying often results from the knowledge that there are many points of view out there, many different sources of evidence, and many different ways to interpret the evidence.

Have students listen for and look for qualifiers in various messages. They might also find places where qualifiers are needed. Put the qualifiers to be learned into sentences on the wall. Point them out when you use them and read them. Point out areas in student writing where they use qualifiers and should use them.

Grammar-Building Conversation Activities

The following activities help students to acquire grammar abilities that will aid them in their conversations in school and beyond. Many of these activities also foster growth in academic writing.

Talking in Paragraphs with Topic Sentences

This activity trains students to think and speak in paragraphs. Speaking in paragraphs not only improves their oral communication but also supports their writing and reading. This activity also helps students to elaborate, paraphrase, build on ideas, and synthesize. It develops students' abilities to generate an idea and craft it into a strong topic sentence that is followed by additional sentences that support it. The topic sentences tend to be more general and abstract thesis-level thoughts (e.g., *Columbus did not discover America.*). Students get to practice figuring out what they want to say and shaping it into one strong topic statement.

Prepare open-ended (not just short-answer) review questions for students to answer in pairs, or have pairs prepare the questions. The questions should require paragraph-sized answers. The questions should allow the responder to formulate a topic sentence and then support it with other sentences. Partner A asks a question to B and gives B some time to think *without* writing. B thinks up a complete topic sentence and several other ideas to support it. After four to seven sentences (a paragraph), Partner B stops. Then, Partner B asks A a different question. Model this multiple times with different topics. Here is an example:

Partner A: *Why do you think we should study history?*
Partner B: *We should study history in order to understand ourselves. If we don't know what our ancestors have done, or what they were thinking, then we don't know where to go. We keep making mistakes, and learning history will prevent this. For example, we had two world wars.*

If students struggle, they can also use a preconversation graphic organizer with a shape on top in which to put a topic sentence, supported by several columns below (see Figure 6.1). After writing, though, they should cover up the organizer when they talk.

Figure 6.1 Topic Sentence Supported by Other Sentences

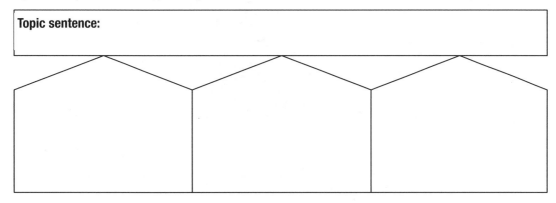

Topic sentence:

Practicing Cohesion Devices with Pro-Con

Cohesion means that the ideas in a message's paragraphs and sentences tie together clearly and smoothly. Cohesion devices make it much easier for the reader or listener to construct meaning. As in academic writing, academic talking uses cohesion devices (many of which are transitions) to link and separate ideas. Learning to use a variety of transitions and cohesion devices helps students to more effectively write, think, read, and speak in all disciplines.

The pro-con activity (adapted from Duffala 1987) can be used to train students to orally use and acquire academic transitions and other cohesion devices. Figure 6.2 shows four categories of cohesion devices that are common in school.

Figure 6.2 Cohesion Devices for Pro-Con

To Compare	To Contrast	To Express Cause and Effect	To Add Ideas and Evidence
likewise	in contrast	therefore	in addition
as	even though	as a result	also
in a similar way	nevertheless	since	and
also	yet	consequently	moreover
similarly	unlike	due to	in fact
equally	however	brought about	besides
as well	on the other hand	if . . . then	equally important
too	despite	consequently	furthermore
in the same manner	conversely	given that	next
	whereas	for this reason	too
	in comparison	thus	finally
		provided that	
		this led to	
		in order to	

In each turn of the pro-con activity, one partner is the "director," names the topic, claps, and says, "Pro!" The other partner (the speaker) thinks of the positive aspects of the topic and quickly says them. The speaker might say, "Traditions are important because they help people connect to their past and to remember people they respected, and . . ." Then the director, after hearing one or two points, interrupts with a clap and says, "Con!" The speaker responds with the negative aspects of the topic. For example, "On the other hand, traditions are a problem because some people live in the past, they don't grow or figure out how to solve modern problems, and . . ." "Pro!" says the partner who is the director, and so on. The turns tend to get briefer as the speaker runs out of things to say. To smooth out the transitions, the speaker uses terms such as those in the second column of Figure 6.2. (Students should not use the word *but* because it is so common in speech and writing.) Then partners switch roles and choose a different topic.

After pair practice with easy topics, give them an academic topic of the day's lesson. After the pairs finish, you can have pairs who performed well model the activity again in front of the class.

One effective variation of the final share-out, used by high school English teacher Patrick Hurley, is a whole-class version in which he has students respond back and forth as he calls their names (e.g., "Leila, Pro!"). They need to use the academic transition to contrast the previous student's comment, or start with a response such as, "I agree with Leila's point about . . . because . . ." A variation that develops listening skills is to have students share what their partners said, either with the whole class or in small groups.

To emphasize thinking skills, student directors can also say "Cause!" and "Effect!" or "Similar!" and "Different!" or "For!" and "Against!" In science, for example, a teacher used the For-Against variation to prompt conversation arguing for and against the use of food preservatives. Students can also use the terms in the fourth column of Figure 6.2 to add ideas during each turn.

Model Sentences

As in many arts and trades, imitation and adaptation are powerful ways to learn language structures. Imitation of model sentences has been found to be an effective way to learn more advanced ways to construct sentences (Ehrenworth and Vinton 2005; Ray 2006).

Repeat-Reword-Discuss

In this activity, students read a text, and as they are reading, they identify long or grammatically interesting sentences. The sentences should also be important to the text. Partner A finds a sentence and reads it aloud to Partner B. Partner B repeats the sentence with help from A, trying to ultimately say the whole thing without help. Then B explains the meaning of the sentence by rewording it and/or giving examples. B then asks A the importance of the sentence in the text, and both hold a brief conversation. After the conversation, B tries to repeat the sentence again. Then A and B can reverse roles.

Sample Sentences

As your class learns about a topic, you and your students can post sample sentences from texts or class discussions that describe big ideas and model academic grammar (see samples in Figure 6.3). You can encourage students in pairs to use the format of the sample sentences as they converse and to come up with similar sentences in their synthesis statements after their conversations.

Figure 6.3 Frequently Used Terms and Sample Academic Sentences

Terms and Purposes	Example Sentences
Dependent Clauses after, even though, as, because, before, even if, in spite of, if, rather than, given that, since, because, unless, until, once, when, where, whereas, whether or not, which, while	*Given that* the sum of the two angles must equal 180°, we can figure out the unknown angle by subtracting. *As* you analyze the structural formulas above, you will see that every carbon atom forms four bonds. *When* Constantinople fell to the Ottoman Turks in 1453, the overland spice trade to Europe was cut off. The author is showing that, *if* each person cannot see the difference between right and wrong, evil will prevail.
Relative Clauses which, who, whom, that, whose, those, whoever, whomever	An exothermic reaction, *which* releases energy in the form of heat, has many practical applications. A triangle's angles and sides have relationships *that* can be proven. José María Morelos, *whose* rebel army won some successes, was captured and executed in 1815. And then the old man, *who* talked only when absolutely necessary, faced the window and cleared his throat.
Prepositional Phrases above, across, after, against, along, among, around, as, behind, below, besides, by, except, for, from, in, inside, near, next to, of, off, on, out, over, regardless, to, under, until, with	*To* calculate the mode of a set of data, count the number of times that the value appears. *By* comparing densities, a person can explain why some objects float in water and why some objects sink. *Despite* the many dangers of the Silk Road, traders risked their lives for the profits they could earn. Dantes remained tenuously bound together *by* threads of human love *until* the death of Abbé Farias.

Adapted from Zwiers 2008.

I Want to Say . . . , and Yet

It is vital for teachers and peers to value the language that each student uses at home and with friends. Yet it is also vital for students be able to automatically "translate" certain language into more academic forms. Often the most expressive language isn't considered to be the best language for school or work settings. We teachers often want to say things in powerfully nonacademic ways, but we hold it back and "translate" these thoughts into more appropriate discourse in front of principals, superintendents, and their ilk. Usually, (a) we realize that the language that is about to come out of our mouths isn't appropriate for academic settings, and (b) we have at our disposal synonyms and other expressions that we can use instead. Students need to do and have both of these things as well: realize what is appropriate and build up a bank of synonyms and expressions that they can use.

In this "activity," students keep an ongoing translation chart of colloquial terms and academic terms. See the example list in Figure 6.4. This can be modeled on an evolving poster on a classroom wall as well.

Figure 6.4 Sample Chart for "I Want to Say . . . , and Yet"

I want to say . . . *(with friends)*	And yet a more academic way to say it is . . . *(in school and at work)*
That's lame! No way! That's stupid! Bogus! You are so wrong!	I disagree because . . . I see it another way.
What's your point? So what?	Can you summarize that for me?
That's shady.	That seems unfair (or unjust, immoral).
That's sick!	That's exceptional (or fantastic, exquisite, excellent).
That's good.	That's appropriate (or proper, acceptable, effective).
Whatever!	I'm not sure that's relevant.

Combine in Twos and Choose

This activity is adapted from sentence combining practice described in Deborah Dean's *Bringing Grammar to Life* (2008). Pairs combine two or more short sentences in two different ways. They then meet with another pair to discuss which of the four sentences is clearest and most effective.

They should not emphasize correctness, but instead should focus on how meanings differ in the sentences and which simply sounds best. After students have worked with the sentences, you can go over how to correct them if they have errors. You do not have to teach the grammar terms.

The sentences that students combine should form part of the academic conversation they just had or will have. For example, they might combine two or more kernel sentences that are based on the text that will become the main conversation prompt. (*Len was sick. He was determined. He changed others.* → *Even though Len was sick, he changed others' lives because he was determined and driven.*) At the end of an academic conversation, students can combine several key points into a final synthesis statement.

You can also introduce new ways of structuring sentences after students combine their own sentences. You can teach gerund phrases (*Eating ice cream can be addictive*), participial phrases (*Worried that the others might be after him, the prince hid in the forest*), appositives (*The ship, a brigantine loaded down with tobacco, sank off the coast of Florida*), and different placements of clauses within sentences. Conversely, you can find complex and multiclause/multiphrase sentences and break them down into basic kernel sentences. As students recombine the kernel sentences, you can then see how close to the original students get.

In cues combining (Dean 2008), students eliminate any words you've underlined in a sentence and use cues you've added in parentheses to combine kernel sentences. For example, you might give students sentences like these: "*The spider was very patient. It waited all day for prey to enter its web.* (Use *-ing*)" or "*The farmers were mistreated and overtaxed. They rose up and revolted against the feudal lord.* (Use *because*)." After they write the sample you've prepared, have students write a similarly structured sentence from their school or home life. They can use this sentence to prompt a short conversation.

Transformations

A variation is to have students practice with "moveable" words, phrases, and clauses. They practice with five to ten sentences that have moveable parts (e.g., *The sun went down before I arrived. Before I arrived, the sun went down; The solution will boil if you turn up the flame. If you turn up the flame, the solution will boil; Nevertheless, the event was very significant. The event was very significant, nevertheless.*) After practicing the transformations, students write their own sentences and attempt to transform them. This also gives them practice in writing longer sentences with multiple clauses.

Sentence Building

This activity, adapted from work by Carolyn Hood (2007), teaches students to build sentences that are more academic. It teaches students to add detail, explanation, and elaboration to each sentence. Along the way, students grow in their metalinguistic awareness of how to move words around to improve clarity.

You and your students can use the graphic organizer in Figure 6.5 and the chart in Figure 6.6 to create a thesis or theme statement. Students work in pairs to craft the statement. The pair starts by using the organizer in Figure 6.5. First they fill in the "Who/What" and "Does/Is" boxes in the "Basic" row. They then upgrade vocabulary and discuss the "How," "Where," and "Why" possibilities in the "Notes for Elaboration" row. Finally, students build different elaborated sentences with the pieces from the "Notes" row and extenders from the extenders chart in Figure 6.6. Pairs can share and discuss their final sentences with other pairs.

Figure 6.5 Sentence Builder Graphic Organizer

	Who/What	Does/Is	How	Where	Why
Basic	Charlie	got mad.			
Notes for Elaboration	Charlie	became furious	suddenly	at the restaurant	others were laughing at the boy
Elaborated Sentences	Charlie became furious suddenly at the restaurant because others were laughing at the boy. Because others were laughing at the boy in the restaurant, Charlie suddenly became furious. Suddenly, Charlie became furious at the people who were laughing at a boy who had dropped dishes in the restaurant.				

You can also have students "go backward" and prune a powerful sentence down into a basic sentence by trimming away the additional information. This offers students practice in determining importance when reading and listening to long sentences. A sample chart of sentence extender words is included in Figure 6.6.

Figure 6.6 Chart of Extenders

Extenders			
Where	**When**	**Why**	**How**
above across beyond beside below between against within	before after until during throughout often while frequently recently simultaneously	so since because due to in order to to for the purpose of	sudden*ly* skillful*ly* gent*ly* effective*ly* fierce*ly* poor*ly* *As if* it were a snowflake Peaceful *as* a painting *Like* a prowling leopard Us*ing* a compass, Leo was able to . . . He wandered, wonder*ing* where he . . .

Academic Vocabulary Development Through and For Conversation

There is a very amorphous set of words that we might call academic vocabulary. The most obvious are the big content words: *democracy, proletariat, imagery, trope, allusion*, and so on. Other words seem like content-specific words, but often have multiple meanings used in other content areas: *radical, revolution, reciprocal, character*, and so on. Others are figurative and idiomatic, which are stretched to describe academic ideas such as *society's decay, the bottom line*, and *a string of events*. Others are general-use academic words that typically describe thinking processes as well as complex and abstract ideas: *interpret, analyze, tip the scales, weigh, feature, foster*, and so on. These tend to be what Beck, McKeown, and Kucan (2002) call Tier Two words, also known as mortar words (Dutro and Moran 2003). Examples of Tier Two or mortar words are found in Figure 6.7.

In many classrooms there is a high emphasis on the explicit teaching of vocabulary. And even though we know about the high correlation between vocabulary and reading comprehension, some classrooms spend too much time learning long lists of words. We have seen loads of class time spent putting words into tables, doing fill-in-the-blank exercises, drawing word meanings, taking quizzes, matching synonyms, and the like. These activities can (and do) fill up entire weeks of instruction, especially in schools that are being hounded to raise test scores. Yet cramming students' brains with a list of new words for Friday quizzes is not the lasting answer. Even if quiz and test scores increased in this way, lasting learning will not.

We must critically evaluate how we teach words and how words are learned. Writing a definition and a sample sentence and drawing a little picture are very common practices, but the half-life of a word's meaning is short after the quiz or test is over. Students must use the new words over and over, in writing and in conversation, in order to build ideas and solidify their varying meanings in the brain. I (Jeff Zwiers) still recognize words that I memorized for the SAT and GRE exams; I knew their meanings around the time of the tests, but not now. A big problem, mentioned in Chapter 1, is that the words on many classroom lists don't connect to one another very well or connect across units. Students need repeated exposures and repeated opportunities to connect and authentically use the new words over time—in writing, in reading, and in talking and listening. Lasting learning needs cohesion and reinforcement. As a student once asked, "Once you know a word, then what?" We must teach students how to use the word.

All this doesn't mean that we shouldn't teach new words or train students to figure out new words. Strategically and selectively, and in concert with loads of real reading, talking, and doing, we should teach the words that help students construct academic ideas (Zwiers 2008). Word meanings tend to stick in the brain longer when used multiple times in real communication, which involves the need and desire to listen, learn, express, or get something done with language. As we all know, many vocabulary exercises are not real: they tend to lack both the need and the desire to use the words to communicate. Many activities such as crosswords, games, and matching exercises remain at the basic definition level of thought—not at the "I need this word to help me build an idea" level of thought. The sections that follow describe several conversation-based activities to help students develop academic vocabulary at deeper and more connected levels of thought.

Figure 6.7 Academic Words

access	core	features	layer	proportion
achieve	corresponding	focus	link	range
acquisition	credit	formula	method	relevant
adequate	criteria	framework	obvious	rely on
administration	cultural	function	occur	resources
alternative	cycle	goals	option	response
analysis	data	granted	outcome	role
approach	debate	hence	overall	shift
appropriate	demonstrate	hypothesis	paradigm	significant
approximated	derived	identify	parallel	source
aspects	design	illustrated	parameter	specific
assume	dimensions	impact	participate	status
benefit	distinction	implement	perceive	strategies
categories	distribution	implication	percent	structure
circumstances	dominant	imply	phase	subsequent
components	elements	impose	philosophy	sufficient
concept	emerged	indicate	policy	support
conclusion	emphasis	instance	positive	task
consequences	ensure	integrate	potential	techniques
considerable	environment	interaction	predict	technology
consistent	established	internal	primary	text
constraints	estimate	interpretation	principle	theory
context	evaluation	investigation	procedure	transfer
contrast	evidence	involve	process	variable
contribution	excluded	issue	project	
coordination	factors	justification	promote	

Decide and Debate Cards

As mentioned in Chapter 4, controversy and considering multiple perspectives on an issue can increase the critical thinking in a lesson. Students want to express themselves well in order to argue with and respond to peers. When we provide, or "prime," students with academic words, they are more likely to take in the words and use them in their own arguments.

Identify a text on a controversial topic. Choose five or six high-leverage academic words from the text based on their likelihood of future use in the discipline, other disciplines, and life. (See Figure 6.7 for examples of these words.) Preteach these words by saying them, acting them out, drawing them, and using them in sample sentences. Then create cards that state positions on an issue and use the words in the descriptions of the positions. Sample cards are shown in Figure 6.8.

Figure 6.8 Sample Decide and Debate Cards

Position A	**Position B**	**Position C**
Guns should be completely *banned* from every state.	*In light of* the constitutional right to bear arms, guns should not be banned at all.	Owning a gun should require *stringent* background checks and ongoing tests.

Students then prepare their arguments, based on the original text and other resources they might find. They meet first with another person who has the same card, then split into groups with different cards. They try to persuade the other(s) using the specified academic words as they talk. Reading the points out loud does not count; they must use the words and phrases in their own sentences as they argue and respond. Finally, students write group and individual paragraphs on what they discussed. Encourage them to switch positions if they were persuaded by other arguments.

Explore One Word

Powerful conversations can revolve around the meaning of one word. Many words carry essential understandings of a discipline, such as *technology, justice, education, society, democracy, happiness, family, evolution, revolution, war, slavery, history, culture*, and *matter*. We can equip students with the skills to have rich conversations that will not only teach them the big idea terms in deep and lasting ways but also empower them to have similar conversations in the future.

We want students to learn the meanings of terms like *endothermic, emancipation, hyperbole, megalithic,* and so on. A vocabulary term's meaning is often seen as the end point of learning. Yet, vocabulary can also be a starting point for thinking and talking. Core terms can be the raw material for deeper thinking. For example, Figure 6.9 provides a range of possible prompts based on thinking processes. Students can generate and respond to these prompts in their conversations. As students converse about the words in cognitively demanding ways, they better learn the vocabulary *and* develop their thinking skills at the same time.

As always, students should use the five core conversation skills as they converse about the word. They can produce a final summary paragraph after the conversation. You can also give different words to different pairs to make the final class discussion more informative and less repetitive. They might even rank the words in order of importance. Students can use some of the following prompts to support the conversations. Make your own class matrix, similar to the one shown in Figure 6.9.

Figure 6.9 Sample Matrix for Exploring a Word and Thinking About It in Depth

Importance of the Term	Why is it important?	Why is it not important?
Connections	To me?	To all of us?
Key Examples of the Term	From texts?	From the world?
What would happen if . . .	. . . it didn't exist?	. . . it still existed?
Compare	How does this term compare to . . . ?	How does this term contrast to . . . ?
Cause and Effect	What causes . . . ?	What are the effects of . . . ?
Perspective	What if you were . . . ?	How did they feel about . . . ?

Use the Best Word

Students should be in the habit of pushing each other to use more challenging and more accurate words over time. Oral messages tend to be less academic than written messages. When you listen to a conversation, you hear many basic words that are repeated.

You can put up a list of overused, boring, and unclear words on a poster. You might already have one up for writing. As students converse, they can refer to the words and politely ask partners questions like these: *Can you clarify what you mean by* good? *Instead of* amazing, *what can we say? How can we best describe . . . ? The word* ___ *comes to mind, but what would be better?* The emphasis is on not being satisfied with hearing or using the same basic, banal words all the time. Conversations are opportunities to challenge and build vocabulary muscles.

Connect-the-Word Cards

This activity (adapted from Zwiers 2008) challenges students to see and verbalize relationships between important vocabulary terms. It becomes a visual way to make connections and remember the words for a long time. Main content words (bricks) go on rectangular cards and connection descriptions (mortar terms) go on diamond-shaped cards.

To model the activity as a whole class, put words on the rectangular cards (put their meanings on the back, if needed) and think aloud to describe the connections between the key words. Write connection notes on the diamond cards. Give a connect-the-words organizer (see Figure 6.10) to student pairs. Have students identify the most important word or phrase in a section of text, and put it in the center oval. In pairs, students should find other important words and write them in the rectangles at the outer corners. They can move the cards around, if they want. Pairs can ask one another, *How does that word relate to this word? How does this word relate to the central word?* Pairs can share their connections with other pairs. If there is time, have students create a written summary.

Figure 6.10 Sample Connect-the-Words Organizer

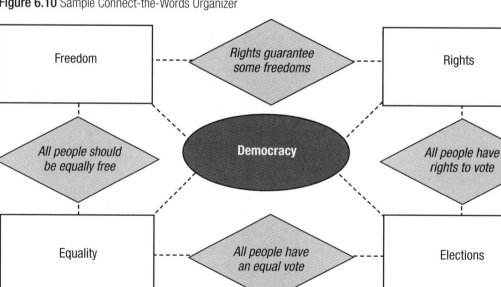

As an option, students can organize the words in different ways and explain their rationale. They might put the words into columns, a sequence, a picture, a Venn diagram, and so on. They can generate additional words and finish by writing a short paragraph using the words.

Semantic Impressions Vocabulary and Prediction Conversation

In this activity (adapted from Richek 2005), you identify several key words and phrases from a text that students are about to read (e.g., *axe, forest, survival, erosion, environment*). Students look at the words and at any other clues from the text that you want to give them, and then they converse in pairs to formulate a quick synopsis of what they think the text will be about. Tell them to be serious about coming as close as possible to the mystery text by using the words and clues given. They can write their idea down, if there is time. As they converse, students should use skills such as elaboration, building on ideas, persuading, and predicting with evidence.

Figure Out and Use Academic Metaphors

Figurative and metaphorical terms are widespread in academic texts and oral messages. Many are subtle and so commonplace that they do not show up on our radar. Terms such as *off the radar, dealing with, struggle, obstacle, access, right track* and other common terms become either obstacles or supports to comprehension and offer students access to expressions used in professions. This activity (adapted from Bean, Singer, and Cowan 1985) is a way to help students develop the habit of listening for and interpreting multiple meanings, idioms, analogies, metaphors, and symbols.

A key skill is the ability to quickly be able to interpret a new metaphor or analogy in the context of what is being said. In many political speeches, for example, speakers use analogies and other metaphors to colorfully illustrate an idea. The analogy or metaphor might come from sports, science, literature, history, or popular culture.

Read several speech transcripts, excerpts from plays (Shakespeare, for example), and editorials to show students how people use metaphors to make their points. Think aloud when you come to a new metaphor to show how you figure out the meaning from context. Write the metaphor on a sticky note and the meaning of it on the back. Put them up on the wall. Students can also put them in their notebooks. The chart in Figure 6.11 offers sample metaphors and ways to understand their meanings.

Have students come up with their own metaphors for academic and abstract concepts. In their conversations, when they hear an abstract idea (e.g., perseverance, adaptation, culture), they can ask their partners for an analogy. You can scaffold this in a mini-lesson by having students act as your collective partner who asks you for sample analogies and figurative explanations when you mention a concept.

Figure 6.11 Chart for Understanding and Using Academic Metaphors

Academic Metaphor	Why the Metaphor Works	What It Means
School is like a factory.	Factories produce the same product over and over.	The author wants to emphasize that current schooling just wants to produce the same kind of student.
An argument doesn't hold water.	It's like a weak bucket that has holes in it.	The argument doesn't have convincing enough evidence; it is weak.
We see eye to eye.	Two people the same height are like two similar views.	Two people have the same perspective or opinion.

We hope that this chapter has provided some ideas for improving students' oral academic grammar and vocabulary. As Lobeck (2005) states, "Students will need more than by-the-book grammar to succeed in the world. They will need to be innovators and creative thinkers, problem solvers, and pioneers, or else they risk being marginalized again, condemned to the ranks of the functional" (87).

Reflections

1. Discuss the meaning of the concluding quotation by Lobeck.
2. What types of grammar do students need to know in order to read texts in your lessons and discipline?
3. What types of grammar problems arise when you look at students' writing? Or when you listen to them talk?
4. How have *you* learned the key vocabulary terms in the content area(s) that you teach?

Chapter 7
Conversations in Language Arts

Finally, after years of preparing for tests on the stories we read, I was asked to share what I think about them.

–Sixth-grade student

This chapter describes how conversations can fortify language arts and English classes. Teachers of English language development and world language classes will also find the ideas in this chapter to be useful. As in Chapters 8 and 9, we first present several key thinking processes and topics that good readers and writers tend to talk about. Then we describe conversation activities for conversing about literature and about composing analytical and persuasive essays.

While language arts and English courses seem to be the most natural place to develop oral language and thinking, often the heavy emphasis on reading, writing, and test preparation can squeeze out high-quality oral language time. You already know that oral language is a foundation for literacy and thinking, but putting it into practice is a challenge. Fortunately, an added bonus of classroom conversations for many students is that oral language activities are more interesting and engaging than reading and writing exercises. One student said, "Talking seemed to help me read and write better. I like talking a lot, even about stories. I read them better when I knew we would talk about them. But if it was just to answer questions, I just skimmed to answer the questions. I did pretty well on quizzes but didn't remember much."

Conversations fortify the understanding of literature in multiple ways. Before reading, conversations provide extra background and "idea seeds" for what students are about to read. After reading, conversations allow students to fill in any holes of understanding and solidify what they just read. Conversations during reading build the types of thinking and vocabulary that help students understand the reading on multiple levels. And many "conversations" actually happen inside one's head.

Reading literature fuels conversations. Besides the advanced grammar and vocabulary that accumulate inside readers' minds, reading literature provides students with a range of ideas, opinions, and themes for rich conversations. We must teach students how to best use their reading to converse. One teacher describes her experience: "At first I thought it [academic conversation] was a stand-alone activity; but when students' skills became more automatic, I wove conversations into and between reading activities. Over time I think they began to understand the texts much better because they talked about them so much." Conversation activities can make lessons and objectives more engaging. It helps to ask yourself, "Would *I* want to talk about this? Would *I* want to learn this if I were eight years old [or 10, 16, and so on]?"

No two people understand a work of literature (e.g., novel, story, song, poem, film) in the same exact way. This is what makes talking about literature so rich and rewarding. Students might explore dozens of different ideas about one story in one classroom. Because of students' diverse backgrounds, they will often generate, if given time and encouragement, a variety of new interpretations. These interpretations are raw materials for a variety of ways to build language and thinking.

It's important to think about what happens in good conversations between literary critics, between authors, between two people who have read the same book. In observing many good conversations about literature, we have noticed several helpful language arts thinking skills that support and deepen conversations (see Figure 7.1). We zoom in on four in this chapter: evaluating importance, taking multiple perspectives, interpreting, and persuading. Not surprisingly, these skills are also prevalent in most state lists of language arts standards and lists of skills desired by employers. Teachers can help students develop these skills for and with a variety of works of literature and engaging topics throughout the year.

Many of the skills in this chapter are also found in resources that describe collaborative strategies such as book clubs (Raphael, Florio-Ruane, and George 2001), literature circles (Daniels 2002), Socratic seminars (Moeller and Moeller 2001), and instructional conversations (Goldenberg 1991). These are strategies that have made significant strides in getting students to converse in deeper ways about what they are reading.

Comprehension Habits and Thinking Skills in Language Arts

Fortunately, many schools have made progress in identifying and teaching key comprehension habits (also called strategies) such as predicting, inferring, questioning, connecting to background knowledge, and figuring out words (see Keene and Zimmermann 2007). Yet it gets muddier when you realize that students must use these habits *along with* other thinking skills such as evaluating, inferring cause and effect, interpreting, applying, comparing, analyzing, and taking multiple perspectives. For example, right now, as you read this paragraph, you might be summarizing this section, questioning how you can use this in your classroom, comparing it to other books on the topic, and considering how to apply it to the texts in your content area. This is the type of mental multitasking (parallel processing) during academic reading that students must learn to do before they converse about texts. The process gets even more complex when you layer in the conversation skills.

Figure 7.1 provides prompts and response starters for different thinking skills that are commonly needed for success in the texts, tests, and tasks of language arts. We suggest that you create posters that show the skills, prompts, and response starters that fit best with your curriculum and students.

Figure 7.1 Language Arts Thinking Skills, Prompt Frames, and Response Frames

Core Thinking Skills in Language Arts	Sample Prompt Frames	Sample Response Frames
Evaluate importance, role, contribution	What role did the character play in . . . ? Why is this important to learn? Why was this part included in the story? Can you clarify how that idea is important to the story? What was the most important part? Is this an important story to read/ teach in our society? When it was written, why was it important? How about today?	(Character) was important in the novel because . . . This part of the story is important because . . . This story is important because . . . At that time, they . . . Today, the story is meaningful in that . . .
Take multiple perspectives	What are other perspectives on this? How did she feel? How do you know? Imagine you are (character). Decide how you would . . . Why do you think he did that? What was the author thinking when she added this part? How does the author think the world should work? Can we really empathize with them? Why or why not?	Another perspective is . . . I think he felt . . . because . . . If I were . . . , I would . . . because . . . I think the author was thinking . . . because . . . I can relate to (character) because I . . . Other people might feel that . . .
Interpret and infer	Why do you think the author wrote this? What does the author mean by . . . ? What are some themes that emerged in . . . ? What does that mean? What can we learn from this character? What might be other nterpretations? Based on the fact that . . . , how would you explain . . . ? What can we infer from . . . ? What's this similar to? Is there an analogy?	I think the author wrote this in order to teach us . . . One important theme was . . . because . . . (Character) teaches us that . . . Several parts support the theme of . . . For example, . . . By (action or words), we might infer that the character actually . . .

Figure 7.1 Language Arts Thinking Skills, Prompt Frames, and Response Frames (continued)

Core Thinking Skills in Language Arts	Sample Prompt Frames	Sample Response Frames
Persuade and argue	Take a side on the issue of whether . . . and argue for it. Come up with a solution to whether . . . What would you do and why? Which idea is the best? Which idea has the most weight? How might this author be biased? Do you agree with the author?	I strongly believe that . . . because . . . We think the best solution is . . . We would . . . for several reasons. First, . . . We believe the author is biased because . . . We agree with the author because . . .
Apply and transfer to new contexts	How can we apply this text to our lives today? In the future? What can we learn from this character, part, or entire story? How can you change how you think or live based on this . . . ? Does this text apply to anyone you know or know of? Who should read this? Whose point of view is missing in this story?	The theme of . . . applies to my life in that . . . We have learned to be more . . . I have changed how I think about . . . because in the story . . . We think that . . . should read this and apply it to . . . We believe that . . .'s point of view is missing . . . It is needed because . . .
Compare	Can you compare yourself to any character in any way? How are characters similar or different? How are the two texts similar? How are the two events different?	I am similar to (character) in the following ways: . . . (Character) and (character) are different in that . . . The two texts are similar in several ways: . . .
Consider ethics	Was the character right or wrong in doing that? Should we believe or do what the author is trying to teach us? Is it right, wrong, or is there a gray area? Does culture or time period make a difference? What are the pros and cons of this decision? What is your opinion of . . . ?	We think the character was wrong in . . . because . . . Even though the author argues for . . . we think that . . . We think it is more right than wrong for . . . because . . . It is like weighing apples and oranges because . . . The pros of . . . are . . .

Analyze author's craft	What words did the author use to get the reader to feel a certain way? Why did the author present it this way? How would you have written it differently? Why?	The author used the technique of . . . in order to cause the reader to . . . Even though it was a little confusing, it was effective to . . . I would have written it differently in the following way: . . .
Create and communicate	How can we communicate this idea to others? What would be a good analogy for this? What kind of poster would show what we are thinking? How can we act out the main point of our conversation? Is there a song or poem we know that is similar? Can we write one?	A good analogy for this idea is . . . We could show this visually by making . . . One way to act this theme out is to . . . There is a song called . . . that illustrates this theme. I would write a story about . . . in order to show the theme of . . .

Most conversations will have more than one of the skills in Figure 7.1. Thinking skills often overlap, support one another, and vary in their depth depending on the topic. In language arts, for example, a pair of students—in one conversation—might do all of the following: interpret character actions, compare the ethics of two characters, empathize with each character, persuade one another to take a side, and talk about how to apply the ideas to life.

This section zooms in on the first four skills in Figure 7.1 and how to develop them in conversation. Let's begin by looking at evaluating importance.

Evaluating Importance

A valuable comprehension habit is figuring out what is important in a text. This includes figuring out what is not important. We often hear students ask the question, "How do I know what is important?" and we still struggle to answer it. Importance varies across disciplines, cultures, and individuals. Part of importance is the author's purpose for including something. If the something's purpose is to add descriptive detail and realism, this is often considered less important than a key part that drives the plot, which in turn might be less important than a section that relates to the theme or application to life. We must have many discussions with students on what makes something in a text, film, song, or painting important—and to whom it is important. Fortunately, the importance of something is often an effective topic for conversations.

So, what makes something important or relevant? Fortunately, in nonfiction texts authors tend to use text features such as subtitles, bold words, pictures, topic sentences and guiding questions to help the reader determine importance. However, in fiction a reader must look for patterns in a text, identify possible main ideas and themes, look for supporting evidence of main ideas and themes in events and character actions and words, and look for out-of-place details that might become meaningful clues.

In the following excerpt from a sixth-grade conversation about a short story, notice how Tamra challenges Daniel's assertion that his question is important.

1 *Tamra:*   Are there any questions?
2 *Daniel:*   Is the cow going to die?
3 *Tamra:*   That's not important.
4 *Daniel:*   Why not?
5 *Tamra:*   Tell me why it is, then.
6 *Daniel:*   Well it's a question that I have. What's wrong with that?
7 *Tamra:*   We need to ask questions that matter. For the main ideas, important things. The cow was just mentioned, like background, I think.
8 *Daniel:*   Well, let's write it down at least, because maybe the cow dies and they all get sad, or they become poor, or can't get milk, you know.
9 *Tamra:*   Okay, but we gotta remember the big things as we read.
10 *Daniel:*   A cow is big *[both laugh]* !
11 *Tamra:*   Very funny!

A possible response in line 3 might have been for Tamra to ask, "Okay, how is that important to the plot [or theme]?" We need to train students not to cling to initial ideas if they aren't important or relevant. Daniel quickly comes up with his not-very-reflective question, likely to be humorous, then argues to defend it, not willing to give it up and think more deeply about another question. This is common and tends to waste time. Tamra tries to keep him focused on importance and relevance, but he seems to be more focused on winning the argument than generating relevant questions.

Considering Multiple Perspectives

Another key skill for understanding literature is seeing other perspectives. This is, of course, a powerful skill for life. Readers must empathize with characters, seeing the world through different eyes. In language arts, students need to be able to think and talk about literature from different points of view: characters, authors, literature experts, and other readers. Taking different perspectives allows students to better understand the meaning of others' lives, including characters in stories, authors, friends, and family. Taking other perspectives can get students more engaged in a story and encourage them to think about what they would do in similar situations. In turn, such thinking helps them understand themselves better as they see new routes for understanding other people's opinions and arguments. Perspective taking can even open up new ways for solving social and political problems.

One of the biggest advantages of conversation is that you have a direct link to what another person, your partner, thinks. As students share ideas with different partners in the classroom, they begin to see how others think about life and literature, they get to jointly build their understandings of characters and connect works of literature to life. Moreover, when perspectives differ in a conversation, the process of respectful argumentation and persuasion becomes rich with thought and language.

In order to take another perspective, students should learn as much as they can about the other person (or group, animal, or thing). Students should learn about the person's childhood, relationships, actions, goals, words, successes, and failures. They should consider how these factors affected this person's actions and personality. Students must try to filter out the many thoughts and feelings from their own experiences that bias their perceptions of others. In this endeavor, students are trying to put together a puzzle that will never be complete, asking lots of questions, such as: *If she knew that . . . then why would she . . .* or *What do those words mean in that time and place?* or *What did loyalty mean in that setting?*

For example, Patrick Hurley, English language development teacher at Mountain View High School in California, modeled a modernized dialogue between Juliet and her mother to teach perspective and theme in *Romeo and Juliet*. Here is an excerpt in which Patrick wove in paraphrasing, a conversation skill that he also wanted to model at the same time.

Lady Capulet:	Let's agree that we won't yell at each other and that we will listen to each other.
Juliet:	Okay. I can agree to that. Can we also make sure that we agree to reach a conclusion and not walk out of this room mad?
Lady Capulet:	Okay. I can agree to that. Now your father and I want you to marry Paris because you are getting older and he is very rich and good looking.
Juliet:	Yes. That is true.
Lady Capulet:	But you think you are too young to get married.
Juliet:	Yes, I want to have more time to find the right man. *Does that make sense?*
Lady Capulet:	*It sounds like you think that* you can make the best decision for yourself in choosing a husband.
Juliet:	Yes. That is right, I would add that I am only thirteen and he is quite older. I want to marry someone closer to my age. Can you tell me why you think Paris is the right man for me?
Lady Capulet:	He is rich. And you wear such fancy clothes and only a rich man can afford to pay for them.
Juliet:	*Let me see if I heard you right.* You want me to marry someone who can buy me expensive clothes?

The class then created a table of viewpoints and sample controversial statements from *Romeo and Juliet*, such as "Teens are too young to fall in love," "Parents should never decide whom their teens should date," and "Life isn't worth living without the one person for whom you were meant." Finally, students took on roles to converse from different viewpoints.

Interpreting

The interpretation of literature helps readers understand what it means to be human. Literature offers brief windows into the worlds of others. Through literature we can see into the thoughts of many different people, present and past, near and far, in order to learn how they lived and thought about life. By looking closely at characters and metaphorical language in literature, we also better understand our own thoughts and feelings.

Interpretation means to use text clues combined with background knowledge to come up with meanings that we think the author intended, but did not explicitly give. Often the theme comes from events in the story and character actions, words, or changes. Themes might be different for different readers, and even the same reader might see different themes when reading the text at different points in life. The deepest themes in life tend to solidify when readers construct them on their own, usually connecting the themes to their own lives.

Getting "underneath" the text and extending its ideas into the realm of the complex and abstract—without getting too far out on a tangent—is a tricky task. We want students to creatively interpret, apply, extend, and connect, but not so creatively that the lesson's or text's ideas are lost. In metaphorical terms, we want students to dig, but not to tunnel miles away from the text. Figuring out a theme should not be the goal—it should be a beginning.

Teach Students to Interpret Everything

Life is a story full of themes. Often we teach students to look at literature first and then to think about how literature themes connect to real life. We can also train students to have an ongoing eye on themes in life. They can look at past and present events and feelings as forming a story with themes. In other words, we can train students to see their own lives as works of literature, as a story, and to interpret themes that come up. And others around us and throughout the world also are stories. The past and present are full of interpretation—if, that is, we allow and train students to observe and to reflect on the facts and information for greater purposes than just knowing. Students can converse about these questions in order to consider themes and meanings in real life and connect them to literature:

- Who are important people who shaped who you are?
- What is a significant event in your life? What if it hadn't happened?
- How would you like to change the world?
- What brings you meaning in life?

- What are three key themes in your life?
- What will your life be missing if you don't read this?
- How will the themes in this story add to your life?

Train students to notice themes in life and notice stories with similar themes. Usually, teachers ask students to read a story and find themes in the story that can apply to life. Another type of thinking involves "reading" life and identifying themes, then connecting the themes to written stories. A powerful strategy is to encourage students to write their own stories that show those themes. Students in the class can then read and converse about the themes in classmates' stories (see the section titled "Academic Conversations for Writing" found later in this chapter).

Common Themes in Literature

You and your students can build an evolving list of themes that emerge in literature (and movies, TV, and art). Figure 7.2 provides a sample list to get you started. Posters of such themes are helpful because students can use them to spark insights. Even if the theme seems off base, the process of defending the theme with evidence from the text is extremely valuable for students.

Figure 7.2 Common Themes in Literature

- Noble goals and causes are worth extreme sacrifice.
- True friendship/love involves deep commitment.
- True beauty is on the inside.
- Diverse ways of thinking and living should be respected.
- Certain symbols in the story represent the main character, and represent us.
- Being yourself takes courage.
- Expressing your beliefs and opinions is important.
- Differences are needed to make life interesting.
- Freedom is everyone's right.
- Some people are afraid of change and differences.
- Young people want to belong.

- People are destroying nature and themselves with uncontrolled technology.
- Society and a person's inner nature are always at war.
- Social influences determine a person's final destiny.
- You can't change who you are.
- Few friends will make extreme sacrifices.
- A child must go through a series of obstacles before becoming a grown-up.
- Everyone has an inner child. Sometimes it holds us back; sometimes it brings us happiness.
- A person grows by facing obstacles.
- Enjoy life now because we all die too soon.
- By the time we understand life, there is too little left to live.

Figure 7.2 Common Themes in Literature (continued)

- Memories are a large part of who we are.
- Immigration changes nations and individuals.
- Do not give in to peer pressure.
- Many people in the world struggle to survive.
- Many stories are based on earlier stories, myths, legends, and so on.
- Bullying is wrong.
- Nonviolence is the best way to solve problems.
- There is more to life than making money and being comfortable.
- Cleverness can be more effective than brute force.
- Life is short and every day is precious.
- We must preserve the environment.
- Envy and jealousy are destructive.
- People can change.
- There are many types of heroes.
- Standing up for what is right is often difficult and even dangerous.
- Helping others is itself a reward.
- Teamwork is often necessary.
- All languages and cultures are valuable.
- We should respect nature's power and beauty.
- Good and evil are not always clearly separated.
- Death is part of living, giving life its final meaning.
- Sometimes people do stupid things to impress other people.
- Honesty is always the best policy.
- Sometimes it is necessary to lie.
- Family is the most important thing.
- Faith is the most important thing.
- Don't judge a book by its cover.
- Things aren't always what they seem.
- We can change the future.
- Every action has a reaction.
- The fittest are most able to survive.
- With freedom comes responsibility.
- It is important to be your own person.
- Love is stronger than hate.
- Good is stronger than evil.
- It is important to be yourself.
- Losing a loved one is challenging.
- There is hope even when things seem hopeless.
- Peace is possible.
- Set goals and work hard to reach them.

The following conversation about theme occurred during the theme chart activity, described later in this chapter. The two students are discussing the theme of a short story. Notice how Arturo, in line 3, acknowledges Brenda's opinion in line 2, but then gets back to the theme. Arturo then asks for elaboration in line 5. Brenda then asks how to apply the ideas to life in line 8, leading to the topic of racism and studying hard to make changes.

1   *Arturo:*   What do you think the author's message is?
2   *Brenda:*   Well I don't think it was fair that the principal changed the rules about the jacket, you know, to pay for it.

3	*Arturo:*	Me too, but what was the lesson from the story?
4	*Brenda:*	Maybe it was to stand up for what is right.
5	*Arturo:*	Can you elaborate on that?
6	*Brenda:*	Well, she was sad at first and then talked to her grandpa who told her he could pay, but wouldn't. Maybe this helped her see that it would be, like, wrong to just give in and pay. What do you think?
7	*Arturo:*	Yes, I agree. I think Martha changed 'cause maybe at first, if she had the money, she would've paid. But, however, her grandfather made her think and show the school people that they were wrong.
8	*Brenda:*	So how can we apply this to our life?
9	*Arturo:*	Maybe we can make sure bullies at school don't get away with bullying.
10	*Brenda:*	And maybe it has to do with racism, like we talked about in class, how people bully people based on their skin color, like we saw in history class.
11	*Arturo:*	How do we stop racism, though?
12	*Brenda:*	Maybe study really hard to be lawyers.
13	*Arturo:*	Okay, how can we sum this up?
14	*Brenda:*	We can say that the author wanted to teach us to stick up for what is right, even when more powerful people change the rules. And we should study more.

Persuading

Persuasive thinking is engaging. Students enjoy getting others to take their side of an issue. There tends to be more drama, more tension, and more energy in a persuasive situation than other learning activities. When students see that their thinking (and writing) has a dynamic purpose, such as to change another's mind or make a decision, they are more interested in making extra efforts to back up their side with evidence and to see other perspectives. This thinking contrasts with many static "right-back-at-you" responses that tend to simply show learning (or fake it).

Persuasion is, figuratively speaking, tipping another person's scale of reason to your side of an issue. You show them that the evidence and reasoning for your side outweigh the reasons on the other side(s). Many issues, of course, require highly subjective comparing, evaluating, and weighing of the reasons and criteria used. For example, a story might have the theme of defying or following family traditions and cultural customs. In this case, one must weigh tradition against the main character's right to defy tradition in pursuit of the woman he loves, for example. Students must learn what it means to compare apples and oranges, a common expression used throughout life. And along the way students need to develop two subskills: not to be persuaded by illogical yet convincing tricks of the persuasion trade (often used by advertisers), and to allow themselves to be persuaded to change their minds by the logic of the other side's argument.

Persuasion provides some hefty thinking to fuel rich conversations. Persuasion often requires and builds other thinking skills, such as analyzing, comparing, synthesizing, and problem solving. It also can be used to convince others to evaluate importance, see perspectives, and interpret literature in the way that you do. All of these things can happen in conversations. Students might also talk about typical persuasion topics that come up in other classes, such as opinions about world events, controversies, school uniforms, and so on. And in language arts classes, the writers of most literary responses and analysis essays are persuading readers to believe the main thesis of the essay by supporting it with evidence and explanations.

Assessing Literature Conversations

To assess students' academic conversations, you can use the rubric shown in Figure 7.3. Refer to Chapter 10 for ideas on how to use the rubric for both summative and formative purposes. You and your class should be extra clear on the descriptors in each box. Model and analyze conversations that have and lack the elements, and ask students to help score them. Students can also use the rubric to self- and peer-assess. Add or take away elements in order to fit your curriculum and unit objectives.

Figure 7.3 Sample Academic Conversation Rubric for Language Arts

	At or Above (3)	Approaching (2)	Below (1)
	(T) Think and talk like literature experts. - Interpret themes and apply them to life. - Connect to characters and other texts. - Critique texts and author techniques. - Use literature terms and complex syntax.	Make some connections, use some complex sentences and literature terms, and show some deep thinking.	Use short sentences and only social language (slang), make few connections, and take on few perspectives.
	(F) Stay focused. - Build on comments. - Connect ideas to topic well. - Negotiate conflicting ideas and word meanings. - Offer few, if any, tangential thoughts.	Stay mostly on topic; show some idea building and negotiation; go on some tangents and deviations; show some confusion.	Rarely connect or build on ideas; go on many tangents and give unrelated information; demonstrate no negotiation of differing ideas.

	(S)	**Support** ideas and opinions with examples from text, life, and previous lessons; clearly explain and elaborate on ideas.	Offer some prompting for and support of ideas with examples and clarifications.	Offer little or no support of ideas and reasons; show lack of appropriate prompting.
	(P)	**Paraphrase** partner ideas to clarify, deepen, and stay focused; synthesize key points or steps at end.	Offer some paraphrasing and synthesizing of key points or steps.	Offer little or no paraphrasing and synthesizing.
	(C)	Use **communication** behaviors; actively listen (eyes and body); take turns; value partner comments; be respectful.	Show some appropriate listening and turn-taking behaviors.	Show little eye contact or listening; interrupt; dominate talk or do not contribute at all.

Literature Conversation Activities

The following sections describe how to fortify literature lessons and activities with conversation work. Activities are organized into the categories *before reading*, *during reading*, and *after reading*. Activity descriptions within these categories progress from those that are more appropriate for early grades and beginning levels of English language development to activities that are more appropriate for middle and high school English courses. Yet many teachers at both ends of the grade-level spectrum have found ways to use all of them.

Before Reading

Conversation before reading, although underutilized, can prime students to better comprehend difficult texts. It can also build their interest in the text and help them make better connections as they read.

Conversing About Images: Interpreting and Persuading

In this activity, students analyze and interpret images such as advertisements, paintings, murals, and so on and converse about the messages intended by the creators of each image. Remind students that advertisers tend to target students because they think young people are easily duped into using products at a young age (e.g., cigarettes, soda).

Give one or two images to each pair. To conduct their conversations, students can use sentence starters like these:

The artist _____ in order to give viewers a sense of _____.
This ad uses this phrase with this image because it makes the viewer _____.
The ad writers were trying to persuade people to buy the product by _____.
This is an effective ad because it _____.
This painting contains powerful symbolism, such as _____.
The mural's underlying message is _____.
Their persuasion strategy is to make a viewer think that_____.

A variation of this activity is to use children's picture books and wordless books as artifacts for conversation. This can be done in all grade levels. For example, you might use a folktale (e.g., *The Three Little Pigs*) and have students analyze and discuss how characters represent humans and why such tales have endured so long.

Quotation Café

The quotation café, similar to the tea party activity (Beers 2006), gives pairs a chance to predict, synthesize, and interpret. As they converse, students use academic terms to support their ideas (*makes me think that, I believe that, because of a quote I heard from, if we consider the title and this line here, therefore, we can assume, we will likely learn about*).

The first step is to choose important quotations from the text that students will read. Put them on separate paper strips or note cards. You might choose six to eight different quotations and put the same quotations on cards of the same color. Distribute a quotation to each student. Then show the title of the text, read the first part of the text aloud, and/or show an image or two from the text.

Explain to students that the purpose of the activity is to form an idea of what the text will be about as they talk to different partners. Students should circulate and find one partner at a time with whom to discuss each quotation and predict what the text will be about. They should find three partners with different quotations and one partner with the same quotation. After this initial circulating discussion, have students get into pairs or groups to analyze the cards and synthesize their ideas. Predictions and inferences will improve as they hear more quotations and predictions from other students. They can then meet with other groups to share what they have discussed and guessed. You might want to have each student "become" the person who said the quotation and share thoughts from a first-person point of view. Students can also guess the sequence of their quotations in the text. Lead a brief whole-class discussion on what students predict the text is about.

For a variation of this activity, create a semantic map with the quotation in the middle and four branches coming out from the middle (see Figure 7.4). A student fills in an interpretation of his or her quote on one branch individually. Then as students pair up and converse, they fill in the other three (or more) possible interpretations for the quotation. They can add more branches for more interpretations.

Figure 7.4 Sample Quotation Conversation Map Card

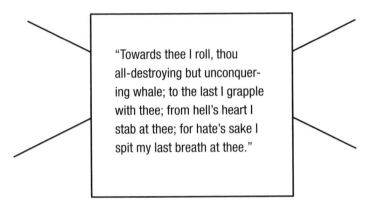

"Towards thee I roll, thou all-destroying but unconquering whale; to the last I grapple with thee; from hell's heart I stab at thee; for hate's sake I spit my last breath at thee."

For another variation, find themes in the upcoming text and do a search for famous quotations about those themes on the Internet. Choose six to eight quotations and split them into two parts. Write the quotation halves on separate pieces of paper or note cards and give each student one quotation half. Each student reads his or her half and predicts what the other half will say. Then they get up and find their other half. They read their half-quotes to one another and discuss whether the two halves fit or not (adapted from Kumar 2010). Once they find their quotation partner, they answer three prompts: (1) What does the quotation mean? (2) Do you agree with it or not? Give examples. (3) What do you think the upcoming text will be about?

Paired Gallery Walks

In a typical gallery walk activity, you put up posters around the room with a text's topics or related images, and students walk around to comment on them. In this variation, pairs walk around to each of four posters and converse about the type of prompt that you give for each turn. The prompts are based on conversation skills, and they accumulate over the four rotations. At the fourth poster students will use all four prompted skills. You prompt all students to work on a certain skill in each rotation. In the first rotation, for example, you might ask pairs to generate elaboration questions about the subject on the poster they are looking at. At the second poster you ask them to ask elaboration questions and come up with opinions and evidence; in the third rotation they ask and answer questions as well as provide counterpoints and other perspectives, and at the fourth poster you prompt them to use the first three skills plus synthesize their ideas. You might do this with eight stations and four different posters. Students can use a graphic organizer like the one shown in Figure 7.5.

Figure 7.5 Gallery Walk Note Sheet

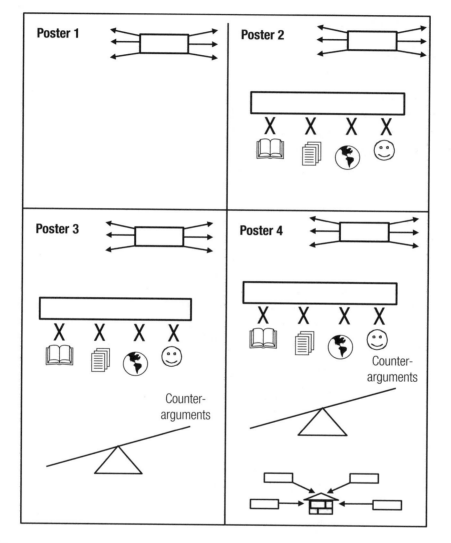

![Pencil on note paper icon]

Two-Sided Information Gap Conversation

This type of activity, popular in English language development and world language courses, gives students conflicting information for an argument-based conversation. It gives students a chance to argue different sides of an issue as they learn key points of the topic. The task is designed so that students need to talk to bridge the gaps in their knowledge.

Provide Partners A and B with note cards that describe points on each side of an issue. Use academic vocabulary in the points, because students will likely use them in their conversations. You can also have students come up with the points for each side; some students generate points for perspective A and others for B. A sample set of cards for *To Kill a Mockingbird* is shown in Figure 7.6. Additional sample cards for other content areas are in the appendix.

Figure 7.6 Sample Information Gap Conversation Cards

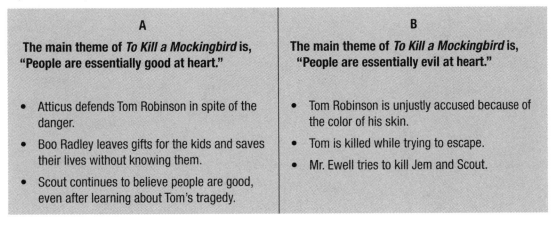

A	B
The main theme of *To Kill a Mockingbird* is, "People are essentially good at heart."	The main theme of *To Kill a Mockingbird* is, "People are essentially evil at heart."
• Atticus defends Tom Robinson in spite of the danger.	• Tom Robinson is unjustly accused because of the color of his skin.
• Boo Radley leaves gifts for the kids and saves their lives without knowing them.	• Tom is killed while trying to escape.
• Scout continues to believe people are good, even after learning about Tom's tragedy.	• Mr. Ewell tries to kill Jem and Scout.

Model the use of sentence stems such as: *That is an important point, but does it outweigh . . . ; But in the long run . . . ; Then again, . . . ; Even though . . . , we believe that . . . ; If it requires . . . , then . . . ; Why is that important?; Which is more important?; Yet what about the influence of . . . ; Tell me more about why . . . ; How does that example support your argument?; and So, how should we synthesize our conversation?* (You can include these frames on each card below the evidence points.)

Partners read their own cards, try to memorize points and use them to support their side of the argument, respectfully persuade each other, and in the end decide to choose a side or to compromise. A third person can mediate or take notes. Students come to an agreement of the synthesis that they will write up to turn in.

During Reading

Conversations during reading are also underutilized, but they support students' practice of core comprehension skills when they need to happen most. Conversations can help students clarify difficult texts, take a break to process the information, and motivate them to finish reading.

Comprehension Target Talk

As indicated previously, not all ideas are equally useful for comprehension. The comprehension target talk activity (Zwiers 2010) helps students to evaluate the relevance and usefulness of their ideas to a main topic of discussion. It helps students discuss and filter out the less important ideas. You can choose important reading skills (as shown in Figure 7.7) to put into a target visual, with the main topic or focus in the center. Students then evaluate the usefulness and relevance of ideas that come up in conversations. The more useful the idea, the closer it goes to the center. Disagreement about the usefulness of an idea is fine. It forces students to negotiate their values, clarify thoughts, support their ideas with evidence from the text, and use logical reasoning.

Figure 7.7 Comprehension Target Visual Organizer

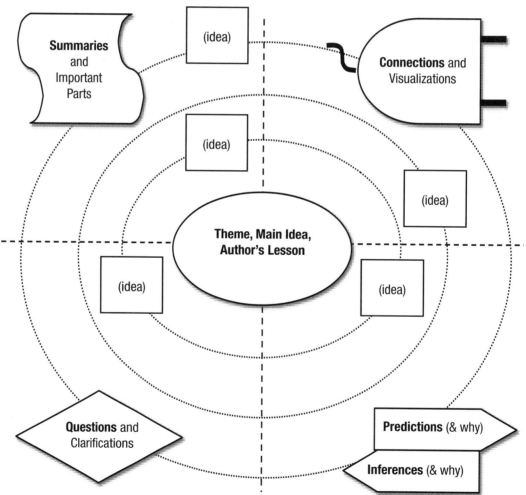

Here is the procedure for the target talk activity:

1. Model how to evaluate ideas with a partner. For example, you might come up with a draft theme (use pencil), and then create a wild tangent about your cousin's trip to the mall and place it way off the paper. Then come up with a valuable connection and put it near the center of the target.

2. Working in pairs or groups, students take turns facilitating after each section of the text that they read. Before reading, students in each pair or group agree on where to stop next, and then silently read.

3. Summaries and Important Parts: The facilitator prompts the pair (or group) to write a summary on a sticky note. Students discuss the value of the summary and its importance to the overall text meaning and place it in the summary quadrant, evaluating where it goes on the diagram (far from or close to the center).

5. Questions and Clarifications: Students prompt each other for questions about the text to clarify vocabulary or deepen concepts. Students decide if the questions are worth pursuing as they put them in the questions quadrant on the target. A good starter for each prompt is, *I wonder why . . .*

6. Connections and Visualizations: Students connect ideas from the text to the world, to other texts, or to their own lives. They also share what they visualized while reading. Students discuss the usefulness of the connections and visualizations and put them on the diagram.

7. Predictions and Inferences: Students predict what will happen next in the text using starters like these: *I predict that . . . because . . .* and *Evidence suggests that . . .* Partners can agree or disagree about the value of the ideas, giving their evidence.

Perspective Anchor Chart

When you take a perspective, you look at something from a particular point of view. This requires understanding and inferring what a variety of other people would think when looking at the same information. They might have different pasts, values, goals, knowledge, and so on. For the perspective anchor chart activity, students focus on a central topic, such as an event in the plot, a character, or a theme, and take various perspectives on the topic. Students converse about possible perspectives and write notes about the perspectives on an organizer like the one shown in Figure 7.8. Encourage students to use the sentence starters for perspective taking found in Figure 7.1.

Figure 7.8 Perspective Anchor Chart

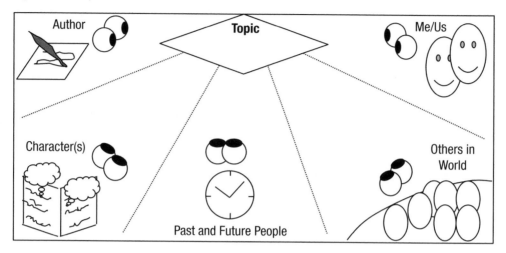

Theme Chart

The theme chart visual organizer shown in Figure 7.9 provides a helpful scaffold for conversing about interpretations of theme. On the surface of the water in the organizer, students write the story's plot, events, and character actions, changes, and words. Underneath the water, students write the theme(s) that emerge from thinking about the story. The arrows help students generate theme ideas. Underneath ideas for themes, students write the evidence and examples that support the themes. Students should use pencil and/or sticky notes, because ideas and themes might change along the way. As students read, they can jot down their ideas. Then they converse about them after reading.

Most literary analysis essays require students to interpret quotations they have chosen and then analyze them. For a variation of the theme chart activity useful for this process, have students find quotations that support a theme, discuss what the quotations mean, and explain how the quotations support the thesis. Theme, support, and explanation roughly correspond to Toulmin's argument model of claims, evidence, and warrants (see Toulmin 1969).

After Reading

Academic conversations after reading can help students synthesize and remember what they understood from the text. Conversations can form important language and content supports for activities such as writing and projects.

Figure 7.9 Theme Chart Visual Organizer

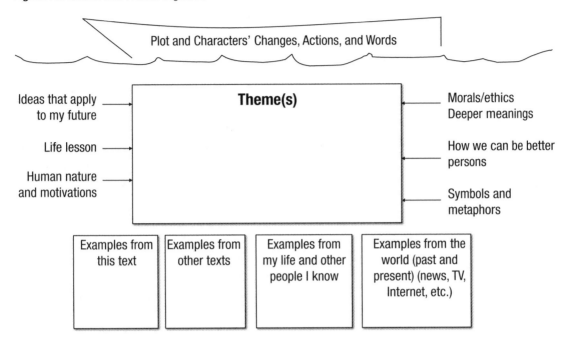

Paired Reading Conference

Like conferences between teachers and students, paired reading conference conversations involve students acting as teachers to one another as they talk in pairs about a story. They ask each other questions such as these: *Who was an interesting character? Has anything like this happened in your life? What could the character have done differently? How would you have ended the story? What was the main message of the story? What did the main character learn? How did the character change? Why did the character . . . ? Did you learn any new words or ideas? What was your favorite part? Would this be a good movie?* This is not meant to be an interview; questions are meant to spark conversations in which conversation skills are used to build ideas. Remind students that they both must ask questions and build on answers.

This activity can also take the form of a conversation between movie critics, such as Ebert and Roeper, who critiqued films and gave different ratings with their rationale. To prepare students, you might want to show them several clips of Ebert and Roeper or other critics and have them analyze what the critics are doing in them. Do they converse? Do they support their claims? Are some things (feelings) unsupportable? If so, are they valid? Such talk could also be used to critique books, short stories, paintings, photographs, documentaries, student writing, class performances, and even a teacher's lessons. In addition, some teachers have students meet in pairs to develop and use rubrics to evaluate works of literature and movies in conversation.

Paired Conversation in Character

In this activity, both partners should pick a character from the text(s) to role-play in the conversation. Knowing who one's partner will be, each student prepares several questions they might ask that character in a conversation. Students should then try to remain on one topic as long as possible. They should start with the most thought-provoking questions. Questions might cover lessons learned from the story, relationships with other characters, motivations, feelings, plans for the future, and so on. After they talk, students can write down a synthesized version of their dialogue (describing the deepest points) as a more permanent record.

Socratic Conversations Plus

Socratic conversations emphasize the power of questioning ideas and negotiating contradictory thoughts. The conversations extend and deepen ideas that students are already forming in their heads. Such critical questioning and the interactions that result help students build upon their previous ideas about life and create foundations for future ideas.

The conversation begins with a general statement of truth, often a universal or abstract theme. Socrates, for example, tended to focus on concepts such as wisdom, discipline, courage, morals, and justice. Speakers then identify other hypotheses by asking questions and eliminating ideas that contradict. Ultimately, partners seek to clarify and discover beliefs, truths, and opinions. The questions are used to scrutinize and critique the consistency and logic of an idea and to explore definitions of key terms. For example, if this theme statement arises from a text: "With freedom comes responsibility," students might first ask what freedom and responsibility mean. Other questions might challenge the cause-and-effect relationship in the statement, find exceptions, and note inconsistencies in logic. Answers and questions are usually followed by more questions. Eventually a clearer or even a contrary theme might develop, such as "Freedom to choose one's path in life makes one accountable to those choices" or "With responsibility comes a lack of freedom." You can mix pairs and groups of four around to serve different purposes. In a pair-to-square structure, pairs have a conversation that prepares them to converse with another pair. In a square-to-pair, groups of four start off and then partners process the ideas in pairs. In mini-fishbowls, one pair observes another pair in conversation and provides feedback afterward. Then they switch.

It is important to develop students' questioning skills before and during the Socratic conversations. One way to do this is to model how to create questions while reading, perhaps on sticky notes, on a visual organizer, or in a reading log. You can teach stock questions, such as *What does that mean? What makes you think that? Why did the author . . . ?* and *How do we see that happen in life?*" Questions should focus on figuring out themes, symbols, metaphors, motives, author style and technique, and underlying meanings in character actions and words. Students should be asking and probing for deeper meanings, truths, and lifelong themes. Students should leave the conversations with as many good questions as new ideas. Asking good questions is a vital life skill. Socrates was also well known for saying that he was ignorant, and that the first step to knowledge is realizing one's ignorance. This relates to having a humble attitude and a knowledge-seeking approach to conversation.

Finally, effective Socratic conversations have the following characteristics: conversations remain connected to concrete and personal experiences; participants strive to understand one another; participants work hard to focus on a fundamental question while being open to exploring different lines of thought; and participants strive for consensus (Saran and Neisser 2004).

Academic Conversations for Writing

Conversations can significantly improve students' writing. As students build interesting ideas in their heads, teachers offer them the chance to make the ideas more clear, permanent, organized, and shareable in writing. But if ideas aren't interesting, aren't perceived as students' own ideas, or aren't worth communicating to others, then writing tasks just end up being words on paper for getting points. When the thoughts are authentic, original, mulled over, challenged, supported, and debated, then they are worth writing down, revising, and even editing.

The main genres of writing that upper elementary and middle school teachers ask students to write are literary analysis, persuasion, autobiographical narrative, and descriptive reports. Different thinking skills are emphasized in each. For example, in literary analysis, writers will tend to use interpretation, supporting ideas with evidence, and analysis. For persuasive pieces, writers will use persuasion, multiple perspectives, analysis, and evaluation of evidence. For autobiographical narrative, writers tend to use cause and effect, identifying importance, and interpretation. For descriptive pieces, writers use analysis, synthesis, identifying importance, and sometimes persuasion. You can train students to think in these ways through oral activities. And the writing process, in turn, can help strengthen students' oral abilities.

Student conversations should be crafted somewhat like the writing you want to see from them. A teacher once remarked how similar the conversation rubric was to the writing rubric we were using. It's true, and semi-intentional, that the types of oral interactions we want students to have will also build up features that are valued in writing. For example, using examples is often needed both in talk and in writing, along with elaboration, summarization, staying focused, and so on. Many teachers have commented that the more students talk before they write (about the content, of course), the better their writing is.

The following activities can help students improve their writing through conversations and vice versa.

Written Conversations

In this activity, students converse on paper to one another. Partner A writes a comment or opinion and Partner B responds. This can be done in class, between classes, or with pen pals across the world. Writing is an excellent chance to work on grammar and to push students to use more advanced grammar to communicate academic thoughts.

Conversation Journals

Conversation journals keep track of one's thoughts for conversations and from them. Students should write before and after conversations. Journals can have a variety of formats. For example, students can draw a picture of a key point or summary of the recent conversation in the middle of the page. They then write around the picture they've drawn (Figure 7.10). Before talking, students can write down their thoughts, questions, and opinions that they want to converse about.

Figure 7.10 Sample Conversation Journal Page

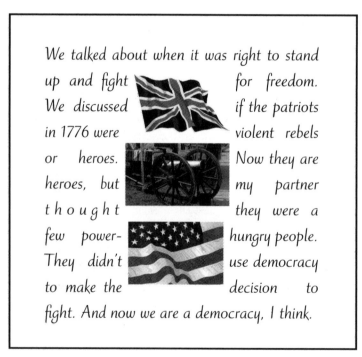

We talked about when it was right to stand up and fight for freedom. We discussed if the patriots in 1776 were violent rebels or heroes. heroes, but Now they are my partner thought they were a few power- hungry people. They didn't use democracy to make the decision to fight. And now we are a democracy, I think.

Persuasive Writing Conversations

As explained early on in this chapter, persuasive thinking and writing are educational and engaging. A common pattern for persuasive essays progresses like this: hook, background, thesis; reasons with evidence and quotations; counterarguments with responses and rebuttals to them; and a conclusion that ties it all together. Conversations can prompt students to think about these elements in preparation for writing, as evidenced in the following conversation between two seventh graders, Lenora and Hilario.

Lenora:	I think guns should be against the law.
Hilario:	Why?
Lenora:	Because the more guns around, the more people get killed. For example, those shootings at schools and in malls.
Hilario:	Yes, but a counterargument would be that we have the right to own guns in the Constitution. What about that?
Lenora:	It should be changed. That's what amendment means. We should amend it.
Hilario:	But if we change that one, we might have to change many more.
Lenora:	Whatever, maybe something that makes it harder to buy guns.
Hilario:	Maybe, but I know a lot of people want one in their house to defend it.
Lenora:	So we need to weigh the right of having a gun and its protection against counterarguments of more people dying from lots of guns around. So, is less deaths worth giving up this right?
Hilario:	How do you know less deaths will happen?

As students have conversations like this, they build ideas and language that they can use in their writing. The process of preparing for and then writing a persuasive piece motivates students to more deeply evaluate evidence, organize thoughts, and think critically about multiple perspectives. Students can borrow some of the persuasive terms in Figure 7.11 for use in their conversations and their writing.

A fun variation of this activity is having students converse about whether or not they should write a persuasive essay. They then write a persuasive essay on whether or not they should write persuasive essays. If they are persuasive enough, they don't have to write the essay, which they just wrote.

Figure 7.11 Academic Terms for Persuading

- We feel that the long run gains outweigh the short run losses because . . .

- Based on the evidence in the story, we believe . . . because . . .

- It is a difficult issue, but I feel that the positives of . . . outweigh the negatives of . . .

- However, there are several reasons to oppose this point of view. First, . . .

- The statistics are misleading, however, because they do not show . . .

- There is a lot of discussion about whether . . . but the crux of the matter is . . .

- It is also vital to consider . . .

- The advantages of . . . outweigh the disadvantages of . . .

- Well, that is only partly the case. The other side of the story is . . .

- Granted, we admit that . . .

- That is a good point, but I think the evidence shows that . . .

- What it seems to come down to is . . . versus . . .

- I understand what you are saying, but I would like to emphasize . . .

- Yet some argue strongly that . . .

- These (facts, reasons, data) strongly suggest that . . .

- Although not everybody would agree, our position is . . .

- Although some people claim that . . .

- They say/claim/maintain/hold that . . .

- Opponents also argue that . . .

- The issue is not so much a question of . . . , but a question of . . .

- On the other hand, there are many who disagree with the idea that . . .

Adapted from Zwiers 2008.

3–D Persuasion Seesaw

This hands-on activity (Zwiers 2004) allows students to literally grasp the process of weighing criteria of two sides of an issue. They can create a working seesaw (scale) with one piece of 8 1/2-by-11-inch paper, scissors, and tape. Copy the blackline master titled "3–D Persuasion Seesaw" provided in the appendix, and assemble the seesaw as shown in Figure 7.12. Create the seesaw by cutting on the solid lines and folding on the dotted lines. You should model this process with a large replica of the scale made out of construction paper.

Here is the procedure for the 3–D persuasion seesaw:

1. Each pair has its own seesaw; partners will be adding to both sides as they converse.
2. Students write the issue in the center box and write each side of the argument at the ends.
3. Students decide on the criteria, or reasons, and put them in the separate "weight" boxes. The larger boxes are for the most important or most valuable persuasive reason and evidence for a side. This prompts students to prioritize and compare reasons, a key skill that supports the larger skill of persuasion. Reasons might include: time, money, danger, lives

lost, ethics, freedom, environmental protection, future impact, health, culture, human rights, human progress, and so on.

4. Students explain to each other the reasons on the cards and evidence that they have found, which can include quotations and statistics. They can put the "weights" on the scale and move their most important (MVP) criterion to the outer slot.

5. Students then converse and compare the opposing reasons and see which one is more convincing and/or has the strongest evidence. For example, a student may have two opposing weight cards with "High cost of universal health care" on one and "Moral right to have good health care" on the other. He or she should have some evidence for each card.

6. Students come to some agreement and then use the ideas to write a persuasive essay.

Figure 7.12 Assembly of the 3–D Persuasion Seesaw

Reason	Reason	Reason	Reason	MVP Reason
Evidence	Evidence	Evidence	Evidence	Evidence
fulcrum side	fulcrum top fulcrum side		fulcrum bottom	MVP Reason Evidence

This position   Issue/question being evaluated: This position

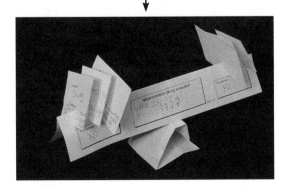

Conversations for Authoring Literature

Sadly, many students, starting as early as third grade, are no longer allowed or encouraged to write literature. As with watching sports instead of doing them, students learn less about writing if they are only told to write responses and critiques to other people's writings. We learn much more about something when we actually do it. How many amazing writers never realize their gifts because they are always only told to analyze another's writing? We must give students of all ages a chance to create, converse, and explore as they put their thoughts on paper for the world.

Before students begin to write their own works or even fill in their prewriting organizers, have them doodle, think, and talk about the potential story, share ideas, and get new ideas from partners. They can answer prompts such as: *What if your cat could talk? What if your house were a boat? What if your teacher were from outer space? What if you could fly? What if you lived underground your whole life? What if you had lived in 1860?* and *What if you were a water molecule?* Students can then fill in visual organizers, such as a story map or theme chart. Then have students, in pairs, talk about what they will write. They might write a joint work or decide to write separate pieces. Students might mix modern issues with famous fairy tales and myths to make a point, or they might write a children's book based on their own life or an interview with family members. In upper grades students can outline a novel, short story, historical fiction, epic poem, or other longer work.

After writing and publishing, students can then have conversations to write written responses to each other's works of literature. Students can also have an author's press conference to share how and why they wrote their work of literature, the different meanings, future projects, book signings, etc.

Converse About a Hook

Give students a funky, eye-catching first line or paragraph of a novel, poem, song, or essay, and have them converse about what they think the whole work is about, or what they would write if they had to use that beginning. If there is time, have them write a story, essay, or outline together that might fit the hook. Offer a choice if you have multiple hooks. A few samples are included here.

» "Many years later, as he faced the firing squad, Colonel Aureliano Buendía was to remember that distant afternoon when his father took him to discover ice." —*One Hundred Years of Solitude,* Gabriel García Márquez

» "It was a bright cold day in April, and the clocks were striking thirteen." —*1984,* George Orwell

» "As Gregor Samsa awoke one morning from uneasy dreams he found himself transformed in his bed into a gigantic insect." —*The Metamorphosis,* Franz Kafka

» "I live my life in growing orbits which move out over the things of the world." —"Ancient Tower", Rainier Maria Rilke

»   "Happy families are all alike; every unhappy family is unhappy in its own way." —*Anna Karenina*, Leo Tolstoy
»   "I am an invisible man." —*Invisible Man*, Ralph Ellison
»   "The moment one learns English, complications set in." — *Chromos,* Felipe Alfau
»   "The human race, to which so many of my readers belong, has been playing at children's games from the beginning, and will probably do it till the end, which is a nuisance for the few people who grow up." —*The Napoleon of Notting Hill*, G. K. Chesterton
»   "The past is a foreign country; they do things differently there." —*The Go-Between,* L. P. Hartley

You can also create quotations that pertain to your unit of study, such as these:
»   "I wandered around for centuries, to the ends of the earth, only to wake up an hour later."
»   "Computers will be the end of us all."
»   "The Civil War is not over."
»   "The planet is a living being."

RESPONSE-to-Literature Acronym

This activity was initially created as a prewriting activity, but it has been successful in scaffolding rich conversations, particularly in upper elementary and middle school classrooms. The conversations can prepare students to write response-to-literature essays as well. Feel free to change the lines to fit your needs.

R   Reflect on why the title was given to this story.
E   Empathize with characters—how they changed or not.
S   See the symbols that keep popping in.
P   Pick out the main problem, challenge, or plot.
O   Observe and critique the author's style and techniques.
N   Notice life lessons or deeper life themes.
S   Support a main thesis with evidence and quotes.
E   Explain how the theme applies to us and the world.

Go through the acronym and have students explain what each line means. Give examples of each. Explain that many of the things that they talk about as they converse through the acronym can be used when they write their response essays. Have students discuss with a partner ideas for each of the acronym lines. The more they talk, the more ideas they will get from others. Have them converse with multiple partners to get more ideas, and have them take notes before and/or after the conversations.

This chapter has described a set of ideas for using conversation-based tasks and skills in support of language arts teaching. In language arts class, language is both the product and the tools. A vital tool is conversation. To conclude this chapter, we provide a sample language arts lesson plan (Figure 7.13) that integrates conversation strategies and tasks into a typical lesson.

Figure 7.13 Sample Language Arts Lesson Plan with Academic Conversations

Topic: Metaphorical language and symbols **Text:** *Seedfolks*, by Paul Fleischman, Chapter 1	*Conversation Integration*
Objective(s)/Vocabulary: - Interpret metaphors in a text and apply them to life - Create own metaphors - Vocabulary: *metaphor, symbol, figurative, support*	*Use examples to support ideas in a conversation*
Assessments: Interpretation paragraph; academic conversation assessment	*Academic conversation*
I. Opening/Modeling: - Introduce the topic and the book title. Ask, "How are people similar to plants?" Pairs talk and share answers on the board. - Semantic impressions activity (see Chapter 6). Identify several key words and phrases from a text that students are about to read (*vacant lot, farmer, memories, vowed, thrive*).	*Think-pair-share* *Semantic impressions conversation*

II. Guided Practice:
- Tell students that they need to do two things as they listen to you read the text aloud:
  1. Listen for the words from the semantic impressions activity. When they hear them, they can raise their hands. Discuss the words if they are important.
  2. When you stop reading, have paired conversations about symbols, metaphors, and possible themes.
- At the end of the chapter, pair-share brainstorm a list of themes that came up as a whole class. As a class, choose three or four and divide them up on different colored strips of paper, enough for one per student.
- Choose a difficult theme or one that students would not likely choose. Model a conversation with a student (or with the whole class acting as your partner). Model how to support your idea with examples from the text, other texts, the world, and your own life.
	
	Brainstorm in pairs and then share.
	
	Modeled academic conversation

III. Practice Academic conversation mingler: Students converse with several partners about the themes on the colored strips (or cards) and support them with the text. - Preparation: Students prepare cards that will help them explain the following in their conversations: the theme, metaphor, and/or symbol and why it is important in life; parts of the text that support this idea, with quotations, if they can easily find them. Students review the AC Placemat in the Appendix to avoid looking at it too much while talking. - Students need to converse with a student who has the same theme and two with different themes. - Students converse and provide different evidence from the text and their own lives.	*Three academic conversations with different partners*
IV. Independent - Review the RESPONSE-to-literature acronym. - Have students focus on R, S, N, and S in their academic conversations to prepare to write their paragraphs about their most important interpretation of metaphorical and symbolic language. - Pairs write their paragraphs and trade with another pair to get peer comments.	*Pairs have final ACs to prepare for writing their paragraphs on theme of their choice; teacher observes five pairs and scores them on the AC rubric.*

Reflections

1. How has conversation influenced your understanding of a work of literature?
2. Create the top row of a conversation rubric (as in Figure 7.3) for your language arts class. Which skills and content concepts are most important to develop this year?
3. What are the biggest challenges your students face in becoming great literature conversationalists?

Chapter 8
Conversations in History

We were still talking about history after class was over!

—Eighth-grade student

Just as history is full of conversations, so should be history classes. History, the events of centuries ago and the breaking news of today, is a dynamic sea of debate, persuasion, interpretation, application, and abstract ideas. One goal of teaching history is to help students navigate this sea and develop increasingly advanced ways of talking and thinking about history.

Sadly, many textbooks and tests turn history into a boring list of facts, famous people, and events to be memorized in time for Friday's test. As Holt (1990) argues, schooling often causes students to see history as summation, rather than a point of departure for thinking. Fortunately, conversations can help students think of history as dynamic and full of life, drama, mystery, questions, opinions, lies, gossip, and other engaging things that can develop students' historical thinking abilities. Moreover, we can help students see that they can contribute to history. As R. G. Collingwood writes, "Every new generation must rewrite history in its own way; every new historian, not content with giving new answers to old questions, must revise the questions themselves. . . . Historical thought is a river into which none can step twice" (1946, 248). Our students are new historians, and it is our exciting job to help them negotiate this wild and deep river.

No two people understand history and its people, events, artifacts, and documents in the same exact way. This is what makes talking about history so rich and rewarding. Students in one classroom might explore dozens of different ideas about one event or one historical person. Because of students' diverse backgrounds, they will often generate (if given time and encouragement) a variety of novel understandings. This chapter therefore focuses on ways to have rich dialogues by building history conversation skills.

Historical Thinking

Similar to conversations in literature classes, good history conversations usually depend on skills of interpretation, perspective taking, identifying importance, and persuading, which were described in Chapter 7. Rich conversations in history also thrive on other thinking skills, listed in Figure 8.1. In the sections that follow we provide detailed explanations of three skills that contribute to rich history conversations: inferring cause and effect, recognizing bias, and applying and transferring knowledge to new contexts.

It helps to consider the kinds of conversations that historians tend to have. What kinds of history ideas do they talk about when in meetings, in coffee breaks, writing papers, doing research, responding to articles, or arguing over dinner? Which thinking skills do they use the most? Their expertise is not just a result of vast knowledge; it is, as Wineberg (2001) argues, the ability to cultivate puzzlement, get a fix on what you don't know, and generate a roadmap to new learning. Historical expertise means lifelong learning from the past.

We include some key historical thinking skills in Figure 8.1, but we encourage you and your students to develop your own list of skills and prompts. Note that the prompts in Figure 8.1 can be used to form a conversation's initial prompt as well as to maintain and deepen conversations.

This section zooms in on the first three skills in Figure 8.1 and how to develop them in conversation. We begin by looking at inferring cause and effect.

Inferring Cause and Effect

History is full of cause-and-effect connections. Some are obvious and many are not. Students must learn to notice when a text implies or assumes causes and effects and try to understand and/or challenge the alleged connections. In order to infer historical causes and effects, students must have knowledge of the many different ways in which nature and humans influence events and vice versa. Most causes and effects in history fall under one or more categories: racism, fear, religion, desire for wealth, compassion, desire for power, desire for knowledge, lust for fame, desire for truth, desire for freedom, and natural events. If students keep these categories in mind, they can make more logical inferences about causes and effects. For example, in considering why Christopher Columbus crossed the Atlantic, which cause categories would you infer? Notice several suggestions in the following conversation.

Alex:	Why did Columbus sail the ocean blue?
Sandra:	To prove the world wasn't flat?
Alex:	I don't know, though. One thing we read said he used maps that showed American land on them.
Sandra:	Can you explain the map part more?
Alex:	Well, if he had maps, then he knew he wouldn't fall off the earth.
Sandra:	And he brought religion to them, too. That was a reason I read, but maybe it was just an excuse.
Alex:	I think he wanted gold. What do they call that, when you just want money?
Sandra:	Greed.
Alex:	Yeah, he was greedy.
Sandra:	Can you elaborate on that?
Alex:	He came and asked for gold bracelets and stuff.
Sandra:	But, however, maybe he also wanted to find a shorter way to Asia.

Alex: But why did he want that? 'Cause of greed, I think. And he turned people into slaves, right? Greed.

Sandra: So why is he so respected, if he was greedy and made slaves?

Figure 8.1 History Thinking Skills, Prompt Frames, and Response Frames

Core Thinking Skills in History/Social Studies	Sample Prompt Frames	Sample Response Frames
Infer cause and effect *(causation vs. correlation)*	Describe the role that (person or event) played in . . . Identify the primary causes and effects of the war. Was it causation or correlation, in the case of . . . When was the turning point? What brought this on? What were the long-term effects?	We believe that she played a key role in . . . because . . . The primary cause seemed to be . . . It was more of a correlation than causation because . . . Most likely the long-term effects were . . .
Recognize bias	Was this author biased? Why? What did the author have to gain by writing this? If it wasn't meant for future history students, why was this written? Whose voice is missing? What do you think really happened? How can we support the fact that the film/book was biased? Where did this artifact or evidence come from? Was a person or group of people harmed by this artifact/source/event?	The author was likely biased because . . . It was written because . . . A missing perspective is that of . . . We think what really happened is . . . because . . . Because of this . . . the author was able to . . . Certain groups were harmed because . . . The truth was covered up by . . .
Apply & transfer to new contexts	So how can we apply this idea to our lives in the future? What can we learn from this character/part/story? How can you change how you think or live based on this . . . ? Does this text apply to anyone you know or know of?	The idea that . . . applies to our lives today in that . . . I learned that we should . . . We should . . . from now on because . . .

Figure 8.1 History Thinking Skills, Prompt Frames, and Response Frames (continued)

Core Thinking Skills in History/Social Studies	Sample Prompt Frames	Sample Response Frames
Interpret 	Why do you think the author wrote this? What are some themes that emerged in . . . What does that mean for us today? What can we learn from this event? What might be other interpretations? Why is this important to learn? How was this important in history? What should we remember from this . . . ?	We think the author wrote this to . . . Several themes we found were . . . Even though this occurred long ago, we are still . . . Other interpretations might be . . . We should learn this because . . . It is an important part of history because . . .
Take different perspectives; empathize 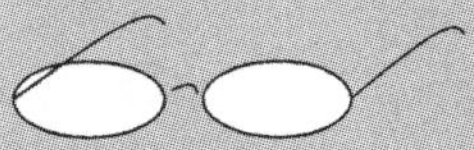	How did they feel during that time period? How do we know? Imagine you are . . . What would you have done? Why do you think they did that? Can we really empathize with them? Why or why not? What is missing from this account?	I think that they felt . . . because . . . I would have . . . because . . . We think they were motivated by . . . I would like to know what they were thinking about . . .
Compare; recognize inconsistencies 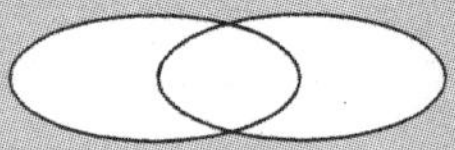	Can you compare yourself to any person in any way? How are the two historical figures similar or different? How are the two accounts similar? How are the two events different? How do the sources compare to one another? Are they consistent?	I can be like . . . because . . . They are similar in that . . . They also differ in several ways. First, . . . There seems to be a pattern of . . . The two accounts are inconsistent in that . . .
Evaluate 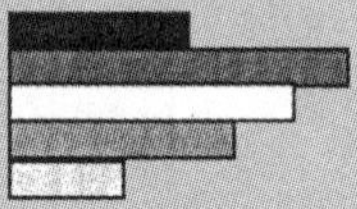	Evaluate this Web site (text) for its bias, accuracy, and usefulness. What criteria would you use to evaluate this account? Prioritize, in order of value, the examples used to support the argument. Critique the author's omission of the . . . perspective.	This Web site seems biased because . . . We should use the following criteria to decide how true it is: . . . This example seems to support our argument the most because . . . We believe that the author omitted her perspective because . . .

Recognizing Bias

One of the most interesting aspects of history is how wrong it can be—as far as we know. It is often wrong because people, usually with something to gain or lose, significantly skewed their recordings of what happened in their favor. This still happens every day. For this reason, students must be trained to recognize bias and be critical of information from books and all other forms of media. This skill is highly useful not only in school but also in life. Students need to look for how words are used and abused to shape the accounts of history. In the following conversation about a primary source account of the Boston Massacre, notice how the students look for bias and its role in history.

Elisa:	Why did the author write this?
Brian:	To tell us about the Boston Massacre. But what I don't get was why it was called a massacre if only seven people were killed.
Elisa:	What do you mean?
Brian:	Well, the people weren't so famous, and a massacre usually means lots of people die.
Elisa:	Maybe the people reporting it wanted to make it sound really bad.
Brian:	Maybe they wanted to get people all mad in order to rebel, like, to start the Revolution. At that time, not everyone wanted to rebel.
Elisa:	Oh like the teacher said, a lot of times the newspapers—I don't think they had radio or TV back then—would make up stuff . . .
Brian:	You mean *exaggerate*?
Elisa:	Yeah, they would exaggerate things or focus on things or not print things to influence people.
Brian:	So calling it a massacre made the English look really evil?
Elisa:	Maybe. How about today? How can we apply these ideas to today?
Brian:	Like, in commercials they only talk about good parts. And reporting on the war in Iraq might be biased, depending on the source.
Elisa:	But why?
Brian:	Maybe to influence voters to vote to get troops out.
Elisa:	So news can be biased?
Brian:	Yeah, how history is reported can make a big difference.

Students also need to recognize their own bias as they look into the past. We are all biased. Our interpretations of history are products of our own backgrounds and opinions about how history, people, and the world work. We are highly present centered and need to realize how limited our views become through such lenses (Wineberg 2001). Students should self- and peer-critique their biases as they converse.

Primary Source Analysis

It brings tears of joy to our eyes when students ask, "How do we know this textbook is right?" Students need to realize that even expensive history textbooks are full of bias, especially with respect to what is included and not included. They can ask an array of questions about why this or that was included and why other pieces, events, and people were not. Such questions foster rich conversations.

Fortunately, there has been much more emphasis on using primary source documents in recent years. Despite the reading challenges primary sources usually pose, analyzing these documents allows students to be historians and engage in conversations similar to those historians might have about what the documents say and do not say. Students might analyze letters from a soldier, for example, and compare them to related accounts in the textbook. Students might then discuss the roots of biased accounts and how similar practices might be happening today.

Applying and Transferring Knowledge

"Why are we learning this?" and "How will we use it?" are common questions asked by history students. Admittedly, some of the knowledge taught consists of facts that students just simply need to know to participate in society. Knowledge allows students to build more complex concepts over time and to develop thinking skills.

Application takes ideas and other thinking skills to a more practical and often personal level. Applied learning means that a student is able to match a concept or skill to a life situation or problem. As much as possible, teachers must put students in situations where they attack problems as historians would, showing their understanding as they wrestle with ideas and evidence. For example, students might apply the concept of democracy to analyze and critique the current electoral college system; they might apply their knowledge of the economy in 1930 to present-day economic challenges; or they might apply their skill of recognizing bias to analyze historical accounts of the last days of World War II.

In the following fifth-grade conversation, notice how Jacqui and José apply the themes that emerge from their initial topic based on inferring causes and effects.

Jacqui: So why did the Pilgrims come over to America?

José: They say religious freedom. But maybe it was to take over, for power, too.

Jacqui:	Can you elaborate that?
José:	They came and moved into Native American villages, 'cause they had died. Then little by little they, like, forced the Native Americans further and further.
Jacqui:	Can you give an example?
José:	Like in the *Sign of the Beaver* book, they kept moving away from the white people.
Jacqui:	I add to that idea that maybe not the first Pilgrims, but later people probably wanted their own country.
José:	I think most people who came wanted all the land for themselves. That's human nature. To keep wanting more and more. People never have enough land, money, power.
Jacqui:	So you are saying that you think all of us want to own more and more?
José:	Yes, but the Native Americans weren't like that. They share the land, I think it says.
Jacqui:	Yeah, but Europeans thought way different. And they lied and stole lands.
José:	So how can we apply this to our life?
Jacqui:	I don't know. Maybe we should share. What would the world be like if we shared more?
José:	And what about all the lands that the Native Americans had before Europeans arrived?
Jacqui:	Maybe people on them should pay rent to tribes that had the land before.

Applying history to life is a rich topic for conversation because of the many possible applications that might emerge. It is engaging to make ideas and theories useful in the real world and in one's own life. It is also challenging because it creates extra layers of thinking that go deeper than the initial learning or thinking skill (and deeper than tests can assess). For example, initially one might understand the feelings (empathy/perspective thinking) that caused (cause/effect thinking) certain freedom fighters to rebel. Other layers of thinking are involved in comparing and applying those feelings and causes to other times and places in history, including the present.

Figure 8.2 provides ideas for applying and transferring historical thinking skills and knowledge. These are effective prompts for paired conversations.

Core History Themes

Core history themes are big ideas and processes that recur throughout history. They can be applied to many different time periods and settings. In order to understand the static and dynamic forces that make up human history, students should learn to explore the following themes and narratives, from the National Council for History Education:

Figure 8.2 Task Ideas for Applying Thinking Skills Used in History

Thinking Skill	Task Ideas for Application and Transfer
Analyze	Prepare a newspaper article that informs the public of how this community started.
Compare	As advisors for the current president, create a visual that clearly and quickly shows the president the differences of two opposing approaches for economic growth; refer to historical lessons.
Classify	Design the perfect society and include descriptions of economics, jobs, education, law enforcement, art, and so on.
Cause/Effect	Design a simulation that will teach younger students about supply-and-demand forces in the economy.
Problem Solve	Write a proposition—for voter approval—that would help jobless people.
Persuade	Write a letter to the school board that asks for money to buy primary documents to supplement the biased textbook.
Empathize	Create a journal entry (or blog or social network page) from the perspective of a WWII soldier.
Synthesize	Analyze several songs written during the Civil War and synthesize their contents into a letter to President Lincoln.
Interpret	Write a simulated autobiography from the point of view of a slave (or slave owner, slave trader, modern-day slave, and so on).
Evaluate	As the Commission for Historical Accuracy, evaluate Christopher Columbus's actions and decide how he should be described in history texts. Create a master list of the ten biggest mysteries of history and explain why they are important.
Communicate	Design a training manual for WWI troops that outlines the enemy's weapons and tactics. Design a museum exhibit on the roles of nonmilitary people in the American Revolution.

- Civilization, cultural diffusion, and innovation

  The evolution of human skills and the means of exerting power over nature and people. The rise, interaction, and decline of successive centers of such skills and power. The cultural flowering of major civilizations in the arts, literature, and thought. The role of social, religious, and political patronage of the arts and learning. The importance of the city in different eras and places.

- Human interaction with the environment

  The relationships among geography, technology, and culture, and their effects on economic, social, and political developments. The choices made possible by climate, resources, and location, and the effect of culture and human values on such choices. The gains and losses of technological change. The central role of agriculture. The effect of disease, and disease fighting, on plants, animals, and human beings.

- Values, beliefs, political ideas, and institutions

  The origins and spread of influential religions and ideologies. The evolution of political and social institutions, at various stages of industrial and commercial development. The interplay among ideas, material conditions, moral values, and leadership, especially in the evolution of democratic societies. The tensions between the aspirations for freedom and security, for liberty and equality, for distinction and commonality, in human affairs.

- Conflict and cooperation

  The many and various causes of war, and of approaches to peacemaking and war prevention. Relations between domestic affairs and ways of dealing with the outside world. Contrasts between international conflict and cooperation, between isolation and interdependence. The consequences of war and peace for societies and their cultures.

- Comparative history of major developments

  The characteristics of revolutionary, reactionary, and reform periods across time and place. Imperialism, ancient and modern. Comparative instances of slavery and emancipation, feudalism and centralization, human successes and failures, of wisdom and folly. Comparative elites and aristocracies; the role of family, wealth, and merit.

- Patterns of social and political interaction

  The changing patterns of class, ethnic, racial, and gender structures and relations. Immigration, migration, and social mobility. The effects of schooling. The new prominence of women, minorities, and the common people in the study of history, and their relation to political power and influential elites. The characteristics of multicultural societies; forces for unity and disunity. (1988, 10–11)

Cognitive Flexibility

Conversations in history deepen even more when students use additional habits of mind that fall within the category of cognitive flexibility. These skills and understandings include (1) knowing that causes and effects in history are rarely cut and dried and that ambiguity often prevails; (2) noticing the interplay of change and continuity in history; (3) knowing that there will always be many uncertainties, unsolved problems, and unanswered questions; (4) seeing that history's many "lessons" do not always apply to the present; (5) appreciating the influence of the illogical, random, and accidental; and (6) understanding the many blurred lines between fact and opinion in history (National Council for History Education 1988). Notice the flexibility evident in the following eighth-grade conversation.

Elías:	Why did he or they shoot Kennedy?
Tanya:	We might never know. Too much evidence was lost or destroyed.
Elías:	You would think that they could have found something, like in the movies.
Tanya:	It might have been a conspiracy; it might have been a random act.
Elías:	What do you mean?
Tanya:	Some people have studied the assassination for decades. There are lots of opinions but not much hard evidence except for what they found in the building. But people heard other shots and things.
Elías:	If it was a conspiracy, could it happen again?
Tanya:	Maybe. I hope not. It's scary to think that it could happen here.

Even though these habits appear to belong in middle school and beyond, teachers can begin to cultivate them in elementary school by generating questions that prompt each skill, such as *Do we know for sure that this was the main cause? How have things changed and stayed the same over time? Will we ever know the answer to this, for sure? How was thinking very different from ours back then? Could this have been a random accident?* and *In your opinion, was this a fact or the writer's opinion?* Students can generate similar questions, and classes can make posters and graphic organizers that emphasize these habits of mind, similar to the historical thinking lens described later in this chapter.

Assessing History Conversations

To assess students' academic conversations, you can use the rubric shown in Figure 8.3. Refer to Chapter 10 for ideas on how to use the rubric for both summative and formative purposes. You and your class should be extra clear on the descriptors in each box. Model conversations with and without the elements, and ask students to help score them. Students can also use the rubric to self- and peer-assess. Feel free to add or take away elements in order to fit your curriculum and unit objectives.

Figure 8.3 Sample Academic Conversation Rubric for History/Social Studies

At or Above (3)	Approaching (2)	Below (1)
(T) Think and talk like historians. - Connect to own life and other time periods. - Infer causes and effects. - Use history terms and principles. - See biases and perspectives. - Ask big questions. - Use complex syntax and transitions.	Make some useful connections and see some other perspectives; use some complex sentences and history terms, and use deep thinking.	Make few connections; see limited perspectives; use short sentences with mostly social language.
(F) Stay focused. - Build on comments. - Connect ideas to topic well. - Negotiate conflicting ideas and word meanings. - Offer few, if any, tangential thoughts.	Stay mostly on topic; show some idea building and negotiation; go on some tangents and deviations; show some confusion.	Rarely connect or build on ideas; go on many tangents and give unrelated information; demonstrate no negotiation of differing ideas.
(S) Support ideas and opinions with examples from text, life, and previous lessons; clearly explain and elaborate on ideas.	Offer some prompting for and support of ideas with examples, evidence, and clarifications.	Offer little or no support of ideas and reasons; show lack of appropriate prompting.
(P) Paraphrase partner ideas to clarify, deepen, and stay focused; synthesize key points or steps at end.	Offer some paraphrasing and synthesizing of key points or steps.	Offer little or no paraphrasing and synthesizing.
(C) Use communication behaviors; actively listen (eyes and body); take turns; value partner comments; be respectful.	Show some appropriate listening and turn-taking behaviors.	Show little eye contact or listening; interrupt; dominate talk or do not contribute at all.

History Conversation Activities

The descriptions in this section emphasize how the activities can be used to hone conversation skills and how conversations can deepen the learning through such activities. It is important to develop the habit of seeing where to integrate conversations throughout each lesson. Every day, students should have some form of academic conversation about the lesson topic, a current event around the world, or an issue at school.

History Quotation Conversations

Many quotations about history show how vast, important, complex, and biased history can be. Make cards with quotations about history on them. Examples are provided in Figure 8.4. Students converse about a quotation or set of quotations in order to explain their meanings to the class later. Students should think of examples from the past and from the present that might fit the quotation. After they share explanations with the whole class, the class can choose several quotations to go up on the wall to help them frame their historical thinking during the year (and the rest of their lives). You and your students can also select important quotations from the texts used in class throughout the year.

Here is a sample conversation excerpt from a ninth-grade history class. Notice the depth and application of ideas on the part of both students.

Eduardo:	I like Baldwin's quote about people being trapped in history and having history trapped in them.
Tarik:	What does it mean?
Eduardo:	I think it means that we can't escape the processes of history, no matter how hard we struggle.
Tarik:	Or we can't change it. For example, so many people in many countries have been poor for so long. In some places poverty has gotten worse.
Eduardo:	I think it is because of greed. The governments want all the money and don't care about the poor.
Tarik:	But what does it mean to have history trapped in us?
Eduardo:	Maybe we can't change who we are on the inside. We are products of all the good and bad things that happened in the past. We are greedy, too, like governments. What do you think?
Tarik:	Maybe, but it could mean that we will keep on doing things like happened in the past.
Eduardo:	For example?
Tarik:	Like the world wars. We didn't learn from the first one. It's like war is trapped inside of us.

Figure 8.4 Quotation Card Ideas

"History is written by the victors." –Winston Churchill	"Nothing capable of being memorized is history." —R. G. Collingwood	"History is something that happens to other people." —Anonymous
"All modern wars start in the history classroom." —Anonymous	"Those who don't know history are destined to repeat it." —Edmund Burke	"History will die if not irritated. The only service I can do to my profession is to serve as a flea." —Henry Adams
"The past is a foreign country; they do things differently there." —L. P. Hartley	"History is not the accumulation of events of every kind which happened in the past. It is the science of human societies." —Fustel de Coulanges	"Understanding the past requires pretending that you don't know the present." —Paul Fussell
"History is filled with the sound of silken slippers going downstairs and wooden shoes coming up." —Voltaire	"People are trapped in history, and history is trapped in them." —James Baldwin	"History consists of a series of accumulated imaginative inventions." —Voltaire
"History is the most dangerous product evolved from the chemistry of the intellect. . . . History will justify anything. It teaches precisely nothing, for it contains everything and furnishes examples of everything. —Paul Valery	"History consists, for the greater part, of the miseries brought upon the world by pride, ambition, avarice, revenge, lust, sedition, hypocrisy, ungoverned zeal, and all the train of disorderly appetite." —Edmund Burke	"My own conclusion is that history is simply social development along the lines of weakest resistance, and that in most cases the line of weakest resistance is found as unconsciously by society as by water." —Henry Adams

Historical Source Analysis Table

The historical source analysis table helps pairs to critically think together about history books and other sources.

Students read a text together and fill in the columns on the chart, not necessarily from top to bottom. To complete the table in Figure 8.5, for example, ninth-grade world history students analyzed the textbook and letters from Napoleon to Josephine. Questions should be based on big ideas and not easy facts. In their conversations, students can decide how "right" or "wrong" the answers are. Students must justify their ideas and support them with evidence. Several terms that they might need for this activity include *purpose, hypothesize, bias, significant, perspective, turning point, in their shoes, empathize, conflicting accounts,* and *might have led to.*

Figure 8.5 Sample Historical Source Analysis Table

	Events, Persons, Sources		
	French Revolution	**Napoleon**	**Letters**
Questions	*Why did it start? Why is it important?*	*Did he do more good or bad?*	*Why did he write them?*
Hypothesized Answers	*People were mad. People were freed.*	*More bad because he caused wars.*	*So people would know his feelings*
Purpose and Importance	*Got people thinking about freedom and rights*	*Spread revolutionary ideas around*	*Showed that he was a real person with feelings*
Empathy Notes	*I would have fought if treated like that.*	*I would like all that power, but would not abuse it.*	*I feel his pain about being away from a loved one.*
Possible Biases	*Lots of people not talked about in text*	*What did Napoleon write about himself?*	*These were a small part of the war.*
Causes and Effects	*People were fed up with monarchy.*	*Teased as a child; Corsican revolution*	*Showed feelings for Josephine*
Application and Lessons	*Ideas still around; church and state separation?*	*Many modern leaders are like him.*	*War changes people; some for better; some worse*

Cause-Effect Diagram

This activity allows students to think about possible causes and effects of an event or condition. The activity also lets students infer and evaluate how much influence the cause had and, similarly, how much influence the condition or event had on the effects. A sample diagram is shown in Figure 8.6, and a sample conversation that used the diagram as a scaffold follows the description of the procedure.

Figure 8.6 Cause-Effect Diagram Example

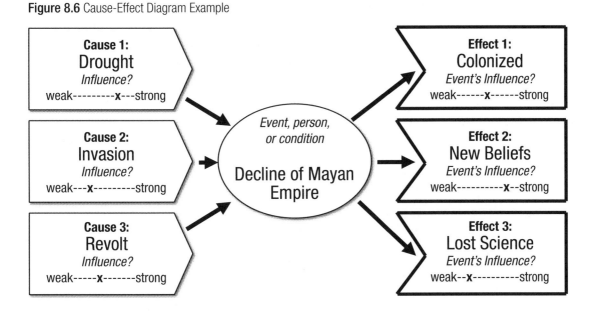

1. Choose a well-known event or person. Model how you would brainstorm possible causes for the event or condition, and then pick three causes to put on the left side of the diagram. You can also model with more challenging topics, such as the Boston Tea Party, World War II, the fall of Rome, and so on. Think aloud to model the influence of the cause and where you would place the *X* on the scale below each cause. Do the same with effects.
2. Have a student in each pair draw the empty diagram (Figure 8.6), then give them or let them choose a topic (event, person, or condition) for the center oval.
3. Pairs fill in their top three causes and discuss how much they think each cause influences the topic and why. They put an *X* on the scale to indicate whether it had a strong or weak influence. They refer to the text to support the placement of the *X*. Each partner can write with a different color to show where they agree and disagree.

4. Pairs brainstorm various effects of the event/condition. These can be other events or effects on people involved or related to the future. Pairs should try to come up with both positive and negative effects.

5. Pairs rate the influence that the event/condition had on each effect and place an *X* at the appropriate place on each scale. Then, they generate reasons and evidence for the rating. They can each use a different color to show where they agree and disagree.

6. Pairs share syntheses with the whole class.

Kyle:	I would put the X on the strong side for invasion because invasion tears everyone down.
Tomás:	Yes, but how many invasions were there? I think the evidence of drought is strongest because no water, no food. When you die or move away, life goes downhill.
Kyle:	And then you might revolt, too. So we can draw an arrow from drought to revolt.
Tomás:	Okay, so what about effects?
Kyle:	They got new beliefs, I think.
Tomás:	Why?
Kyle:	I don't know; I wasn't there. But maybe because they thought their old gods let them down?
Tomás:	Works for me. And then they got colonized by the Spanish. They might have fought the Spanish off if they had not declined.
Kyle:	So we can say that two big effects of the decline were they were colonized and they got new beliefs.

Fact-Thought Combinations

As mentioned in this book's introduction, students do need to learn facts and concepts in all disciplines. Students need to remember key ideas, dates, people, and so on, not only to converse but also to think. This simple activity trains students to attach a deeper thought to a basic, not so exciting, yet important fact. The activity helps students to be critical, take a different perspective, and question the accepted line of thinking. It also helps students remember the important fact or concept.

Train students to take a fact that they need to know, such as, *In 1919 the Nineteenth Amendment was passed to give women in the United States the right to vote*, and then respond to the fact using thinking prompts such as, *Why did it take so long?* or *Why that year?* or *How do women's votes make a difference?* It can help if students put the fact in the middle of a semantic map and surround it with deeper thoughts and questions. You can do this process with three facts, gradually allowing students more responsibility for producing the thoughts. They then choose a fact and a thought prompt or two and hold an academic conversation. Have students report out their syntheses to the whole class. Here is a sample conversation with elaboration, links, application, and deep questions:

Marissa:	Okay, we know that women finally got to vote in 1920. So why did it take so long before 1920? Were women considered to be people back then?
Shayla:	I don't know. Maybe a lot couldn't read. I don't think many girls went to school back then.
Marissa:	Well, if not, why not? That is worse.
Shayla:	Can you elaborate?
Marissa:	Not giving a girl an education means she can't work or compete with men. Or even teach her children at home. Did they just think women should cook and clean and take care of babies?
Shayla:	I think so. I think it is still that way in many countries. I read about women in Iran and Afghanistan; in lots of places they threaten girls who go to school. They burn schools that teach girls.
Marissa:	Why the heck do they do that?
Shayla:	Religion, I think. But I don't know why a religion would want to keep women from education.
Marissa:	Or why people wouldn't want women to vote for, how many? One hundred forty years of being a country? We are supposed to be a democracy, right?

Tackle History's Mysteries, Controversies, and Big Questions

History's mysteries and controversies are many, yet for some reason they seldom make it into textbooks. Many a conversation has been fueled by the zeal to solve a historical mystery. For this reason, look for mysteries, controversies, and big questions within the material that you are teaching. Have students generate their own big questions and seek to answer them. Students can then converse to solve the mystery, or make a plan for doing research that will get them closer to solving it. Here are examples of some enticing historical mysteries:

- » Is there anything valid to the conspiracy theories about Kennedy's assassination?
- » What happened to the *Mary Celeste*?
- » Was Mozart murdered?
- » Who was the Man in the Iron Mask?
- » Why was Stonehenge built?
- » Was there really a Trojan War?
- » Who was King Arthur?
- » Why did the Mayan civilization decline?
- » What was the "sign" that helped Joan of Arc become a leader?
- » Did Shakespeare write all of his plays or not?
- » Did Hitler murder his niece?
- » Was Mikhail Gorbachev part of the August Coup?

» Did Edwin M. Stanton, secretary of war at the time, betray Lincoln?

» Why was the Viking settlement at L'anse aux Meadows in Newfoundland abandoned?

» Did Atlantis exist?

» Was the Alamo a setup?

A variation of this activity is to have students consider "What if . . . ?" questions. What if Lincoln had not been assassinated? What if Cortés had been defeated by the Aztecs? What if disease hadn't decimated the original inhabitants of North America? Such questions offer students a chance to hypothesize, link causes and effects, and wonder.

My Image of and in History

It can be helpful to have an artifact or image act as a foundation for a conversation. In this activity (adapted from Drake and Nelson 2005), students create their image of history on paper. This can be done at the beginning and end of the school year. First, ask students something like, "Draw your image or vision of history on one sheet of paper. Include yourself in the picture." When most students are finishing their pictures, have them pair up and choose from the following questions about their images. The conversation can start with one partner asking the other about his or her image.

• Describe your picture to your partner. Is it one time period, multiple, or all of history? Why did you include these things?

• Does your picture depict big events with famous people or mundane events with normal people?

• Does your picture include symbols? Of what?

• Does your picture include politics, government, or national, and/or local concepts?

• Does your picture contain vital themes of culture, civilization, innovation, environment, values, beliefs, conflict, cooperation, patterns, change, continuity, human nature, and so on?

• What is your role in the picture? Are you just observing or are you changing history around you? What should be your/our role?

• Is there bias in this image? Cause/effect? Empathy? Are there questions?

• How do our two images compare and contrast?

Students can modify the images as they talk, if they want. Optionally, afterward, the two students can create a shared, synthesized image of history that combines their two images and the ideas that surfaced in their conversation. The class could even create a mural or poster to modify and anchor their learning throughout the year.

Movie Critics and Writers

Wineberg and colleagues (2007) described the value of having students analyze historical movies or other texts and "stretch them or call them into question" (68). Popular history-based movies fill the mind with images and words that are supposed to be historically accurate. Students need to refer to other sources, consider biases, and think about how the producers depicted the events or people in the movie. And when differing opinions arise, students should be encouraged to sort them out in their conversations. Show the most relevant clips from historical movies. Movies worth criticizing include *Pocahontas, Mulan, JFK, Pearl Harbor, Patton,* and *Gandhi,* to name a few. A sample conversation follows:

Silvia:	I don't think King Arthur was real.
Todd:	Why?
Silvia:	The movie, *Arthur,* says he was, like, just a Roman soldier.
Todd:	That was just a movie.
Silvia:	But maybe the movie is more true than the famous legends. So I looked up a little, and lots of articles said Arthur was a myth. Some talk about a Roman soldier who won the Battle of Badon. He was a hero.
Todd:	Well, maybe, but what about Merlin, the sword, and all that?
Silvia:	Does it matter? As the teacher said, what about the themes and the inspiration? Arthur was a hero. He was a just king.
Todd:	Maybe the idea of him helped inspire the British people to unite. Maybe even to be more democratic. You know, that whole Round Table stuff.

Partners can also work together to write a historical fiction movie script or documentary. Agree on the criteria for a high-quality film as a whole class, and have students peer-assess along the way.

History Time Capsule

For this activity, students, in pairs, decide which objects should be included in a box to be buried and opened in fifty years. You can decide the dimensions of the box. Students must discuss the importance of and prioritize objects and information, including images and videos. You can set parameters, such as not allowing computers, but allowing DVDs, books, and photos in hard copy. Pairs can meet with other pairs to discuss/argue the inclusion of certain items.

It is helpful to create an anchor chart of "Guidelines for Historical Significance," which can be used in such conversations and class discussions. Some guidelines might include the following:

influenced many people's lives, solved a major problem in history, shaped national boundaries, was a hero/heroine to many people, is a warning to the future, and so on.

Choose the Best Image

In pairs, have students look at three or four pictures from an event or time period. They need to jointly decide which picture best shows what happened or shows the most important part of that period, person, or event. They must discuss the positives and limitations of each image and then argue for the image that they choose in front of another pair or group of four other students. They should consider such things as bias, empathy, importance, cause, effect, and connection to the present. They should bring up what they know about the time period and what they need to know to make a more informed decision. They should do extra research, if there is time. Here is a sample conversation:

Daniel: We should choose this image because it shows how people were feeling during that period.

Tarah: But does it? We know that some people were unhappy with the taxes and all that, but was this the majority? Did the majority want to fight a revolution? I think this other image that shows some people happy and others mad is better. For example, if you had a family and had food and shelter, would you support the revolt?

Daniel: Maybe, if I wanted my kids to not live under the English king.

Tarah: I don't know. We see the famous ones as heroes, but they also ended up with the power in the new government. Some still had slaves. So, this picture.

Daniel: Sure, but I think we should look up more about how it all really started.

Paired Role-Play Stations

For this activity, make cards that describe important characters and underrepresented people from the historical period you are studying. The cards should be prepared in pairs—the people on them should represent two different perspectives from the same time period or during the same event. On each card, give a brief description of the character, telling what the character likely wanted, felt, thought, and so on. (After some practice with such cards, students should make their own cards, based on reliable sources, of course.) An example is shown in Figure 8.7.

After students read their cards, they play the parts of the characters on the cards and have a conversation about a hot topic of that time period. They can look at the cards, but should try to face the partner and converse as much as possible. Situations and topics for discussion might be reviewing an article or film; preparing for a debate; deciding to go to war or not; deciding what to include in a future history textbook; or solving a problem from that time period.

Figure 8.7 Paired Role-Play Cards

John Smith: You helped to establish the first permanent North American English settlement in Jamestown, Virginia. You briefly interacted with the Native American girl called Pocahontas during an altercation with her father, Chief Powhatan. You encouraged people to colonize the New World. You said, "Here every man may be master and owner of his owne labour and land . . . If he have nothing but his hands, he may . . . by industrie quickly grow rich." This and similar messages brought millions of people to North American in the centuries that followed.

Chief Powhatan: You were the high chief of the Powhatan tribes. There were an estimated 14,000–21,000 native Powhatan people in eastern Virginia in 1607, when the English established Jamestown. After being captured, John Smith was brought to you. An account by Smith tells that your daughter, Pocahontas, prevented you from executing Smith. When you were being crowned as a vassal of the English, you were forced to bow down, but you followed two rules: "He who keeps his head higher than others ranks higher," and "He who puts other people in a vulnerable position, without altering his own stance, ranks higher."

Ideas for card pairings include Columbus and a Taino chief; two presidents; historical figures from different time periods or different parts of the world; historians with differing theories; Native Americans being removed in 1831 and Andrew Jackson; a slave and slave owner; authors of biography and historical fiction; a liberal and a conservative.

After they finish role playing, partners can put the cards down and talk as historians might talk about the role-play conversation, the issue, its importance, and how it might apply to modern day. They might take two different sides of the issue and try to come to an agreement.

Another option is to have students be in roles as they prepare a speech, presentation, or product for a certain audience. Ideas include a speech at a civil rights rally; a keynote address at a conference; a news broadcast; a song that depicts key events and feelings; a presidential candidate speech; or a video persuading viewers to vote a certain way.

For another variation, have students create a talking wax museum. Two students become the same historical person. First, they converse to understand what the person did and felt and how the person would describe himself or herself briefly. When they finish this discussion, they move to different parts of the room. Each student stands in an important pose, waits for a passerby to "press a button," and then starts talking about the historical person's life in first person. For example, partners might become a person from the American Civil War era, such as Abraham Lincoln, who explains some of his rationale for his decisions and elaborates on some of his contradictory quotations. You might want to make this a performance-based assessment.

The Sample History Lesson Plan shown in Figure 8.8 refers to the Connecting and Applying History graphic organizer (Figure 8.9), which helps students to write down connections between and applications of historical ideas before, during, and after academic conversations.

Figure 8.8 Sample History Lesson Plan with Academic Conversations

Topic: Trail of Tears Text: Fifth-grade textbook, Jackson letters, *Trail of Tears* by Joseph Bruchac	*Conversation Integration*
Objective(s): - *Content:* Know the causes of the Trail of Tears and removal policies; argue if they were constitutional or not; connect and apply the concepts to modern life. - *Language:* Concession language *(Even though, despite, given that)*; focusing on a topic - *Reading:* Skills for reading long sentences: identify main subjects and verbs	*Connect ideas to focus on and deepen a topic in a conversation*
Assessments: - Quiz on events and key people - Persuasive letter - Academic conversation	*Academic conversation*
I. Opening/Modeling: - Tell students that the principal has decided that he or she wants to use our classroom as an office and that we need to hold class in the hall (or in a very small room) from now on. - Students quickwrite their reactions, converse in pairs, and then share out. Tell them this is what happened to Native Americans in the 1830s and that the questions we all will try to answer in class today are, *But was this removal legal?* and *What should we do now?*	*Think-pair-share*
II. Guided Practice: - Read *Trail of Tears* (Joseph Bruchac) aloud. Stop for comments, questions, etc. Have a quick paired conversation on the question of whether Jackson was right, was a hero, and/or should be on the $20 bill. Tell students that Jackson is not here today, but we are about to take him and others involved to court. - Show copies of the *Declaration of Independence* and the *U.S. Constitution* (or abridged versions) and look for relevant parts as a class. Have them take notes for their conversations. Model the start of a conversation. Students then hold paired academic conversations (with different partners than before) on the questions: *Was this removal legal?* and *What should we do now?* Have them share their syntheses with the whole class.	*Paired conversation* *Model a conversation* *Analyze and discuss documents in pairs and converse about question(s)*

III. Practice	
- Have pairs in one half of the room prepare arguments for the Jackson side, and the other half prepare for the Native American perspective. Students share their points. Write them down on the board. As a class, evaluate the weights of each argument.	*Preparation of arguments in pairs*
- Connecting and Applying History organizer (Figure 8.9). Using this graphic organizer, students learn to connect and apply concepts from history to different dimensions of their life (past, present, future). Students learn the power of history to teach them important lessons.	*Students hold academic conversations based on the graphic organizer*
Procedure: (1) Model with a student in a fishbowl how to converse in pairs about a sample topic (use one that they are familiar with but are not going to use today, e.g., freedom of speech), then have students choose the topic or give the topic to them (e.g., "Discuss ideas of land ownership and the forced removal of people, and how they connect to and apply to modern life. You might think of an analogy, too."). (2) Partners silently fill in their connect-apply tables. (3) Students converse to compare their notes, challenge others' ideas, and come to a synthesis. Observe and support conversations. (4) Pairs write down their final synthesis paragraph together. (5) Whole class converses and writes a whole-class negotiated paragraph on the overhead, if time.	
IV. Independent	
Students have conversations to prepare to write persuasive letters on their choice of topics, including, if they need prompting, (1) Write a letter to President Jackson about the removal policies. Include a description of the *Trail of Tears*; (2) Write a letter to the current president about what to do about the injustices that occurred in the 1830s; (3) Using *Trail of Tears* as an example, write a letter to argue against similar treatment in the past or present around the world. Students should be reminded to include counterarguments and support claims with evidence.	*Final ACs to prepare for writing their letters* *Teacher observes five pairs and scores them on a rubric*

This chapter has provided activities for building students' historical critical thinking skills through and for conversation. Each student is unique, with his or her own unique history, and conversations allow students to make sense and learn from events and people across time.

Figure 8.9 Connecting and Applying History Organizer

Connecting and Applying History
Connect to past/current (and/or create an **analogy**)
Apply this concept to the future in order to learn from it and improve; ask questions
TOPIC: *Removal of Native Americans*

Connect/ Analogy		Apply
Like someone kicking us out of our house	Your life, family, house	If they move us from apartment, we fight it in court.
One time our room was needed and we met outside.	Your classroom	We should not be forced to move seats!
If they found oil under our school, they would move us.	Your school	We should have the right to choose our teachers and our classes.
There were Native Americans here until others moved in.	Your community	House prices are forcing many people to leave. Is that fair?
We thought the Constitution prevented this.	Your nation	Still on reservations; should they get their original lands back?
Colonies in Africa	The world	The UN forces makes it so people don't get moved from home lands.

Adapted from an eighth-grade history lesson on the removal of Native Americans in the nineteenth century.

Reflections

1. How is history unique in its potential to develop student minds?
2. Which history skills do your students most need to develop?
3. Generate three history conversation prompts that *you* would most like to talk about with a partner. Write an excerpt (actual or created) from the conversation and analyze it.

Chapter 9
Conversations in Science

> Science wasn't very interesting until we started talking about it.

—Fifth-grade student

Science has its own thinking, language, and conversations. This chapter is about how to build students' scientific skills and understandings through conversation as well as how to build conversation skills through science learning. The following pages highlight how to converse about scientific inquiry and experimentation. Examples of scientific thinking skills are found in Figure 9.1 and are described in subsequent sections. Different scientific thinking skills are emphasized in the different branches of science being taught (biology, physics, earth science, etc.).

As Jay Lemke, a noted researcher in the area of science education, points out, "We have to learn to see science teaching as a social process and to bring students, at least partially, into this community of people who talk science" (Lemke 1990, x). Of course, talking science means thinking science, so one of our teacher tasks is to consider the thinking processes that beginning scientists need to use and then emphasize them in teaching and conversation activities. Students can practice translating scientific language into colloquial terms and vice versa. Gradually, in their conversations, we scaffold them to use scientific terms and grammar.

Understanding Through Uncovering

We want students to understand and to show their understanding of science through conversation. But what does it mean to understand science? One level of understanding is knowing the structures and functions of things, such as a cell, a glacier, a proton, or a spring. Students need to learn basic facts and processes that happen in science, and many of these must be learned directly, building on previous science discoveries throughout history. Students must be trained to see connections between current and previous concepts and connect them over time.

Yet a much deeper level of understanding happens when students get involved in scientific inquiry, analysis, and experimentation. Students need to learn science by doing science. Too many materials and lessons have "cookbook science," in which labs are just simple recipes to follow. Students follow the recipe, describe what happened, and forget most of the science because they never asked questions or pondered their own ways to experiment. We must be careful not to over-scaffold, because if we do, students will miss key opportunities to inquire and discover. For example, we have seen teachers not directly tell students the objectives for a lesson, and instead let students discover what they were to learn or not learn that day through inquiry-based activities.

Types of Science Conversations

We have observed several types of high-quality conversations in science classrooms. In these conversations, student pairs talk about how to do the following:

» Solve a problem or answer a tough question.
» Design an experiment.
» Write up a lab (describe, explain, communicate, support conclusions with results).
» Explain or teach a process or concept to other students.
» Apply the science learning to real life.

Science Thinking Skills

In most science conversations, partners will use multiple thinking skills. Some of the most common thinking skills in science are listed in Figure 9.1, with corresponding conversation prompts and responses. We encourage you to create your own chart with the prominent skills and language that you are working on in class. Detailed descriptions of the first three of the core scientific thinking skills listed in Figure 9.1, including sample conversations, follow. As in Chapters 7 and 8, we focus on these skills and how conversation can develop them across science classes.

Figure 9.1 Science Thinking Skills, Prompt Frames, and Response Frames

Core Thinking Skills in Science	Sample Prompt Frames	Sample Response Frames
Observe some aspect of the physical or natural universe	What did you observe? What do we see happening? What does that mean? Why did that happen? What can we learn from this phenomenon? Why is this important?	I notice that . . . I observed that . . . We have all seen . . . Look at the way that the . . .
Ask questions about the observations	What questions do we have about what we observed? What do you wonder? What don't we know about this?	I wonder why . . . Where does the . . . come from? How does it . . . ? What kind of reaction could cause that? What caused . . . to happen?

Generate a logical hypothesis that attempts to answer the question(s)	How can we investigate the possible reasons for . . . ? What do you think will happen? Why do you think that happened? What if we . . . ? What do we hypothesize? Which principles apply here?	If we add . . . then maybe . . . I hypothesize that . . . because . . . I think that it will . . . because . . . Based on . . . I think that . . . Most likely, it will . . .
Design experiments or research to test the hypotheses; identify and isolate variables	What if we changed the variables? How can we isolate this variable? What do you think will happen? Why? What will not happen? How could we prove this? What might be other interpretations? How can we design an experiment to measure our hypothesis? How can we prove that . . . ? But what about the effects of . . . ? Which variables do we isolate? Is there a control group?	If we isolate the variable . . . then we can see . . . Several variables come into play . . . We also need a control group. We need a microscope to see how . . . We need to change the . . . to see how . . . reacts. We need to consider the effects of . . .
Perform experiments and do research; gather data, interpret it, and organize it	How can we quantify our observations? What data do we have? What does this data mean? How do we organize the data?	The control group doesn't get treatment. The data should go into a table because . . . We need to measure the . . . As the . . . increases, the . . . decreases. There is a correlation between . . . and . . .
Make conclusions about experimental data, its validity, and its support of the hypothesis	What are the data telling us? What evidence supports our conclusions? What does that mean? How can we extrapolate from the data? Is this set of data valid? What might critics argue about this data?	The data show that . . . We discovered that . . . Our data were not valid or reliable enough to make solid conclusions about . . . We found a negative correlation between . . . Based on these numbers, it is likely that . . . Our research has demonstrated that . . . The results seem to indicate that . . .

Figure 9.1 Science Thinking Skills, Prompt Frames, and Response Frames (Part 2)

Additional Thinking Skills in Science	Sample Prompt Frames	Sample Response Frames
Analyze patterns and relationships	What patterns do you notice in . . .? How do these two . . . relate? What does the data show? What are the different components, factors, dimensions that . . .? What do we see if we keep on breaking this down?	I notice that each time . . . I think this . . . is affecting the . . . It is composed of . . . If we break this down, we see that . . .
Use scientific principles and laws	Is that possible? Why wouldn't that work? Which rules or laws can we apply here? How should we use what we learned about . . .? What do we already know about this . . .?	It shouldn't be possible because . . . We know that . . . We can apply the law of . . . We need to remember that . . .
Apply (to real world and future) and transfer to new contexts	So how can we apply this concept to life? What can we learn from this experiment? How can you change how you think or live based on this . . . ? Does this text apply to anything in the world you know of? How could this improve the world? How can these results apply to our lives? Why is it important? How is it useful to us?	An application to our lives could include . . . I believe that the results from this study have implications for our lives, such as . . . This process is important because . . . We can use this in the future . . .
Compare	How does what we saw in the experiment compare to our hypothesis? How are the results similar or different? How are the two labs similar? How are the two occurrences different?	Compared to what we hypothesized, what did we see? These results surprised us because . . . We found differences between . . .

Analyze ethics	Is it right, is it wrong, or is there a gray area? What are the criteria for right and wrong here? Does the usefulness outweigh the ethical questions? What are the pros and cons of this decision? Why is this controversial? What is the moral dilemma?	This would be unethical because . . . An important criterion is . . . because . . . It is more ethical to . . . The moral dilemma is . . .
Problem solve; make a decision	What information is needed to solve this problem? What do we need to find? What is the question really asking? What information don't we need? How can we make a plan to solve this? What steps can we take? What are different ways to solve this? What are the consequences of each? Which is the best solution? What do you estimate the answer will be? Why? How can we draw it?	We need to know . . . because . . . We should start by . . . We should be asking . . . One consequence of doing that is . . . We think the best solution is . . . We might show that by drawing . . .
Identify causes and effects (causation vs. correlation)	Describe the role that . . . played in the reaction. Identify the primary causes and effects of the phenomenon. Was it causation or correlation, in the case of . . . What caused the . . . to . . . ? What are the short and long-term effects?	The . . . appeared to cause . . . because . . . The main effect was . . . It was more of correlation because . . . The long-term effects are likely . . .

Observing, Inquiring, and Hypothesizing

Students must learn to authentically observe, inquire, and hypothesize as scientists do. They can learn some science with a book, but real scientific thinking is founded upon observing a phenomenon, asking questions about it, and thoughtfully hypothesizing answers or ways to get answers. Science is fueled by wonderings and guesses—and students need to engage in such thinking as much as possible. Unfortunately, many texts and tests cannot or do not emphasize these core skills, and therefore they are neglected in many science classes. Conversations can help students focus and develop these skills. Look at the thinking and language that emerges in the following conversation in an eighth-grade science class.

Ana:	What did you observe?
Ben:	Um, the higher the ramp was, the further the car went.
Ana:	Why do you think that happened?
Ben:	I don't know. We just read about potential energy in the book. So, maybe the higher the ramp, the starting point, the more energy it had and it made it go further.
Ana:	Yeah, I think the cars that went further had more energy because we had to lift the cars higher. We used more energy for them, even though we didn't feel it.
Ben:	But what if we had to push real cars up a hill? Then we would feel it.
Ana:	Yeah. I did that once and used up a lot of energy. I guess I gave it to the car. And every time I go up the stairs, I give myself potential energy, I think. I'm tired at the top.
Ben:	And what about the graph we made? Here we can connect the points and it makes a line, more or less.
Ana:	So what?
Ben:	Well, as the teacher showed last week, we can extra . . . polite . . . (looks up on word wall) extrapolate the data. That means we can predict by using the line. So if the ramp is 500 inches tall, . . .
Ana:	. . . We could predict how far the car would go?
Ben:	But we would have to make up a formula or something, since we can't experiment with a ramp that high. So, if the height, *h*, is something, we want to know the distance, *d*?
Ana:	Well, each time the distance increases, the height is multiplied by around 4, so *d* could equal 4 times *h*, more or less.
Ben:	Okay, but so what? Why is it important? How is it useful to us?
Ana:	We can learn how to predict when things make a line on a graph like this.

In this conversation, the students use a large amount of academic grammar and vocabulary, such as *the higher the . . . , the more . . . ; potential energy; formula; extrapolate; if . . . then; each time . . . so . . .* They hypothesized two ideas: that the cars have more energy from being higher, and that they can use a linear formula to predict cases that are too difficult to produce in the lab.

Experimenting, Identifying Variables, and Interpreting

After observing and hypothesizing, scientists design and perform experiments to better understand what they are observing and to verify their hypotheses. Experiments are designed to confirm or disconfirm a hypothesis, which usually relates a cause to an effect. In most experiments, scientists identify variables and keep all of them constant except the one that denotes the hypothesized cause. This isolated variable is the independent variable—the one that changes. The dependent variable is the result each time the independent variable is changed.

For example, in observing that a lightbulb changes intensity as different materials are used to complete the circuit, two students might hypothesize that only metals conduct and that all metals are the same. The students converse about the variables that need to remain constant, such as batteries, wires, connections, temperature, and the bulb. As they think about metals that might have similar but not the same conductivity, they decide that they want a more precise way to measure voltage than just looking at the bulb. They ask the teacher for a voltmeter. They then design a series of trials with different materials.

During and after the experiment, students must interpret the results. Interpretation means attempting to explain what happened between variables. It is also a way to critique the validity of the experiment. For example, if a sponge with water conducts some electricity, then students need to identify another way to see if it is the water or the sponge that conducts the electricity or both. They make a table and analyze it against the periodic table of elements. They see that aluminum is a poor conductor compared to other metals. They speculate why and do further research.

Even if the experiment is not possible at the school (e.g., living in outer space, life around an oceanic thermal vent, etc.), just having students think about and design experiments is worth the time. For example, you might have students design an experiment that scientists could do to understand the influence of carbon emissions on the atmosphere.

Labs are also common in many science classes. They are typically already organized with steps and procedures for students to follow. They are less flexible and develop fewer inquiry and experiment skills, but they can be focused and educational. They can produce a variety of topics for academic conversations and ideas for experiments. For example, after or during a squid dissection lab, students can converse about why the squid developed certain adaptations over time.

Or in a lab on acids and bases, students can converse about the applications of the reactions they observed, as well as the chemical causes and effects.

Much of science involves observing and understanding patterns and relationships. Patterns are found everywhere in the natural world. We see patterns in animal and plant behavior, gravity, combustion, weather, cells, electricity, geological processes, heat, and so on. We might see patterns in data from an experiment. Patterns help us to make hypotheses and interpretations. Scientists often break a complex thing down to its components and figure out how everything fits together. Biologists might analyze how chemicals influence the relationships between neurons; physicists might analyze how electrons behave in a magnetic field. Scientists also infer relationships between two components and design experiments to confirm them.

As student scientists infer and conclude, they must also be able to accurately describe their levels of certainty. Students must be able to differentiate strong from weak data patterns and be able to objectively describe the strength of the conclusions that they make from such data.

Using Scientific Principles and Laws

A vital yet often overlooked and under-taught skill in science is using previously-learned principles and laws to learn new concepts. For example, we would want students to use the principles and laws on gravitational forces that they have already learned in order to understand a new unit on orbits. They might have learned last year that gravity is an attraction between two objects. They need to use this knowledge to understand new and more advanced ideas about gravitational forces between objects in space.

We need to train students to refer to "umbrella" principles and laws in their conversations. Even the question, *How does that work?* can prompt a partner to bring up foundational principles of the discipline that apply. The partner, for instance, might refer to principles of adaptation during and after a dissection lab. During a design challenge, students might use Newton's laws to maximize the distance their invention will travel. Students might also collaboratively analyze textbook sections and articles to identify the processes, questions, and controversies that relate to principles, theories, and laws.

Throughout science activities, students should develop the habit of challenging their own and others' conceptions and misconceptions. In the following conversation, students converse about why two objects of different masses fall at the same rate in a vacuum. They refer to several ideas and laws they had learned previously.

Naia: So, why did the feather and the rock fall at the same speed in that tube?
Chris: I don't know.

Naia:	Well, the tube had no air, a vacuum, so the air didn't affect the feather, like it would out here.
Chris:	Can you elaborate?
Naia:	Well, the air molecules push up more on the feather, because it is much lighter.
Chris:	So, why wouldn't the feather land sooner if it is lighter?
Naia:	But we learned that acceleration of Earth's gravity is 9.8 meters per second per second for everything. This means the two things should fall at the same time, right? And there is Newton's law of inertia, or something like that. It says that if something is bigger and more mass, there is more attraction to it. But it also has more inertia to stay where it is. So the rock is more attracted to the Earth, but . . .
Chris:	. . . But it is harder to move because it has more mass than the feather. I bet that's it.
Naia:	We could test it with different objects, maybe even ourselves.
Chris:	In a vacuum? You go first, then.

To build scientific questioning habits, chemistry teacher Derek Ang, of East Palo Alto High School in California, has students use a "So and Why" protocol in which, after starting with an opening question, they build on each answer with so or why questions. They can do this as a whole class, in groups, or in pairs. For example, an exchange in this protocol could proceed like this:

"What happened in this reaction?"

"Heat was released and a solid was formed."

"Why was heat released?"

"Because chemical bonds were broken and reformed."

"So how can we apply this?"

As students continue to ask so and why questions, they think more and more as scientists.

Assessing Science Conversations

To assess students' academic conversations in science, you can use the rubric in Figure 9.2. Refer to Chapter 10 for ideas on how to use the rubric for both summative and formative purposes. Make sure that you and your class are extra clear on the descriptors in each box. Model a variety of conversations that have and don't have the elements in the "At or Above" column, and ask students to help score them. They should also use the rubric to self-assess and peer-assess. Add or take away elements in order to fit your curriculum and unit objectives.

Figure 9.2 Sample Academic Conversation Rubric for Science

At or Above (3)	Approaching (2)	Below (1)
(T) Think and talk like scientists. - Observe and hypothesize. - Propose ways to experiment; isolate variables; use evidence. - Refer to science principles and laws. - Use science terms and syntax. - Apply science to real life.	Make some connections; use some complex sentences and science terms; make some applications.	Use few connections or scientific reasons; use short sentences and mostly social language.
(F) Stay focused. - Build on comments. - Connect ideas to topic well. - Negotiate conflicting ideas and word meanings. - Offer few, if any, tangential thoughts.	Stay mostly on topic; show some idea building and negotiation; go on some tangents and deviations; show some confusion.	Rarely connect or build on ideas; go on many tangents and offer unrelated information; demonstrate no negotiation of differing ideas.
(S) Support ideas and opinions with examples from text, life, and previous lessons; clearly explain and elaborate on ideas.	Offer some prompting for and support of ideas with examples and clarifications.	Offer little or no support of ideas and reasons; show lack of appropriate prompting.
(P) Paraphrase partner ideas to clarify, deepen, and stay focused; synthesize key points or steps at end.	Offer some paraphrasing and synthesizing of key points or steps.	Offer little or no paraphrasing and synthesizing.
(C) Use **communication** behaviors; actively listen (eyes and body); take turns; value partner comments; be respectful.	Show some appropriate listening and turn-taking behaviors.	Show little eye contact or listening; interrupt; dominate talk or do not contribute at all.

Science Conversation Activities

The following activities can be used in science lessons to cultivate academic conversation skills. Some are activities that you may already use, but these variations emphasize developing conversation skills and critical thinking.

Case Study Conversations

A case study offers a real-world example of a complex issue in science and presents students a chance to act as problem solvers. Students analyze the case by focusing on the key information and identify different possible courses of action. As students converse to analyze the case, they (1) identify the important facts, factors, and variables; (2) identify the main issue or problem, as well as its possible causes and effects; (3) generate possible solutions; (4) evaluate each solution's positives, negatives, and feasibility; and (5) choose the best solution and support their decision. Steps 1 through 5 are not necessarily sequential; they might overlap and support one another. The following are some possible case study topics:

- Biology: dinosaurs' extinction, genetic anomalies, patient illness
- Earth/Space: acid rain, animals predict earthquake, space travel
- Physics: electric cars, black hole energy, safe nuclear power

Here is an excerpt from a seventh-grade conversation about a case study on the feasibility of cryogenic preservation for deep space travel.

Keisha:	What's important in this case?
Aldo:	I think that, I don't know, that the end of the world is important; and how to survive on another planet.
Keisha:	And we would have to sleep, like frozen for hundreds of years, but we can't be frozen.
Aldo:	Can you elaborate on that?
Keisha:	Well, something about ice forming between cells and tissue damage. They can't, don't have technology yet to revive people. They can freeze them, but that's it.
Aldo:	Okay, so the problem is freezing us for travel for a long time. So we can keep life going on another planet.
Keisha:	The problem is waking us up. We have lots of water and it freezes and gets bigger, you know, like bottles of water that freeze and explode.
Aldo:	So it sounds like we need to figure out how to freeze water and keep it from getting bigger.
Keisha:	Hmm. Why does water expand when it freezes?

Ninth-grade science teacher Octavio Rodriguez showed a video of a medical case study that argued for genetic testing. He then provided a text of a different case used to argue against testing. Students paired up and had academic conversations about both sides of the argument in order to prepare for a "taking sides" activity. In the activity students chose a side, moved to the side of the room designated for that opinion, shared with others near them why they chose that side, and then responded to students on the opposite side using sentence frames posted on the board. For example, one student would say, "I somewhat disagree. I believe that genetic testing is necessary to avoid suffering like we saw in the video." If students were convinced by arguments on the opposing side, they were encouraged to change sides and give a reason for moving. For example, one student said, "Eduardo changed my mind when he argued that life is better when you don't know if you will get sick." Students then wrote their final arguments using the target language of the lesson.

Design a Lab, Experiment, or Research Project for the Text

Much of the information in science texts is based on experimental evidence that has accumulated over time. Students can think about a textbook's assertions and come up with ideas for the experiments that led to the principles described in the text. For example, students might read the following excerpt from a science textbook:

> Electric currents move freely through materials called conductors. Metals, such as copper, silver, iron, and aluminum, are good conductors. In a conductor, some of the electrons are only loosely bound to their atoms. These electrons, called conduction electrons, are able to move throughout the conductor. As these electrons flow through a conductor, they form an electric current. (Frank et al. 2001, 354)

The students consider what they are supposed to learn from the text (e.g., materials vary in the looseness of their electrons). Then, instead of just memorizing the information, they codesign a lab or experiment that would yield the key concept described in the text. In their conversation, they might respond to the following prompts: *What science (facts, concepts, procedures) is the text trying to teach us? Why is this important? What could scientists have done to come up with this? What could we do to confirm that this is true (if we had all the money needed)? What tools and materials might we need?* The conversation should develop as students agree on experimental procedures, controls, and variables.

Conversations to Write Up Labs and Reflections

In order for students to write clear and thoughtful lab reports, they should converse about what they learned and how to present it on paper. They should have notes and data in front of them. What should a chat between two lab partners sound like before they write the report? Consider the types of thinking skills needed and the language and sentence starters you would like to hear.

Go around and listen to conversations and write down those expressions that you would like to hear and the ones that you would like to make more academic. Later on, you might say, "The other day I heard someone say, 'The push and pull of the ground makes valleys and mountains.' What other, more science-sounding terms can we use? We could say, 'The forces of compression and tension of the earth's plates create valleys and mountains.'" Continue to scaffold the language that students use as they talk about and eventually write their reports.

Share and Compare Labs

For this activity, have pairs perform different, but related, labs. They use slightly different materials or variables so they can compare their results and conclusions at the end. For example, in a plant growth lab, some pairs might have different types of plants, others might change the amount of light, and others might have different soil or provide different amounts of water. Students converse about their observations, hypotheses, variables, results, and so on.

Encourage students to use science language such as *observe, hypothesize, constant, dependent variable, independent variable, control, gather data, graph,* and *extrapolate*. Other helpful language might include *procedure, increment, adjust, factor, inaccurate, guarantee, inertia, reduce that effect,* and *found that*. Academic grammar might emerge, such as *If we had added more water, then it would have. . . . Because we didn't keep the light amount constant, we don't know. . . .* Prompt students to ask questions as they work, such as *What about if we . . . ? What do you think will happen if . . . ? Why do you think that would happen? So you think it did that because . . . ?*

Role-Based Conversations

Even though students are already scientists, in a sense, it can help for them to play roles of professional scientists. We have seen students use more scientific language when they are not trying to be their cool selves. This happens because many students do not want to sound nerdy, arrogant, or like they are trying to impress the teacher. Acting allows them to try out language without it being seen as theirs.

Present student pairs with a problem and have them act as scientists who converse about it. Students can also write down their conversations. In this conversation from a high school chemistry class, the problem is how to create new and safe energy sources.

Arjan: What about nuclear fusion?

Alicia: Yes, when hydrogen gets converted into helium because of high temperatures and pressure. Like 15,000,000 degrees or something like that. But what could hold that much heat? Wouldn't everything melt?

Arjan: The heat is the smaller problem. The pressures of the sun are very high. We are working on it. They are using magnets to hold the hydrogen stuff, fuel. I think it's like when two magnets repel each other. They don't touch so maybe the heat doesn't melt anything.

Alicia: It says in the book here that because they can't create the pressures here on earth, they need to raise the temperature to 100,000,000 degrees.

Arjan: Whoa, it seems like they will use a lot of energy just to heat the deuterium up. Is it worth it?

Alicia: I think so. Just think about the equation $E = mc^2$ and put 300,000,000 into c. Then when two protons fuse, 0.7 percent of the protons convert to energy.

Arjan: So square c and multiply by .007, you get 630,000,000,000,000 times the mass of whatever was used as fuel. Even just one gram of hydrogen protons has massive energy.

Another more drama-based option is for students to become objects or animals and convey their perspectives in a conversation. They might be two animals that discuss their adaptations to survive. They might be two chemicals that describe how they would interact with different substances; they might be two planets who talk about how the universe began and will end.

Science Museum Exhibits

For this activity, pairs converse as experts who are in charge of setting up a museum exhibit to teach a certain science concept. They are given a budget and informational points that they need to teach to people who visit the exhibit. Their goal is to come up with an outline of the materials that are needed, a description of the exhibit, written or oral instructions at the exhibit, and the procedure for when people visit it. They can also come up with potential audience questions and prepare their answers.

Design-Challenge and Inquiry-Based Lessons

Students learn by doing and construct their own knowledge and understanding by working through relevant tasks that support the learning process. Design-challenge and inquiry-based lessons allow students the opportunity to use their problem-solving skills to uncover important rules or pathways to solutions. Throughout the design-challenge process, students work to solve a relevant, authentic, real-world problem. Student teams apply and reinforce their content knowledge through an open-ended design process that results in an original solution. Student talk is essential to push this process along and build deeper understanding. Students also incorporate peer feedback as they conceptualize and redesign their solutions to the given challenge. With inquiry-based lessons, students ask and answer questions to discover scientific principles that deepen their understanding. Inquiry and design can work hand in hand to help students construct meaning. Both rely heavily on student talk and teamwork to assist in the completion of the tasks and challenges.

The fourth-grade lesson plan in Figure 9.3 shows different ways to use conversations to support the learning of science concepts and vice versa.

Figure 9.3 Sample Science Lesson Plan with Academic Conversations

Topic: Flow of Electricity Through a Circuit Grade Level: Fourth and up	Conversation Integration
Objective(s): Students will make use of their knowledge of insulators and conductors to control the flow of electricity through an electrical circuit by designing and building an electrical switch. **Vocabulary:** *insulator, conductor, circuit, electricity, electric current, switch*	
Assessments: - Light a Lightbulb worksheet - Academic conversations about circuits and switch (informal observation with scoring rubric) - A working switch - Build a Switch worksheet - Flow of Electricity Through a Circuit exit ticket	*Academic conversation*
I. Opening: The purpose of this activity is to apply your understanding about electricity to solve some challenges. You will need to work together, talk, and apply your knowledge and understanding of electricity, circuits, conductors, and insulators to solve the challenges presented.	

Figure 9.3 Sample Science Lesson Plan with Academic Conversations (continued)

Topic: Flow of Electricity Through a Circuit Grade Level: Fourth and up	Conversation Integration

II. Inquiry Warm-Up:
Light a Lightbulb
1. Work in teams of two to determine how to light a holiday tree lightbulb using the materials provided: 1 holiday tree lamp with wires exposed and 1 AA battery per team (have materials for switch building available).
2. As a team, draw at least one way to successfully light the bulb and one way to unsuccessfully light it.
3. Share your results with another pair and explain your thinking.
 	
Whole-Class Conversation about Light a Lightbulb:
Suggested teacher prompts:
  - Can anyone share a way to successfully light the light bulb?
  - Would anyone like to add their scientific thinking and scientific vocabulary to this idea? (Encourage the use of the vocabulary words: *circuit, electric current, conductor*—highlight words from vocabulary list as they are shared.)
  - What were some ways that did not light the lightbulb? (Gather all possible answers and draw results on the board.)
 	
Paired Academic Conversation
  - Why did our successful approach to light the lightbulb work?
  - Why did our unsuccessful approaches to light the lightbulb not work?
 	
Whole-class share results of conversation highlights that should emerge: A circuit is a closed loop that allows an electrical current to flow through it. An electric current can only flow through materials that are conductors of electricity.
 	
Written Synthesis
Record explanations on a half-sheet of paper.
	Share results with another pair
	
	Sample whole-class conversation with response frames:
	
	In order to successfully light the lightbulb, we attached the wires to the battery in the following way . . . This worked because . . .
	
	We found a slightly different way to light the lightbulb, which included the use of . . . This worked because . . .
	
	We believe electricity didn't flow because . . .
	
	Paired academic conversation

III. Design Challenge—Design a Switch

Whole-Class Introductory Discussion: *How do you control the lights in your house? How do light switches work?*

Whole-class conversation with response frames

Challenge: Design a switch that will allow you to control your lightbulb by easily allowing you to turn it on and off. Constraints: Your switch must be reliable and easy to use, and you can use only the materials that are made available.

Directions:

1. Work as a team to determine how to build a switch to turn on and off the lightbulb, using the materials provided: 1 holiday tree lamp with wires exposed and 1 AA battery per team, conducting and insulating materials.

Academic conversation for designing a switch

2. Draw your switch and label the parts. Show them in the open and closed positions.
3. Share your results with another team and explain your thinking.
4. Redesign switches based on conversation.

Whole-class share response frames:

Whole-Class Demonstration of Switches:

- Teams demonstrate their switches simultaneously, following teacher prompt (Optional: Sing or play a song while controlling the lights on the beat of the song.)

We built a switch to control the electric circuit for our light in the following way: First we . . . , then we . . . This worked because . . .

- Prompts for explaining the switches:
  - *Please turn to your partner and have a quick conversation about your results from this design challenge. Discuss this question:* How did our switch work to control our lightbulb?
  - *Can anyone share how their team created a switch to control the electric circuit for their light? Did any team find a different way to build a switch?*
  - *Record your explanation.*

We found a different way to control the electric circuit for our light in the following way: First we . . . , then we . . . This worked because . . .

IV. Independent Assessment

Exit Ticket: Demonstrate knowledge and understanding of how electricity flows through a circuit.

Notice the use of academic language in the following sample conversation from the lesson in Figure 9.3. You will also see the conversation skills of paraphrasing and elaborating.

Ruben:	Why did our approach to light a lightbulb work?
Rosalia:	Well, I think it worked because we completed a circuit.
Ruben:	What does completing a circuit mean? Please elaborate.
Rosalia:	Okay. We attached one wire of the lightbulb to the top of the battery and the other wire to the bottom of the battery. So we closed the circuit and let the energy light the lightbulb.
Ruben:	So you are saying that we closed the circuit by touching the wires to the opposite sides of the battery and that allowed the energy to flow in a circuit.
Rosalia:	Yeah, that sounds right. Can you tell me why the unsuccessful approach to light the lightbulb didn't work?
Ruben:	Yes. Our unsuccessful approach didn't work because we didn't close the circuit.
Rosalia:	Can you elaborate on that?
Ruben:	Uh huh. We didn't close the circuit because we attached both wires to the top of the battery. That didn't let the energy flow at all. It has to go from one side of the battery to the other side of the battery. From the positive to the negative, you know?
Rosalia:	I see your point. And I would add that to complete the circuit the electric current has to flow in a circle from one side of the battery to the other side of the battery. If we don't do that then the lightbulb doesn't light up.
Ruben:	I agree.

Direct Instruction

Not all science lessons need to be inquiry based or design challenges to foster good conversations. In fact, some of the best direct instruction lessons are prime candidates for academic conversations. These lessons need to be broken up by student talk even more than hands-on lessons because of the amount of information presented. Students need the opportunity to process what they have learned so that they can construct their own understanding of the material. The following conversation is an example of eighth-grade students using the ideas and language of a lesson to respond to a question based on the lesson's focus on benefits, limitations, and differences of series and parallel circuits.

Kendra:	What are the benefits and limitations for series and parallel circuits?
Ashleigh:	Well, I think a benefit for parallel circuits is that all the lights burn brightly. But that is not a benefit for a series circuit. That is actually a limitation for a series circuit.

Kendra:	Can you expand on that idea about series circuits?
Ashleigh:	I'd be happy to! The series circuit is in a chain, like a daisy chain, and every time you add another light to it all the lights get dimmer. What do you think?
Kendra:	Well, I agree with your point about series circuits, and I would add that they also have a benefit.
Ashleigh:	What is the benefit? Can you remind me?
Kendra:	Yes, the benefit is that they use less power, so the batteries don't run out.
Ashleigh:	Oh yeah, I forgot about that. But that reminds me of the limitation of parallel circuits. They use a lot of energy!
Kendra:	But I think that's okay since everything gets the same amount of energy.
Ashleigh:	So, would you rather have your house wired in series or parallel circuits?
Kendra:	Parallel, definitely.
Ashleigh:	Yeah, me too! It would be hard to do anything in a house wired with series circuits!

We hope that this chapter has provided a set of ideas that will get you started in helping students have more conversations like that of Kendra and Ashleigh. Science can and should be full of rich conversations, which, as you just saw, deepen students' understandings and fuel their motivations to learn.

Reflections

1. Just as science has changed throughout history, it evolves in each person each year. Consider how you want your students to evolve this year with respect to their knowledge and skills in science.
2. Have a science conversation with a colleague and reflect on the terms you both used and the thinking involved.
3. Choose an activity from this chapter you would like to use and write a model conversation that you would like to hear from your students during the activity.

Chapter 10
Academic Conversation Assessment

> Conversations are as diverse as
> the people who hold them.

—Middle school teacher

Consider how much you can learn about people from your conversations with them. Likewise, we can learn a lot about our students from their conversations. Conversations can show us what students have learned, how they actually use what they have learned, and their abilities to work and negotiate meaning with others. Conversations show us students' communication behaviors, higher-order thinking skills, academic language proficiency, and content understandings. They often provide a better window into students' thinking than written work or tests.

Conversations can complement a wide variety of other assessments, such as projects, lab reports, persuasive essays, presentations, and research reports, to name a few. One of the goals of assessment is to show students' knowledge and skills, as much as possible, in discipline-realistic situations. Multiple assessments help to "triangulate" the data, making what is learned about a student's learning much more valid than just looking at one score on one type of assessment. Another goal of assessment is to teach—with the assessment, not just before it. Conversations can do both—assess and teach at the same time.

You might have heard of the man who lost his watch at the end of an alley. A friend walked by and saw him looking for the watch on the corner where the streetlamp was. He asked the man, "Why are you looking over here? I thought you lost it down the alley." The man responds, "I did, but the light is much better over here." In our case, the "watch" is priceless: our students learning. Yet many systems tend to look for it as cheaply and conveniently as possible. It is vital that we keep looking in the right place, not just where it is convenient. Like looking for a priceless watch in a dark alley, assessing oral language and thinking is a big challenge for several reasons. First, a conversation is highly influenced by what a partner says. Because it is unrehearsed, the wide range of comments can send a conversation in different directions, some productive and some unproductive. One clever question at the right time, for example, can trigger a great conversation.

Preassessment of Academic Conversation Skills

In the beginning of the year it is important to assess students' conversation skills in order to know where to start. You can use a checklist or rubric from this or other chapters and provide some basic prompts. Preassessment also helps to show students that talk is important in your classroom, both as a tool for learning and for showing learning. These preassessment survey questions might be helpful as well:

- » How have you learned from talking with another person?
- » What skills are important when talking with another person?
- » What conversation skills would you like to work on this year?
- » What problems can come up when talking with others?
- » What would you like to converse about this year?

No Surprises: Alignment of Objectives, Assessment, and Instruction

"No surprises!" is our motto for encouraging a continual push for alignment of objectives, assessments, and instruction. Students should never be surprised by the prompts on an assessment. This means that the teaching must prepare them for success on it. Nor should students ever be surprised by their scores on an assessment. And when looking at an assessment, we should not be surprised by a list of objectives it is supposed to assess. If we are observing instruction, we should not be surprised by the assessment that will be given. And if we have an assessment in front of us, we shouldn't be surprised by the instruction we observe. In other words, it should all line up. In order to align conversation objectives, assessment, and instruction, we use the chart in Figure 10.1.

Conversation Assessment Challenges

Conversations are highly unpredictable. A seemingly poor prompt or response might eventually spark a profound conversation, or vice versa. You can never know all the alternative paths a conversation could have taken, or might still take. Consider Figure 10.2. The partner who prompts listens to whatever came before, and she decides that Prompt B is the best prompt at that moment. Another person might have chosen D, F, or A. The responder hears Prompt B and decides that the best response is W. If he had chosen a different response, such as S, the conversation would have taken a very different path. Answers are seldom clearly right or wrong.

Figure 10.1 Alignment of Conversation Objectives, Assessment, and Instruction

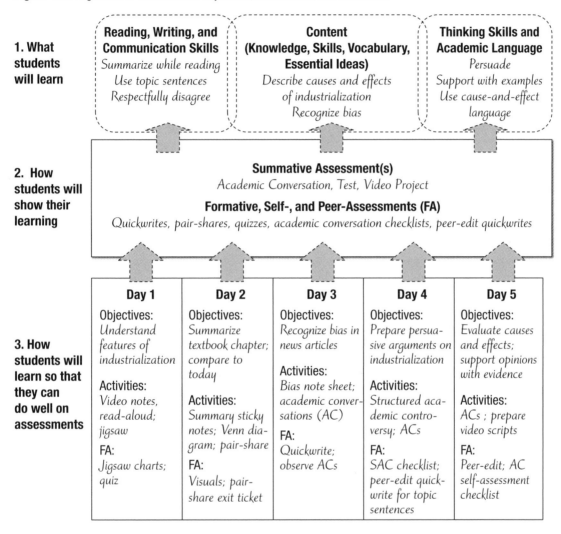

	Reading, Writing, and Communication Skills	**Content (Knowledge, Skills, Vocabulary, Essential Ideas)**	**Thinking Skills and Academic Language**
1. What students will learn	*Summarize while reading* *Use topic sentences* *Respectfully disagree*	*Describe causes and effects of industrialization* *Recognize bias*	*Persuade* *Support with examples* *Use cause-and-effect language*

	Summative Assessment(s) *Academic Conversation, Test, Video Project* **Formative, Self-, and Peer-Assessments (FA)** *Quickwrites, pair-shares, quizzes, academic conversation checklists, peer-edit quickwrites*
2. How students will show their learning	

	Day 1	**Day 2**	**Day 3**	**Day 4**	**Day 5**
3. How students will learn so that they can do well on assessments	Objectives: *Understand features of industrialization* Activities: *Video notes, read-aloud; jigsaw* FA: *Jigsaw charts; quiz*	Objectives: *Summarize textbook chapter; compare to today* Activities: *Summary sticky notes; Venn diagram; pair-share* FA: *Visuals; pair-share exit ticket*	Objectives: *Recognize bias in news articles* Activities: *Bias note sheet; academic conversations (AC)* FA: *Quickwrite; observe ACs*	Objectives: *Prepare persuasive arguments on industrialization* Activities: *Structured academic controversy; ACs* FA: *SAC checklist; peer-edit quickwrite for topic sentences*	Objectives: *Evaluate causes and effects; support opinions with evidence* Activities: *ACs ; prepare video scripts* FA: *Peer-edit; AC self-assessment checklist*

Figure 10.2 The Unpredictable Path of Ideas in a Conversation

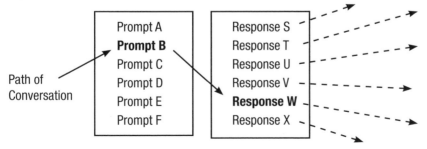

Path of Conversation

Prompt A
Prompt B
Prompt C
Prompt D
Prompt E
Prompt F

Response S
Response T
Response U
Response V
Response W
Response X

The "path" or structure of a conversation greatly depends on the two individuals. As Mercer and Littleton argue:

> Speakers will not usually know in advance exactly what they are going to say. A conversational interaction depends on the participants having some knowledge in common, that they can take for granted: the basis of common knowledge upon which their shared understanding depends is constantly being developed as they interact. The nature of the shared, contextualizing knowledge being invoked in any dialogue is therefore potentially quite complex. (2007, 121)

In other words, conversations are moving targets, morphing all the time. This being the case, we must figure out ways to assess what we want to assess, despite the variations.

A second challenge of assessing a conversation is the subjectivity of conversation and of analyzing it to assign values. Unlike short-answer and multiple-choice tests, in conversations there are no clear-cut right or wrong answers to count up. How do we "score" the quality of a thought-provoking question at the right time? How do we "score" appropriate silence and keep-talking tactics (e.g., *Uh huh, I see, Go on, Wow, Right, Hmm, Interesting, Really? Seriously?*) that deepen a conversation? How do we "score" a thoughtful response that meanders and repeats? Every utterance has a purpose, and it is up to the assessor (and the listener) to figure out what it is *and* its value to the conversation.

A third challenge is maintaining high validity. High validity means accurately assessing what you want to assess. What can we see and hear in a conversation that shows the learning we want to see? How do we evaluate the quality of a turn, a paraphrase, or a counterargument? What does it look like when students learn well? Or when they don't learn well? These questions are important to consider as we assess with conversations.

A final challenge is that conversations can last days, months, and years. That is, the slice of conversation we see today might be a continuation of many other slices on the same topic during the year. These conversations might be between two people or between one student and different partners throughout the year. We often don't know what came before, at school, at home, or somewhere else. We must do what we can to understand students' thinking based on the slice that we observe. Imagine watching just two minutes of a two-hour movie you have never seen. Those two minutes are all you get in order to evaluate the movie's plot, acting, message, and quality.

And yet, despite all the challenges, we can notice strengths and weaknesses in conversations that help us to identify what we need to work on in our teaching. This chapter offers ideas for both formative and summative assessment of conversation as well as ideas for using conversation to assess reading, writing, and content understandings. Given that conversation-based assessments will tend to be short and focus only on one or two ideas, we focus on making every second count.

What Do We Want to Assess with Conversations?

Conversations are useful for assessing how students use the knowledge they have learned as they think with others to negotiate and construct ideas. Several dimensions of learning that are worthy of assessing with conversations are described in the following sections.

Core Content Standards and Essential Understandings

Conversations can be powerful ways to see content understandings or holes in students' understandings. You can see the big ideas in a properly designed conversation assessment. For example, students might be able to define the term *historical bias* on a test, but they might not be able to apply it or explain it in more realistic situations, as suggested by the following conversation about a recent protest described on the news. Guess who scored higher on the test.

Nellie:	Did you hear what happened yesterday? The rallies with the people holding racist signs.
Ron:	Yeah, they shouldn't allow those meetings.
Nellie:	What do you mean?
Ron:	They are supporting racism by bringing those signs. It'll get violent.
Nellie:	But this is a democracy. Meetings are allowed. And what if it is just a few people? Maybe they are even people there who are holding signs to sabotage the meetings and make them all look racist.
Ron:	It doesn't matter. It's on TV and it shows those people. The meeting leaders aren't kicking them out.
Nellie:	But TV doesn't show everything. Just what they want us to see. Kinda like what we saw about winners of wars writing history to make themselves look good.
Ron:	This isn't history. This was yesterday. And with all the news and photos and Internet these days, things are less biased than back then. It's harder to lie.
Nellie:	Are you serious? The Internet has more bias and hate and lies than anywhere!
Ron:	Only if you don't know where to look.
Nellie:	Whatever.

The end of this conversation wasn't very academic, but it showed that Nellie, who didn't score well on the test, could adeptly apply her knowledge to a real topic. Ron, like many students, scored well on the test but failed to use his learning beyond the exam (at least in this conversation).

Thinking Skills

In preceding chapters we provide samples of conversations with higher-order thinking. In the rubrics in this chapter and in previous chapters, the first row includes the discipline's key thinking skills and their language (see "Think and talk..." row in Figure 9.2, for example). It is important to be familiar with the thinking skills and language that students need to use to read the texts, do well on tests, write essays, perform labs, and show their learning of objectives. (For more ideas of assessments based on thinking skills, refer to the chart titled "Conversation-Worthy Performance Tasks by Discipline" in the appendix.)

It is important to assess the ability to transfer skills and ideas from one area or discipline to a new situation. For example, can a student transfer reasoning strategies learned in language arts to debate a topic in history? Can a student transfer the skill of balancing equations in math from the beginning of the year to solve a problem in science at the end of the year? Can a student transfer the use of perspective developed in history class to write a character analysis in language arts? Can a student use skills learned at school out in the real world? We can ask many similar questions, most of which involve transfer across time and across subject areas, a notion that defies the highly compartmentalized approach that says, "They got 80 percent on the last test and therefore they learned it—time to move on." Yet it is this transfer, retention, extension, and real-world application that the future will require of our students.

Academic Language: Turning Language Demands into Language Objectives

Academic language is the lifeblood of success in school. Most of the tasks, texts, and tests in school use and require language that students tend not to encounter in home and social settings. The matrix in Figure 10.3 helps a teacher identify the academic language demands of learning activities and assessments. The first step is clarifying the content objective(s) for the unit or lesson(s). In the first column are four core dimensions of a lesson: assessments; teacher modeling, lectures, and directions; texts; and activities and tasks. Think about the specific parts of the lesson that might be linguistically challenging for students and describe the challenges in the second column. Parts might be quizzes, lectures, or group projects, and the language challenge might be a function, thinking skill, or communication issue. For example, a quiz might ask students to empathize with a historical character.

Figure 10.3 Language Demands and Objectives Planning Table

Lesson's Content Objective(s): *Students will be able to compare the positive and negative outcomes of industrialization and argue for one side over the other.*		
Lesson Dimension	**Linguistically Challenging Part** *(and its thinking and communication skills that students will need to use to learn and to show learning)*	**Language Needed for Thinking and Showing Thinking** *(e.g., text organization; abstract vocabulary; prosody; nominalization; syntax: subject-verb agreement, pronouns, gerunds, adverbs, noun phrases, prepositions, participle phrases, verb tenses)*

Assessments: *(formative assessments look at skills and knowledge needed for summative assessments, which are based on objectives)*	- *Exit ticket asks students to provide evidence for opinions and see both sides of an issue.* - *Think-pair-share requires students to persuade partner* - *Need to soften "all or nothing" comments*	- *Use transitions such as* **although, despite**, so that, *and on* **the other hand** *to start clauses.* - *Opinion terms :* Support your opinion Based on the research that . . . Opponents argue that . . . - *Use qualifiers and hedges to soften message, to show humility, and to question and propose.*
Teacher modeling, lecture, and directions	- *Teacher modeling of choosing quotation and describing how well it supports an argument*	- *Abstract support terms:* Look for a quotation that supports . . . Decide which points weigh the most and offer the strongest support. Explain how the quotation supports your point.
Texts	- *Long sentences in the chapter*	- *Complex sentences that start with embedded clauses:* "Given that the studies were done so long ago, they . . ." "Seeking to hide the truth from the world, they proceeded to . . ."*
Lesson activities and tasks	- *Students choose and evaluate supporting quotations* - *Students explain how quotations support either side of the issue; they compare quotations*	- *Use concession and rebuttal language:* Granted, it is true that . . . , but . . . We concede that the benefits of . . . , yet . . . In spite of the big short-term gains, we must consider . . .

Language Objective(s): *Students will explain how quotations strengthen a side of an issue by using example expressions and abstract vocabulary such as* support, weigh, issue, given that, strengthen, evaluate, *and* point.

Assessment of language objective(s): *Exit ticket with rubric; academic conversation; persuasive essay*

In the third column, identify specific types of academic language that students will need to be successful in the things described in the second column. Identify the most important language needed to support the content objective(s) and use it to create language objectives. Use a format that includes what students will do and what language they will use to accomplish it. The needed language might be a type of grammar and/or specific terms (see the top right box of Figure 10.3 for more ideas.) For example, you might come up with the following language objective: "Students will support opinions by using complete sentences and transitions of example (*for example, for instance*, etc.)." As you teach, you emphasize this language in mini-lessons that prepare students for academic conversations and other tasks, texts, and tests. Eventually, the process of filling in this table to identify key language should become automatic—and less time consuming.

You can use a rubric to assess the types of grammar a student is using when conversing. (See Chapter 6 for more detailed descriptions of academic grammar.) You can make a simple rubric or checklist, like the one in Figure 10.4, that focuses on the grammar you would like to hear. Give mini-lessons beforehand, and have students score oral messages that you model so that they see what they are supposed to do. Then have students practice in pairs with an observer. They can peer- and self-assess.

Figure 10.4 Sample Rubric for Assessing Grammar During Academic Conversations

	At or Above (3)	Approaching (2)	Below (1)
→	Uses varied academic transitions appropriately (*however, in addition, therefore*).	Shows some use of simple transitions such as *so, and*, and *but*.	Uses few or no transitions.
▼	Avoids universal statements; uses hedges and softens opinions (*likely, most, could, might, possible*).	Shows some use of hedges and some universal statements.	Uses few or no hedges; uses many all-or-nothing statements.
-?-- ----- It	Does not overly assume that the audience follows use of pronouns. Pronoun use is clear.	Some unexplained pronouns create confusion.	Overuses pronouns such as *it, this, that*, and *he* without referencing, which causes much confusion.

Academic Communication Skills and Behaviors

One of the most important dimensions of learning that we need to assess is the set of academic communication skills and behaviors emphasized in this book. These are often neglected in schools that favor the focus on more test-focused snippets of knowledge and isolated skills. The ability to use different skills and tools to communicate and negotiate ideas is paramount. The rubric in Figure 10.5 (which you may recognize from Figure 7.3) includes these objectives in rows 2 through 5.

Figure 10.5 Sample Academic Conversation Rubric for Language Arts

	At or Above (3)	Approaching (2)	Below (1)
	(T) Think and talk like literature experts. - Interpret themes and apply them to life. - Connect to characters and other texts. - Critique texts and author techniques. - Use literature terms and complex syntax.	Make some connections, use some complex sentences and literature terms, and show some deep thinking.	Use short sentences and only social language (slang), make few connections, and take on few perspectives.
	(F) Stay focused. - Build on comments. - Connect ideas to topic well. - Negotiate conflicting ideas and word meanings. - Offer few, if any, tangential thoughts.	Stay mostly on topic; show some idea building and negotiation; go on some tangents and deviations; show some confusion.	Rarely connect or build on ideas; go on many tangents and give unrelated information; demonstrate no negotiation of differing ideas.
	(S) Support ideas and opinions with examples from text, life, and previous lessons; clearly explain and elaborate on ideas.	Offer some prompting for and support of ideas with examples and clarifications.	Offer little or no support of ideas and reasons; show lack of appropriate prompting.
	(P) Paraphrase partner ideas to clarify, deepen, and stay focused; synthesize key points or steps at end.	Offer some paraphrasing and synthesizing of key points or steps.	Offer little or no paraphrasing and synthesizing.
	(C) Use communication behaviors; actively listen (eyes and body); take turns; value partner comments; be respectful.	Show some appropriate listening and turn-taking behaviors.	Show little eye contact or listening; interrupt; dominate talk or do not contribute at all.

Academic Conversation Rubrics

Put the features that you want to assess into a rubric, and clarify for students what the terms mean and how to get a high score. You can modify the rubrics to suit the needs of your students. All rubrics in this book are similar after the first row, which focuses on the thinking and academic language of that particular discipline.

The rubrics throughout this book are meant to offer ideas that you can use to create your own rubrics with your students. We encourage you to work with students to decide on the icons, the thinking skills, and the language of the rubrics. You can also turn a rubric into a self- or peer-assessment checklist.

Summative Academic Conversation Assessment

An end-of-unit or end-of-term academic conversation assessment (ACA) can help you take an in-depth look at what students have learned. Students often get interested in things that aren't emphasized on traditional tests. And many students don't like to write or give oral presentations. However, many students like to talk, and ACA offers the chance for them to show what they know and are thinking about through conversation. Conversation offers students some choice in showing what they have learned.

An ACA can augment existing performance-based assessments and more traditional tests. Hopefully, you are already using real-world-esque summative, performance-based assessments that motivate students and let them show what they can do with the new content, language, and skills that they have learned. In the left-hand column of Figure 10.6 are a few examples of summative assessments that you might already be using. In the right-hand column are conversation prompt ideas that would complement the assessments on the left.

Academic Conversation Assessment Procedure

Academic Conversation Assessments are just academic conversations that are assessed. The teacher observes two students as they converse about a topic. Other students might be conversing or doing other work at the time. It generally takes three days to complete the ACAs with all students in one class. Here is the basic procedure:

1. *Rubric.* Students should be very familiar with the rubric. Throughout the unit, go over the AC rubric for your discipline (kid friendly or other) with students and give examples of responses that score well. Put on a fishbowl conversation and have students score it with the rubric.

Figure 10.6 Product-Based and Performance-Based Summative Assessments That Involve Conversation

Summative Assessment	Possible Prompts for Academic Conversation Assessment
Debate	Discuss the details of the issue, state your opinions, and negotiate a conclusion.
Panel Discussion/Talk Show	Practice being an audience member and panel member who disagree on the topic.
Historical Fiction Piece, Movie Script, Short Novel, or Children's Book	Be two coauthors of a historical fiction story for younger students. Plan what to include and not to include. Cowrite a sequel to the story/novel that we just read.
Editorial Letter	Consider two different sides of the topic and decide which side you agree with. Plan the organization of the letter.
Literature Analysis Essay	Be two literary critics and discuss the interpretation of the author's work.
Dialogue Between Two Characters	Be two actors or directors and discuss the next scene of a movie, book, or play; write the dialogue; and practice it.
Lab Experiment	Before or after the lab, discuss the purpose of the lab, the variables, the hypothesized results, and the possible practical applications. After the lab, discuss the results and conclusions.
Math Test	Be two business owners who write a math test with real-world examples for potential employees.
Public Service Advertisement	Be two citizens who identify local problems, argue which one is most urgent, and design an advertisement.
Museum Exhibit	Be two museum curators who create an exhibit for the current unit of study. Discuss and write up short descriptions and floor plans.
Informational Poster/Mural	Decide on several key points from the topic or text and negotiate the clearest visual way for an audience to remember the points.
Magazine/Newspaper (past or present)	Be two editors who outline a magazine or newspaper. Decide the sections, articles, and columns to include; then outline the lead article together.

2. *Topic/Prompt.* As you work with students to prepare for their ACA, emphasize that the topics of conversation should be new (something learned from the current unit), usable in other units and in the future, interesting, important, and challenging. You can generate a list of topics and themes during a whole-class session and then edit it to focus on the essential understandings and skills you would like to highlight or ones that don't show up on other assessments.

3. *Practice.* Have pairs choose a topic or prompt and prepare notes. They then should practice their conversation and self-assess it, using the rubric.

4. *Observation.* Choose a pair that is ready, and remind them of the rubric skills that you are looking for; you might even emphasize one or two, depending on the students. Have them converse about their topic; encourage them to focus on each other and try not to use notes. Take notes on the rubric (you can add two columns on the right side of the rubric, one for each student).

5. *Written synthesis.* Have students synthesize their conversation orally first, then work together to write a paragraph or two that synthesizes their conversation. They should recall key points, disagreements, negotiations, and so on.

Scoring Academic Conversations

Most likely, you will not have time to code each line of a pair's conversation, and you will have even less time to record and transcribe conversations. But you can get a sense of how to listen for thinking, language, and content understandings by looking at some sample scorings (see Figures 10.7, 10.8, and 10.9). The codes are from the rubric in Figure 10.5: T (think/talk), F (focus/build/connect), S (support with examples), P (paraphrase and synthesize), C (communication behaviors). As in the rubric, a 1 is for below the standard, 2 is for approaching the standard, and 3 is for at or above the standard.

Figure 10.7 Sample Language Arts Conversations with Scores (Fifth Grade)

		Maria	Alex
1	*Alex:* What did you notice about human nature in the story?		T3
2	*Maria:* I noticed that the man wasn't happy in the end. People hated him. He had money but not friends.	T3	
3	*Alex:* Can you elaborate on the part about people and money?		S3

4	**Maria:** Well, you know, people are more important than money because we need them more. Lots of poor people are happy.	S1	
5	**Alex:** I agree. Like in the story the man got a lot of money but lost all his friends along the way. I mean, we need money, but we also need friends to spend time with.		T3, F3, S3
6	**Maria:** And laugh with and talk with. Like, I need to talk with my friends all the time. Yesterday we talked a lot. You couldn't pay me enough to get rid of my friends.	T1, F1, S2	
7	**Alex:** What do you talk about?		F2, S2
8	**Maria:** Things you wouldn't understand (both laugh). School and stuff. Now, back to the idea of friends and people. They, like, are more important than money because, well, we get bored without others. There's poor people who are happy 'cause they spend time with friends and laugh.	F3, S2, T2	
9	**Alex:** So you are saying that others can make us happy, even if we are poor, right?		P3
10	**Maria:** Yes, well, I don't know. But people are important.	P3	
Overall Communication (based on observation)		C3	C2

Figure 10.8 Sample History Conversation with Scores (Tenth Grade)

		David	**Mei**
1	**David:** What was the most important result of the Civil War?	F3	
2	**Mei:** I think it was the United States staying unified. One nation.		T2
3	**David:** Why was that so important?	F3	
4	**Mei:** Because if it split up, then it would have been weak. Maybe not been able to defend themselves in future wars.		S2

Figure 10.8 Sample History Conversation with Scores (Tenth Grade) (continued)

		David	Mei
5	**David:** Like which?	S3	
6	**Mei:** Like against England and France, who I think still wanted to take over; and maybe even World War I and II. Who knows?		S3
7	**David:** Good point. But I think the most important effect was the end of slavery. We might still have slavery if they hadn't fought it.	T3, S3	
8	**Mei:** Why is that more important than the nation staying together?		F3
9	**David:** There were millions of slaves, treated worse than animals. Imagine if that were you. Would you care if the nation were divided? You would just care about freedom. The Pilgrims started the country on freedom, and the Constitution talked about it too.	S3, F3	
10	**Mei:** I guess it depends on your perspective. Maybe both made the country stronger. Freedom encouraged people to work hard, and then lots of people immigrated.		T3, S2, F3
11	**David:** Or did slavery make the country stronger? There was lots of free labor. We will never know. Anyway, I think both were important, too.	S3, P2	
12	**Mei:** So we can say that the union—unification—was important for military and economic reasons. And the abolishment of slavery was important for human freedom reasons.		F3, P3
Overall Communication (based on observation)		C2	C3

Figure 10.9 Sample Biology Conversation with Scores (Fourth Grade)

		Ken	Julia
1	**Julia:** I hate bats, but what would happen if a disease killed all the bats in this ecosystem?		T3

2	**Ken:**	I hate them, too. One time I saw one by my house, and it freaked me out. I threw rocks at it.	T1, S1, F1	
3	**Julia:**	Okay, but what about my question? What would happen?		F3
4	**Ken:**	Well, they wouldn't be around to scare us and eat up all the bugs, I guess. I don't like bugs either.	S2	
5	**Julia:**	I agree. But, do you think it would have an effect on the ecosystem?		T3, F3
6	**Ken:**	Um. Well, I think it would be weird not to have them around. Maybe we'd have more bugs.	T2, S3	
7	**Julia:**	So are you saying that there would be more insects because the bats wouldn't be around to eat them?		P3
8	**Ken:**	Yes. I think we need bats to eat the bugs. If something happened to bats, we would probably have too many bugs, and that could cause problems because bugs eat stuff too.	T3	
9	**Julia:**	I agree with your ideas, and I would add that we might have more people getting sick because some insects carry diseases. So, can we say that our hypothesis is that if the bats decreased, then the insects would increase?		T3, P3
10	**Ken:**	Yes, and if the insects increased, we might get sick or other bad things might happen to our environment.	P3	
Overall Communication (based on observation)			C2	C3

This type of scoring is highly subjective, and the scores are not meant to be added up. These examples are meant to give you a rough picture of the types of responses that score high and low, and to offer feedback to students. For example, you might tell Ken that on several occasions, he went off on a tangent and didn't focus on the conversation topic. You might tell Julia how much you valued her skills of focusing the conversation on the topic. You can gather some excerpts from your class, or even have students write them down, to practice scoring them. Eventually, you will be able to listen for high-scoring and low-scoring moves that students make as they converse.

Teacher-Student Conversation Assessment

In addition to observing conversations between students, you can also engage in a one-on-one conversation with a student and get an even better understanding of what the student is learning and thinking. In a teacher-student conversation, you don't just ask questions; instead, you engage in conversation, sharing some of your thoughts about the topic as well. The trick is to encourage students to take the lead in the conversation. You can ask "wonder" questions or ask the student to elaborate and give examples, and so on. The student can choose the prompt and help to keep the conversation focused. You should also share some examples from your life, your interests, and your wonderings. Here is an excerpt from an eighth-grade history teacher-student conversation:

1   *Student:*   So, I was wondering why they left lots of people out of the *Declaration of Independence*. It said that all men were created equal, but what about slaves?

2   *Teacher:*   Good question. I wonder that, too. I think Jefferson had slaves, and he wrote that line.

3   *Student:*   So what did "all" mean to them? I think they didn't think of slaves as human; but more like animals.

4   *Teacher:*   Can you elaborate on that idea?

5   *Student:*   Well, they made them work like animals for just food. They chained them up and punished them. They didn't have rights for life, liberty, and happiness, if you ask me.

6   *Teacher:*   Or what about if they knew they were human, but the owners' selfish and greedy side won them over?

7   *Student:*   So you think they believed the idea of all men are equal, but they didn't want to lose money from it? I think people are like that today.

8   *Teacher:*   How so?

9   *Student:*   Well, like politicians say a lot of things to get them elected, but it usually doesn't happen. For example, they say all people should have jobs, have health care, but it doesn't happen. I think, like you said, their greed wins over. Because big businesses are putting pressure on them, they wimp out.

10   *Teacher:*   So, what should we conclude?

11   *Student:*   So maybe both are true? Some saw slaves as not human and others looked the other way because of greed.

This student successfully used these conversation skills: initiating with an interesting prompt (line 1), probing and elaborating (lines 3, 5), paraphrasing (7), providing supporting examples (9), connecting ideas and staying focused (9), and synthesizing (11). The student used some hedging (*maybe* in line 11) and complex vocabulary (*rights, greed*) and grammar (clause starting with *because*). As this example shows, it is important to tell students the types of thinking and language you would like to hear in their conversation and then let students practice such conversations with one another (and/or with you) before the final assessment.

Formative Assessment and Feedback

Formative assessment informs the teacher and the students of what students have learned and where to go next. Before students are assessed with the more summative ACA just described, they need to practice conversing about a wide range of topics with different partners. Throughout a unit, you can formatively assess and provide feedback to hone their skills. A formative assessment might be a short pair-share or a practice conversation for their final ACA. Students need to prepare for their ACAs. But they also can be assessed during any conversation they have throughout a unit.

Students should constantly be aware of the ideas, skills, and language you are looking for in a good academic conversation. A chart like the one in Figure 10.10 can remind you and your students what to look for and do during conversations. You can share this form with students after conversations by using a document camera, interactive whiteboard, or overhead projector.

Figure 10.10 Conversation Skills and Thinking Skills with Student Language Samples

Conversation Skill	Student Comments	Thinking Skill	Student Comments
Elaborate, clarify	*It means that she probably lied because of all she had to gain by saying that he left.*	Interpret	*I think that the story was about the problem of being full of pride, stuck up.*
Support ideas with examples and evidence	*For example, I had to move from my village to the big city. I was also excited but worried.*	Persuade	*Many might argue that we should allow the market to decide, but research has shown that we should . . .*
Focus and build on ideas	*Related to Silvia's point about the changes in the fruit fly, I think it is a result of . . .*	Empathize; see other perspectives	*If I were in her shoes, I would go talk to the official and demand the money back.*
Paraphrase	*So, you think that we should not have gone to war; that the evidence of weapons was not strong enough.*	Infer cause and effect	*Watching his siblings suffer led him to start that movement.*

Figure 10.10 Conversation Skills and Thinking Skills with Student Language Samples (continued)

Conversation Skill	Student Comments	Thinking Skill	Student Comments
Synthesize	*I think that King Arthur was based on a real person but the magic stuff was made up.*	Problem solve	*What is the main issue between the two groups of people? What are possible solutions?*
Ask probing questions	*What does that expression mean these days?*	Evaluate	*How much money is one person's life worth? It is like comparing apples and oranges.*

You can use more abridged versions of the chart in Figure 10.10 to record the academic language used in student conversations. You can generate the chart's categories by considering what you want students to think about and meanings you want them to construct. It helps to think about the language you would hear if you had a conversation with a highly verbal student who had learned the material very well. As you look at the overall picture of student language, you will notice areas worthy of mini-lessons and other areas worthy of celebration. You might notice a lack of evidence, lack of synthesis, exceptional elaboration, and so on.

After analyzing close to 8,000 studies, Hattie (1992) wrote, "The most powerful single modification that enhances achievement is feedback. The simplest prescription for improving education must be 'dollops of feedback'" (9). So, how can you provide feedback as you listen to students talk and construct meaning?

The first dimension of conversation feedback is helping students with the clarity of their messages. You might, for example, explain to a student how and why his or her comparisons weren't clear. The second dimension of feedback is clarifying what students should keep doing and/or what they should change (Marzano, Pickering, and Pollock 2001). You might tell the student that he or she should use transition words such as *on the other hand* or *however* when comparing ideas to make the differences clear. Conversation feedback should be immediate, specific to student utterances, focused, not overloaded with information or things to think about, and nonevaluative. Feedback should assume students will have other opportunities to use the revised language. Feedback should model target language such as *I liked how you supported your opinion with specific parts of the text and examples from your life.* This is one way to model academic language—language that has meaning to that student in the moment.

Observing and providing feedback on conversations allows teachers to be supportive coaches who listen to what students are thinking. Such an environment with helpful and encouraging feedback emphasizes that students don't have to learn everything today for tomorrow's test—that many important things in life are learned over time, negotiated, argued, shared, mulled over. Students should get multiple chances to learn as much as they can. Each step along the way, teachers are there to scaffold students' thinking and model the work of the discipline.

During conversations, you can gather language data on a chart like the one in Figure 10.10. You can use it to provide specific feedback to students about their conversation skills and other learnings. For example, you might respond to a science student with, "Well done, Luís! When you talked about what you thought would happen to the solution, you used your background knowledge of bonding to hypothesize what will happen when we add the acid." In history you might comment, "Interesting interpretation of this person's motives to pass this bill. You used what you know about the person's past to see his perspective." In language arts, "I heard you say that the author wrote the poem to teach us about fear and love. And then you gave examples from life. Well done." You cannot provide such feedback every day to every student, but these moments make a world of difference over time.

Several strategies for helping you to assess and provide feedback during conversations follow.

Converse About a Practice Quiz/Test

In this formative assessment and instructional activity, give each partner half of the practice quiz questions. The asker reads each question aloud. When a partner answers a question, the asker makes sure the answer is complete. The asker can probe for elaboration and examples. Mini-conversations can begin when two partners need to negotiate meaning, define terms, and clarify on more open-ended prompts. The asker can also evaluate and score the response, justify the score to the partner, and then take a turn answering a question. You can also provide answers to guide the asker. When the asker helps (provides the answer), he or she should not read it out loud. It needs to be covered up and explained in the asker's own words.

Paired Paragraphs

Rather than doing individual quickwrites, students pair up and talk about what they learned in class and then put it on paper together. They have to negotiate meanings and write a coherent synopsis of the learning of the day. You can go around and assess their conversations as they work, and you can assess their writing products afterward.

You might give directions like these: *You and your partner will use your conversation's ideas to write a seven-minute paragraph composed of five to eight sentences, with a topic sentence, key details, and evidence. Use at least two complex sentences. For example, . . . And use at least three key vocabulary terms. You will peer-edit this paragraph with another pair after seven minutes.*

Written Controversy Conversations

Two partners can write their conversation in two different colors on the same piece of paper. This allows you to see what each partner wrote to provide feedback. This also allows you to have all students "conversing" at once and then evaluate their conversation skills and content learnings on paper later. Some teachers even share some of the conversations as models.

A variation is having partners create a written conversation about a controversy (e.g., cell phones at school, social networking sites, legalization of drugs, cloning, etc.). Each person tries to convince the other person to take his or her side. Students should do some reading on the topic and use ideas from them in their written conversations. You can also assign students to take different sides of the issue.

Paired Cloze

In this activity, both students work together to fill in a cloze passage. They negotiate the words they think are most appropriate for each blank. The use language such as *This term is more appropriate because it describes . . .* They should also use examples from the text and other lessons to help them choose the best words.

Podcasts

Students converse to prepare an audio podcast on a topic of interest to the world. They might make up a speech, a dramatic conversation, a critique of a book or movie, an editorial, a monologue, or an interview. They can also prepare a conversation to be recorded.

Student Self-Assessment

Students can self-monitor their conversations using checklists (see Figures 10.11 and 10.12) and rubrics based on those found in this and other chapters. Students can fill in their self-assessments individually or in pairs.

Here are some additional prompts that students can respond to after their conversations.

- Give an example of an idea you learned from the conversation that you probably would not have learned by yourself.
- How did your conversation help you learn the ideas?
- What did you notice about yourself as a learner?
- Suggest a change that you and your partner could make to have a better conversation next time.
- Did you both talk about the same amount?

Figure 10.11 Self-Assessment Checklist for Conversation Work

Symbol	Conversation Skill	Scale	Comments
In our paired conversation, how often did I/we . . .			
	Stay focused on an important topic?	Rarely Sometimes Often	
	Build on each other's ideas?	Rarely Sometimes Often	
X X X X	Support big ideas and opinions with examples or evidence?	Rarely Sometimes Often	
	Negotiate an idea (respectfully), when we disagreed?	Rarely Sometimes Often	
	Maintain good eye contact and use good conversational body language?	Rarely Sometimes Often	
	Choose the most academic ways of talking? (vocabulary, mortar terms, long sentences)	Rarely Sometimes Often	

Figure 10.12 Alternative Self-Assessment Checklist for Conversation Work

Observed		Conversation Moves
		Prompt partner to share
		Have equal talking time
		Elaborate on ideas
		Provide examples
		Build on partner's ideas
		Paraphrase ideas
		Summarize conversation

Figure 10.12 Alternative Self-Assessment Checklist for Conversation Work (continued)

Observed		Conversation Body Language
	☺⊏⊐⊏☺	Face partner
	👁	Use eye contact
	ᷧ ᷨ	Lean forward
	☺⌐	Use gestures and nod
Compliments and Suggestions:		

Peer Feedback

At times it is helpful to have a third student assess a paired conversation and provide feedback. The third student can use a class-developed checklist, similar to those in Figures 10.11 and 10.12. The observer takes notes and provides constructive feedback after the conversation. Before providing feedback, the observer lets the two partners reflect on how they think the conversation went. See a sample checklist in Figure 10.13.

Figure 10.13 Sample Checklist for Monitoring Conversations

Productive Behaviors	Notes	Nonproductive Behaviors	Notes
• Gives reasons and evidence for opinions • Uses academic expressions • Politely disagrees • Asks helpful and thoughtful questions • Leads the group toward a goal		• Interrupts others • Makes fun of others' comments or dismisses them • Distracts others • Does not listen • Takes discussion off topic • Dominates the discussion	

Assess Sentence Length and Complexity

You know that many students talk plenty. But many others don't talk enough, and having them work toward more talk, especially academic discourse, is needed. Some students, for example, might speak long utterances with many simple sentences. They need to learn how to use clauses and combine sentences as they converse. One strategy, described in Chapter 6, is to increase the length of students' sentences, which increases their complexity and cognitive load. Using oral and written samples, you can calculate the mathematical mean of the length of each sentence.

You can then have students listen and read longer and longer sentences during the year, and you can challenge them to produce them in writing and in conversations. The better students are at listening to and processing long sentences with multiple clauses and phrases, the better they can understand complex texts and messages.

Evaluating and Improving the Effectiveness of Academic Conversations

Intuitively, we all might see the value of academic conversations. But we also need to see (and hear) significant results in order to continue using them and in order to modify how we use them. Teaching students to and through talk is highly complex and full of social, cultural, cognitive, curricular, and linguistic variables. We must be action researchers, engaged in a cycle of inquiry as we evaluate and improve our teaching.

A helpful model for action research is shown in Figure 10.14. The cycle revolves around a central question, such as *How can I use academic conversations to improve students' skills of supporting their ideas with evidence in their essays?* In the first stage, "Teach and Assess," you teach conversation skills and gather data on student progress. In the next stage, you analyze the evidence to see patterns and needs. Then in the last stage, you reflect on the evidence and adapt your teaching to bring about improvement. This cycle can be done individually or with a small team of teachers.

Figure 10.14 Reflective Inquiry Cycle

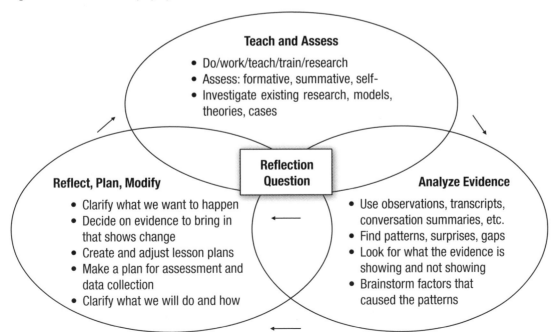

Assessments are not just destinations for learning—they are also vehicles. Assessments can teach. We owe it to students to make the thinking and language that we desire for them to learn as clear and explicit as possible. We also owe it to them to make the learning activities and assessments as aligned and engaging as possible. As we assess *we* must be advocates for students, rather than their judges (Tierney 1998). We must help and encourage students to challenge themselves to show what they know, to take risks, to help one another, and to push themselves to use new language and thinking skills.

Reflections

1. What should students in your classes know and be able to do in a conversation?
2. Why and how do real-world experts of your discipline talk?
3. Design a conversation prompt for a core concept that you teach, and then create a rubric for it. Include thinking and language criteria.
4. Choose a conversation skill, and design a mini-lesson that would help build the language and thinking skills needed for success on the assessment in reflection 3.
5. Describe three general principles that guide your philosophy of how students learn. How do these principles shape your teaching? Where can conversation fit in?
6. Hold a quick academic conversation with a teacher, friend, or student. Jot down some of the language and thinking used.

Chapter 11
Reminders

When we talk to each other, we put our brains together, and we become one big smart!

—*Second-grade student*

Every conversation adds to or changes the grand body of knowledge that has been building since language began. We learn from conversations and pass that learning on to others in conversations. Conversation, whether in a first-grade art lesson or a high-tech company meeting, is both art and science. Conversations are places to create new ideas and see new perspectives, and they are also spaces in which to understand, analyze, and think critically about what we are learning and doing.

This chapter is a brief synthesis of the highlights from the previous chapters. Here we offer some of the key points that we have found helpful to remember when in the middle of planning or teaching or sipping coffee on a cold, early morning commute.

Reminder 1: Conversations Clarify Complex Ideas

Conversations are opportunities to understand and sculpt one another's ideas, values, biases, perspectives, and purposes. Each conversation is a chance to deepen and clarify, slightly more than before, how students think about the discipline and the world. As they clarify meanings with one another, they refine and negotiate their thoughts, pushing one another to use more advanced language and thinking.

Reminder 2: Students Learn Through Conversation

Students tend to learn more deeply and in more lasting ways when they do the following: repeat and reword their ideas ; explain their ideas to a partner; compare their ideas with those of another; support their ideas with examples and experiences from their lives; create new ideas with a partner; listen and have to respond; have their ideas challenged; challenge another's idea; have to figure out new words used by a partner; and reach a level of communication complexity that demands the use of new words and grammar.

Reminder 3: Conversations Should Span Across Grade Levels and Content Areas

We believe that teaching students to converse and teaching them through conversations can and should begin in preschool. Children should learn how to learn through conversation with others, and their conversations should evolve and deepen each year. All students can benefit from conversation-based learning, but linguistically and culturally diverse students *need* to develop academic communication skills in school. The students who lose out the most in the one-way transmission, "trivial pursuit" style of teaching are the students who need the opposite.

Reminder 4: Conversations "Change the Game" of Learning

Each year of schooling shapes how students view learning. If students are to be lifelong independent learners and thinkers, they must be able to learn through conversation. Humans are creatures of habit, and if students get into good habits of deepening, organizing, and supporting ideas through talking with others, then they will be prepared for the future.

Conclusion

We hope that this book has provided ideas for helping your students improve their learning and their lives through conversation. We, like many others, are pleading for major changes in the game: changes in assessment, changes in instruction, and changes in how schools view, value, and treat students.

Knowledge in our world has been building for a long time through oral, written, and visual means. This building started through conversation and will continue to do so. This book was written to help you give your students even more access to the human community and all of its grand ideas by engaging more deeply with the many past and present people who have been sharing and building ideas for thousands of years. As the philosopher David Hume wrote, "They must feel an increase of humanity, from the very habit of conversing together . . ." (1987, 271).

Humanity grows from thinking together about life, solving problems, building relationships, and constructing meaning with others. The world needs our students to become better thinkers and communicators than we are. They will become future parents, teachers, leaders, and problem solvers. Conversations are not the only solution to the complex challenge of how to prepare students for future success in life. However, we believe that academic conversations can play a meaningful role in meeting this challenge.

Appendix

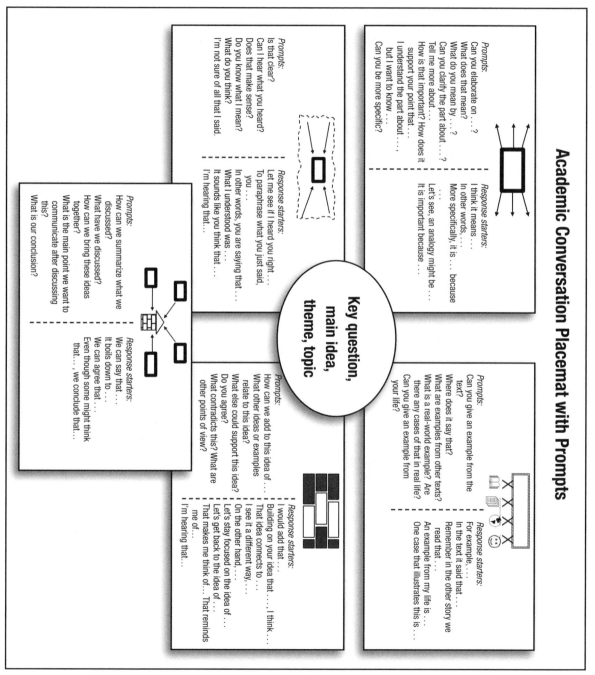

Academic Conversation Placemat with Prompts

Key question, main idea, theme, topic

Prompts:
Can you elaborate on . . . ?
What does that mean?
What do you mean by . . . ?
Can you clarify the part about . . . ?
Tell me more about . . . .
How is that important? How does it
support your point that . . . .
I understand the part about . . . .
but I want to know . . . .
Can you be more specific?

Response starters:
I think it means . . . .
In other words, ...
More specifically, it is . . . . because
it is important because . . . .
Let's see, an analogy might be . . . .

Prompts:
Is that clear?
Can I hear what you heard?
Does that make sense?
Do you know what I mean?
What do you think?
I'm not sure of all that I said.

Response starters:
Let me see if I heard you right. . . .
To paraphrase what you just said,
you . . . .
In other words, you are saying that . . . .
What I understood was . . . .
It sounds like you think that . . . .
I'm hearing that . . . .

Prompts:
How can we summarize what we
discussed?
What have we discussed?
How can we bring these ideas
together?
What is the main point we want to
communicate after discussing
this?
What is our conclusion?

Response starters:
We can say that . . . .
It boils down to . . . .
We can agree that . . . .
Even though some might think
that . . . , we conclude that . . . .

Prompts:
How can we add to this idea of . . . ?
What other ideas or examples
relate to this idea?
What else could support this idea?
Do you agree?
What contradicts this? What are
other points of view?

Response starters:
I would add that . . . .
Building on your idea that . . . , I think . . . .
That idea connects to . . . .
I see it a different way. . . .
On the other hand, ...
Let's stay focused on the idea of . . . .
Let's get back to the idea of . . . .
That makes me think of . . . . That reminds
me of . . . .
I'm hearing that . . . .

Prompts:
Can you give an example from the
text?
Where does it say that?
What are examples from other texts?
What is a real-world example? Are
there any cases of that in real life?
Can you give an example from
your life?

Response starters:
For example, ...
In the text it said that . . . .
Remember in the other story we
read that . . . .
An example from my life is . . . .
One case that illustrates this is . . . .

Thinking Skills and Their Conversation-Based Assessments by Discipline

Thinking Skill	Social Studies	English	Science
Analyze	Prepare a newspaper article that informs the public of the advantages of studying history.	Analyze several high-quality essays and prepare a one-page "cheat sheet" on how to write essays for future students in the class.	Create a poster that shows the process of generating nuclear power and highlights areas where potential dangers exist.
Compare	As advisors for the current president, create a visual that clearly and quickly shows the president the differences of two opposing approaches for economic growth.	Write a letter to an author showing and questioning the incongruities between two of the author's works (or between a book and its movie).	Create a nutrition log that records a weekly diet and then compares it to the recommendations for calorie and nutrient intake.
Classify	Design the perfect society and include descriptions of economics, jobs, education, law enforcement, art, etc.	Devise a way to classify the importance of characters and events in a story.	Generate a new way to classify animals.
Analyze Cause/ Effect	Design a simulation that will teach younger students about supply and demand forces in the economy.	Role play an interview with an author who tells about the life factors that influences themes and choices in a story.	Create a dramatic presentation that teaches younger students about the causes and effects of earthquakes.
Problem Solve	Write a proposition for voter approval that helps homeless people.	An author is having a tough time coming up with a sequel to her novel. Create a list of suggestions and why you think they will touch the hearts and minds of readers.	Clarify the evidence on global warming and propose further studies and possible solutions in a letter to the EPA.
Persuade	Write a letter to the school board that asks for money to buy primary documents to supplement the biased textbook.	Take on the role of an author and persuade listeners to use a certain literary device.	Write an article for the entire school that persuades them to consider being astronauts for a trip to Mars.

Academic Conversations: Classroom Talk That Fosters Critical Thinking and Content Understandings by Jeff Zwiers and Marie Crawford. Copyright © 2011. Stenhouse Publishers.

Empathize	Create a journal entry from the perspective of a WWII soldier.	Create a monologue to act out in front of the class or a small group on the thoughts you have as a main character, dead or alive (e.g., Hamlet), after the story ends.	Write a first-person story from the point of view of a blood cell in the human body.
Synthesize	Analyze several songs written during the Civil War and synthesize their contents into a letter to President Lincoln.	Read several poems or songs by one author and create a TV advertisement to sell the author's work.	Create a dialogue between an anthropology student and a scientist who is explaining the process and accuracy of radiocarbon dating.
Interpret	Create a master list of the ten biggest mysteries of history and explain why they are important.	Take on the persona of an author and create a speech that explains the underlying meaning of a book.	Observe an insect and interpret its actions and physical features with respect to adaptation principles.
Evaluate	As the Commission for Historical Accuracy, evaluate Christopher Columbus's actions and decide how he should be described in history texts.	Create a literary critique talk show (like Ebert and Roeper) that promotes or criticizes a novel.	You have just discovered a new form of energy that is clean and cheap, but could be turned into a bomb. Write a journal entry describing your feelings about announcing it.
Communicate	Design a training manual for WWI troops that outlines the enemy's weapons and tactics.	Read several poems or songs by one author and create a TV advertisement to sell the author's work.	Create a dramatic presentation that teaches younger students about the causes and effects of earthquakes.
Apply	Design a museum exhibit on the roles of nonmilitary people in the American Revolution.	Write a short story that teaches readers about an important human theme or struggle.	Measure the pollution levels in a local stream and prepare a report for local authorities.

Sample Information Gap Conversation Cards

A	B
Using corn for fuel should be encouraged because:	**Using corn for fuel should be discouraged because:**
• it decreases our dependence on foreign oil. • ethanol burns more efficiently than petroleum-based fuels. • it creates fewer gases that contribute to greenhouse warming.	• as ethanol production increases, the price of corn for food goes up. • the price of corn affects the prices of other foods. (Example: In the early 1970s, a sudden rise in grain prices quickly raised the cost of meat.) • food insecurity for poor families is likely.
A	**B**
Viruses are not alive because they:	**Viruses are alive because they:**
• do not have all the parts that make up cells: nucleus, membranes, cytoplasm. • require living cells in order to reproduce. • do not possess a metabolic system, which means that they do not grow. • do not require food.	• have genes made with DNA or RNA, the codes for life. • evolve into different forms. • adapt in order to survive (they can build up resistance). • can rebuild their parts in order to reproduce.
A	**B**
Radical Republicans' plan for dealing with Southerners during Reconstruction:	**President Johnson's plan for dealing with Southerners during Reconstruction:**
• Southerners should be punished for rebelling. • People who used to be rich slave owners should lose their land. The land should be divided among blacks and poor whites in the South. • No one who was in the Confederate government during the war should be able to serve in government again.	• The North should help the South because that will help the country heal faster. • Southerners who rebelled need to ask for forgiveness (a pardon) if they want to participate in government. • Southerners need to agree that slavery is over.

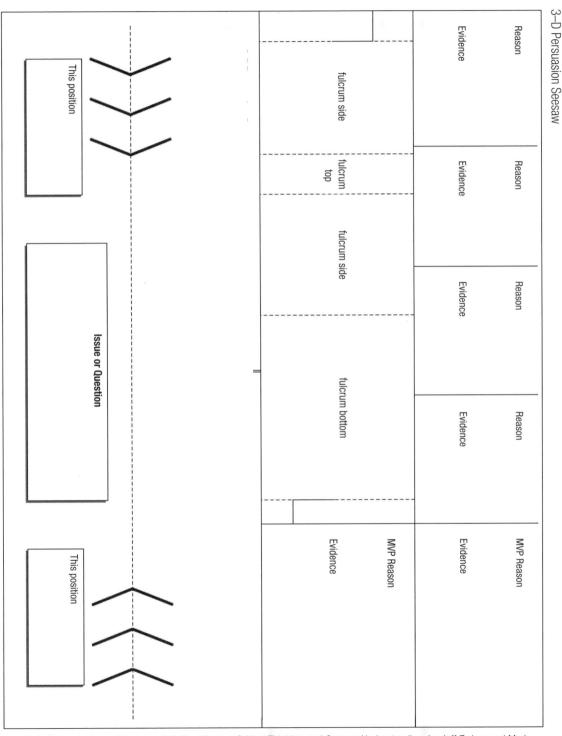

3–D Persuasion Seesaw

References

Almasi, J. F., K. Garas, H. Cho, W. Ma, L. Shanahan, and A. Augustino. 2004. "One Cohort's Social, Cognitive, and Affective Development Across Grades 1–3." Paper presented at the 54th Annual Meeting of the National Reading Conference, San Antonio, TX.

Alvermann, D. E., D. Fl. Dillon, and D. G. O'Brien. 1987. *Using Discussion to Promote Reading Comprehension*. Newark, DE: International Reading Association.

Arreaga-Mayer, C., and C. Perdomo-Rivera. 1996. "Ecobehavioral Analysis of Instruction for At-Risk Language-Minority Students." *Elementary School Journal* 96, 245-258.

Bakhtin, M. (1981). *The Dialogic Imagination*. Austin: University of Texas Press.

———. 1986. "The Problem of Speech Genres." Trans. V. W. McGee. In *Speech Genres and Other Late Essays*, ed. C. E. M. Holquist. Austin: University of Texas.

Barnes, D., and F. Todd. 1977. *Communication and Learning in Small Groups*. London: Routledge and Kegan Paul.

Barron, B., and L. Darling-Hammond. 2008. "How Can We Teach for Meaningful Learning?" In *Powerful Learning: What We Know About Teaching for Understanding*, ed. L. Darling-Hammond, B. Barron, P. D. Pearson, A. H. Schoenfeld, E. K. Stage, T. D. Zimmerman, G. N. Cervetti, and J. L. Tilson. San Francisco: Jossey-Bass.

Bean, T., C. Singer, and S. Cowan. 1985. "Acquisition of a Topic Schema in High School Biology Through an Analogical Study Guide." In *Issues in Literacy: A Research Perspective*, ed. J. Niles and R. Lalik.. Rochester, NY: National Reading Conference.

Beck, I., M. McKeown, and L. Kucan. 2002. *Bringing Words to Life: Robust Vocabulary Instruction*. New York: Guilford.

Beers, K. 2006. "Tea Party." Minnesota Council of Teachers of English. http://www.mcte.org/resources/beers.html.

Bloom, B., M. Englehart, E. Furst, W. Hill, and D. Krathwohl. 1956. *Taxonomy of Educational Objectives: The Classification of Educational Goals. Handbook I: Cognitive Domain*. New York, Toronto: Longmans, Green.

Brookfield, S., and S. Preskill. 2005. *Discussion as a Way of Teaching: Tools and Techniques for Democratic Classrooms.* 2nd ed.. San Francisco: Jossey-Bass.

Bruner, J. S. 1978. "The Role of Dialogue in Language Acquisition." In *The Child's Conception of Language,* ed. A. Sinclair, R. Jarvella, and W. J. M. Levelt. New York: Springer-Verlag.

———. 1986. *Actual Minds: Possible Worlds.* Cambridge, MA: Harvard University Press.

Calkins, L. 2000. *The Art of Teaching Reading.* New York: Addison-Wesley Longman.

Casner-Lotto, J., and L. Barrington. 2006. *Are They Really Ready to Work? Employers' Perspectives on the Basic Knowledge and Applied Skills of New Entrants to the 21st Century U.S. Workforce.* New York: The Conference Board.

Cazden, C. 2001. *Classroom Discourse: The Language of Teaching and Learning.* Portsmouth, NH: Heinemann.

Chapin, S., C. O'Connor, and N. Anderson. 2009. *Classroom Discussions Using Math Talk in Elementary Classrooms.* Sausalito, CA: Math Solutions.

Collingwood, R. G. 1946. *The Idea of History.* Oxford: Clarendon.

Common Core State Standards Initiative. 2010. "English Language Arts Standards—Introduction—How to Read the Standards." Common Core State Standards Initiative. http://www.corestandards.org/the-standards/english-language-arts-standards/introduction/how-to-read-the-standards/.

Corden, R. E. 2001. "Group Discussion and the Importance of a Shared Perspective: Learning from Collaborative Research." *Qualitative Research* 1(3): 347–367.

Cotton, K. 1989. *Expectations and Student Outcomes.* Portland, OR: Northwest Regional Educational Laboratory.

Coxhead, A. 2003. "The Academic Word List." School of Linguistics and Applied Language Studies, Victoria University of Wellington. http://www.victoria.ac.nz/lals/resources/academicwordlist/.

Cummins, J. 1994. "Knowledge, Power, and Identity in Teaching English as a Second Language." In *Educating Second Language Children: The Whole Child, the Whole Curriculum, the Whole Community*, ed. F. Genesee. Cambridge, UK: Cambridge University Press.

Daniels, H. 2002. *Literature Circles: Voice and Choice in Book Clubs and Reading Groups,* 2nd ed. Portland, ME: Stenhouse.

Dean, D. 2008. *Bringing Grammar to Life.* Newark, NJ: International Reading Association.

Dewey, J. 1963 [1938]. *Experience and Education.* New York: Macmillan.

Drake, F., and L. Nelson. 2005. *Engagement in Teaching History: Theory and Practices for Middle and Secondary Teachers.* Columbus, OH: Pearson.

Duffala, J. 1987. *The Teacher as Artist.* Santa Rosa, CA: Author.

Dunn, P., and K. Lindblom. 2003. "Why Revitalize Grammar?" *English Journal* 92(3): 43–50.

Dutro, S., and C. Moran. 2003. "Rethinking English Language Instruction: An Architectural Approach." In *English Learners: Reaching the Highest Level of English Literacy*, ed. G. García. Newark, NJ: International Reading Association.

Ehrenworth, M., and V. Vinton. 2005. *The Power of Grammar: Unconventional Approaches to the Conventions of Language.* Portsmouth, NH: Heinemann.

Fairclough, N. 2003. *Analysing Discourse: Textual Analysis for Social Research.* New York: Routledge.

Frank, D., P. Kahan, J. Little, J. S. Miller, J. Pasachoff, and C. Wainwright. 2001. *Focus on Physical Science.* Upper Saddle River, NJ: Prentice Hall.

Freire, P. 1970. *Pedagogy of the Oppressed.* New York: Herder and Herder.

Freire, P., and D. Macedo. 1987. *Literacy: Reading the Word and the World.* Westport, CT: Bergin and Garvey.

Goldenberg, C. 1991. *Instructional Conversations and Their Classroom Application.* Educational Practice Report 2. Santa Cruz, CA: The National Center for Research on Cultural Diversity and Second Language Learning.

Hansen, R., and K. Hansen. 2009. "What Do Employers Really Want? Top Skills and Values Employers Seek from Job-Seekers." Quintessential Careers. http://www.quintcareers.com/job_skills_values.html.

Hattie, J. A. 1992. "Measuring the Effects of Schooling." *Australian Journal of Education* 36(1): 5–13.

Heath, S. B. 1983. *Ways with Words: Language, Life, and Work in Communities and Classrooms.* New York: Cambridge University Press.

Hernandez, A. 2003. "Making Content Instruction Accessible to English Language Learners." In *English Learners: Reaching the Highest Level of English Literacy,* ed. G. García. Newark, NJ: International Reading Association.

Holt, T. 1990. *Thinking Historically: Narrative, Imagination, and Understanding.* New York: College Entrance Examination Board.

Hood, C. 2007. Handouts of Creating Powerful Writers workshop. West Coast Literacy Conference, San Diego, CA, May 17–19, 2007.

Hume, D. 1987. "Of Refinement in the Arts." In *Essays Moral, Political, and Literary,* ed. E. F. Miller. Indianapolis: Liberty Fund.

Johnson, D., and R. Johnson. 2009. "Energizing Learning: The Instructional Power of Conflict." *Educational Researcher* 38: 37–51.

Keene, E. O., and S. Zimmermann. 2007. *Mosaic of Thought: The Power of Comprehension Strategy Instruction.* Portsmouth, NH: Heinemann.

Ketch, A. 2005. "Conversation: The Comprehension Connection." *The Reading Teacher* 59(1): 8–13.

Krashen, S. 1985. *The Input Hypothesis: Issues and Implications.* London: Longman.

Kumar, P. 2010. Unpublished lesson plan.

Lemke, J. 1990. *Talking Science: Language, Learning, and Values.* New York: Ablex.

Lingard, B., D. Hayes, and M. Mills. 2003. "Teachers and Productive Pedagogies: Contextualising, Conceptualising, Utilising." *Pedagogy, Culture and Society* 11(3): 399–424.

Lobeck, A. 2005. "A Critical Approach to Standard English." In *Language in the Schools: Integrating Linguistic Knowledge into K–12 Teaching,* ed. K. Denham and A. Lobeck. Mahwah, NJ: Lawrence Erlbaum.

Long, M. 1981. "Input, Interaction and Second Language Acquisition." In *Native Language and Foreign Language Acquisition*, ed. H. Winitz. New York: Annals of the New York Academy of Science.

Lowry, L. 2006. *The Giver*. New York: Delacorte Books.

Marzano, R. J., D. J. Pickering, and J. E. Pollock. 2001. *Classroom Instruction That Works: Research-Based Strategies for Increasing Student Achievement.* Alexandria, VA: Association for Supervision and Curriculum Development.

Mercer, N. 1995. *The Guided Construction of Knowledge: Talk Amongst Teachers and Learners.* Clevedon, UK: Multilingual Matters Ltd.

Mercer, N., and K. Littleton. 2007. *Dialogue and the Development of Children's Thinking: A Sociocultural Approach.* London: Routledge.

Moeller, V., and M. Moeller. 2001. *Socratic Seminars and Literature Circles.* Larchmont, NY: Eye on Education.

National Association of Colleges and Employers. 2007. *Job Outlook 2008.* Bethlehem, PA: National Association of Colleges and Employers.

National Council for History Education. 1988. *Building a History Curriculum: Guidelines for Teaching History in Schools.* Washington D.C.: Educational Excellence Network.

National Research Council. 2000. *How People Learn: Brain, Mind, Experience, and School.* Washington, D.C.: National Academic Press.

Nichols, M. 2006. *Comprehension Through Conversation.* Portsmouth, NH: Heinemann.

Nystrand, M. 1996. *Opening Dialogue: Understanding the Dynamics of Language and Learning in the English Classroom.* New York: Teachers College Press.

Nystrand, M., L. Wu, A. Gamoran, S. Zeiser, and D. Long. 2003. "Questions in Time: Investigating the Structure and Dynamics of Unfolding Classroom Discourse." *Discourse Processes* 35(March-April): 135–196.

Palmer, P. 1998. *The Courage to Teach.* San Francisco: Jossey-Bass.

Perkins, D. 1992. *Smart Schools.* New York: Simon and Schuster.

Putnam, R. 2000. *Bowling Alone: The Collapse and Revival of American Community.* New York: Simon and Schuster.

Raban, B. 2001. "Talking to Think, Learn, and Teach." In *Talking Classrooms: Shaping Children's Learning Through Oral Language Instruction*, ed. P. Smith. Newark, DE: International Reading Association.

Raphael, T. E., S. Florio-Ruane, and M. George. 2001. "Book Club Plus: A Conceptual Framework to Organize Literacy Instruction." *Language Arts* 79(2): 159–168.

Ray, K. 2006. *Study Driven: A Framework for Planning Units of Study in the Writing Workshop.* Portsmouth, NH: Heinemann.

Reznitskaya, A., R. C. Anderson, and L. Kuo. 2007. "Teaching and Learning Argumentation." *Elementary School Journal* 107(5): 449–472.

Richek, M. 2005. "Words Are Wonderful: Interactive, Time-Efficient Strategies to Teach Meaning Vocabulary." *The Reading Teacher* 58(5): 414–423.

Rogoff, B. 1990. *Apprenticeship in Thinking: Cognitive Development in Social Context.* New York: Oxford University Press.

Roskos, K. A., P. O. Tabors, and L. A. Lenhart. 2009. In *Oral Language and Early Literacy in Preschool: Talking, Reading, and Writing.* Newark, DE: International Reading Association.

Routman, R. 2000. *Conversations: Strategies for Teaching, Learning, and Evaluating.* Portsmouth, NH: Heinemann.

Sams, C., and L. Dawes. 2004. "Developing the Capacity to Collaborate." In *Learning to Collaborate: Collaborating to Learn*, ed. K. Littleton, D. Miell, and D. Faulkner. Hauppauge, NY: Nova Science.

Saran, R., and B. Neisser. 2004. *Enquiring Minds: Socratic Dialogue in Education*. Stoke on Trent, UK: Trentham Books.

Schleppegrell, M. J. 2004. *The Language of Schooling: A Functional Linguistics Approach.* Mahwah, NJ: Erlbaum.

Schleppegrell, M. J., and L. C. de Oliveira. 2006. "An Integrated Language and Content Approach for History Teachers." *Journal of English for Specific Purposes* 5(4): 254–268.

Scott, P., E. Mortimer, and O. Aguiar. 2006. "The Tension Between Authoritative and Dialogic Discourse: A Fundamental Characteristic of Meaning Making Interactions in High School Science Lessons." *Science Education* 90(4): 605–631.

Smith, P. 2001. *Talking Classrooms: Shaping Children's Learning Through Oral Language Instruction*. Newark, DE: International Reading Association.

Spiegel, D. 2005. *Classroom Discussion: Strategies for Engaging All Students, Building Higher-Level Thinking Skills, and Strengthening Reading and Writing Across the Curriculum.* New York: Scholastic.

Swain, M. 1995. "Three Functions of Output in Second Language Learning." In *Principle and Practice in Applied Linguistics: Studies in Honour of H. G. Widdowson*, ed. G. Cook and B. Seidlhofer. Oxford, UK: Oxford University Press.

Taylor, B. M., P. D. Pearson, D. S. Peterson, and M. C. Rodriguez. 2003. "Reading Growth in High-Poverty Classrooms: The Influence of Teacher Practices that Encourage Cognitive Engagement in Literacy Learning." *The Elementary School Journal* 104:3–28.

Tech Museum of Innovation. 2011. *Simplicity of Electricity*. San Jose, CA: The Tech Museum of Innovation. Available online at http://www.thetech.org/education/downloads/dconline/simplicityofElectricity.pdf.

Tharp, R., and R. Gallimore. 1991. *The Instructional Conversation: Teaching and Learning in Social Activity* (Research Report 2). Santa Cruz, CA: The National Center for Research on Cultural Diversity and Second Language Learning, University of California, Santa Cruz.

Tierney, R. 1998. "Literacy Assessment Reform: Shifting Beliefs, Principled Possibilities, and Emerging Practices." *The Reading Teacher* 51(5): 374–390.

Toulmin, S. 1969. *The Uses of Argument*. Cambridge, UK: Cambridge University Press.

Vygotsky, L. 1978. *Mind in Society: The Development of Higher Psychological Processes*. Cambridge, MA: Harvard University Press.

———. 1986. *Thought and Language*. Trans. A. Kozulin. Cambridge, MA: MIT Press.

Wagner, T. 2008. *The Global Achievement Gap*. New York: Basic Books.

Weber, K., C. Maher, A. Powell, and H. S. Lee. 2008. "Learning Opportunities from Group Discussions: Warrants Become the Objects of Debate." *Educational Studies in Mathematics* 68(3): 247–261.

Whitehead, A. 1929. *The Aims of Education and Other Essays*. New York: Macmillan.

Wilhelm, J. 2002. *Action Strategies for Deepening Comprehension*. New York: Scholastic.

Wineberg, S. 2001. *Historical Thinking and Other Unnatural Acts: Charting the Future of Teaching the Past*. Philadelphia: Temple University Press.

Wineberg, S., S. Mosborg, D. Porat, and A. Duncan. 2007. "Common Belief and the Cultural Curriculum: An Intergenerational Study of Historical Consciousness." *American Educational Research Journal* 44:40. Available online at http://aerj.aera.net.

Ybarra, O., E. Burnstein, P. Winkielman, M. C. Keller, M. Manis, E. Chan, and J. Rodriguez. 2008. "Mental Exercising Through Simple Socializing: Social Interaction Promotes General Cognitive Functioning." *Personality and Social Psychology Bulletin* 34: 248–259.

Zwiers, J. 2004. *Developing Academic Thinking Skills in Grades 6–12: A Handbook of Multiple Intelligence Activities*. Newark, DE: International Reading Association.

———. 2008. *Building Academic Language: Essential Practices for Content Classrooms*. San Francisco: Jossey-Bass.

———. 2010. *Building Reading Comprehension Habits in Grades 6–12: A Toolkit of Classroom Activities*. 2nd ed. Newark, DE: International Reading Association.

Zwiers, J., and M. Crawford. 2009. "How to Start Academic Conversations." *Educational Leadership* 66(7): 70–73.

Index

Page numbers followed by an *f* indicate figures.